MARKETING

ABOUT THE AUTHORS

The late Myron S. Heidingsfield obtained his doctorate at New York University. He was Food Fair Stores Foundation Professor of Marketing in the College of Business Administration of the University of Florida. He was also director of the International Marketing Resource Center at the University, professor of marketing and chairman of the department in the School of Business and Public Administration of Temple University, and served on the faculties of the College of William and Mary and of Columbia University. Dr. Heidingsfield was named Marketing Educator of the Year by the Sales and Marketing Executives-International. He was the author of *Changing Patterns in Marketing: A Study in Strategy* and many articles on business and marketing and coauthor of *Market and Marketing Analysis* (with Blankenship) and *Marketing and Business Research* (with Eby).

A. B. Blankenship earned his doctorate at Columbia University. Currently, he is professor of marketing at Bowling Green State University and research director of the Suburban Newspaper Research Center. Formerly, he was vice-president, an owner, and a director of Canadian Facts Co., Ltd. He has also been director of market research at Carter-Wallace, Inc., vice-president and research director of Ted Bates and Co. Inc., advertising agency, and adjunct professor of marketing at New York University Graduate School of Business Administration. In 1973 he was elected secretary-treasurer of the American Marketing Association. Dr. Blankenship is author, co-author, or editor of four other books in the field of marketing, including *Marketing and Marketing Analysis* (with Heidingsfield). He is a member of the Market Research Council, a Fellow of the American Psychological Association, a Fellow of the Academy of Marketing Science, and a member of the editorial board of its *Journal*.

MARKETING

THIRD EDITION

MYRON S. HEIDINGSFIELD

A. B. BLANKENSHIP

BARNES & NOBLE BOOKS

A DIVISION OF HARPER & ROW, PUBLISHERS

New York, Evanston, San Francisco, London

First BARNES & NOBLE BOOKS edition published 1974.

LIBRARY OF CONGRESS CATALOG CARD NUMBER: 73–19476

STANDARD BOOK NUMBER: 06-460157-9

PREFACE

This *Outline* is designed to give the student (1) a source from which he may obtain a knowledge of the basic principles and practices of marketing, (2) a convenient means of reviewing the fundamentals of the subject, and (3) a helpful companion book to facilitate the study of any other books in this field. In addition, the *Outline*, it is hoped, will aid the businessman to view the entire marketing structure and to reconcile his specific operation with the total picture, a procedure that may prove valuable in forming major policy decisions.

For summaries of related subjects, the reader is urged to consult the following *Outlines* in the Outline Series.

> *Accounting Problems*
> *Business Law*
> *Business Management*
> *Business Writing*
> *Corporation Finance*
> *Dictionary of American Politics*
> *Dictionary of Economics*
> *Modern Economics*
> *Money and Banking*

CONTENTS

MARKETING

1

MARKETING AS A PROCESS

In our economy there are two basic business processes. One is *production*—the creation of goods and services. The other is *marketing*—the activities by which goods and services flow from the producer to the ultimate consumer. The producer, as well as the marketer and the ultimate consumer, performs many of the marketing functions.

The Process of Marketing

Example. Consider the transactions normally involved in the marketing of wheat. Individual farmers (producers) sell the grain to local buyers. After accumulating a supply in their elevators, the buyers sell it to dealers in large markets of midwestern cities which have terminal freight facilities. The dealers eventually sell the supply which they accumulate to millers, to manufacturers of cereal, or to exporters. If some of it is sold to a miller—to General Mills, for instance—the marketing of this portion of the wheat as such has been completed. General Mills uses the grain for the preparation of flour which it may package and sell to wholesalers throughout the country; the wholesalers, in turn, sell it to retail grocers, who complete the marketing of the flour by selling it to the ultimate consumer—the housewife. Alternatively, General Mills may sell the flour to an industrial consumer, such as a baker. Thus the marketing of the flour has been completed, but this step will be followed by the marketing of bread by the baker, either directly to the ultimate consumer or to retail stores.

Broad Scope of the Marketing Network. Some concept of the complex nature of marketing may be derived merely from considering several products—for example, your desk and chair, carpet, lamp, and so on—in the room where you are sitting. In its first stages the wood for your desk and chair may have been transported as lumber from a southern forest to a furniture mill, probably located in the same region. The manufactured products were, in all likelihood, sold directly to the furniture store or the department store from which you purchased them. The carpet may have been made out of fibrous raw material converted from wool grown in the Mountain states. Perhaps it was manufactured by a mill in some eastern state which then sold it directly to a retail store. Various products, such as copper wire and rolled metal, were utilized in the production of your lamp; the raw materials for these were obtained through mining operations in different geographic areas. The manufacturer may have marketed the lamp through a wholesaler who sold it to the retail store from which you purchased it. Similarly with other objects in your room (the glass in the windows, the paint on the walls, and the like), the marketing function involved a variety of processors and sales organizations, in widely separated locations, each contributing to the task of making finished goods and services available to you as a consumer.

The extent of your dependence upon marketing is hard to exaggerate. The fact that you are reading this book is the consequence of the marketing of raw materials, industrial goods, and services, plus the wholesale and retail processes required in order to bring the finished volume from the publisher to you. The chair you sit on, everything you wear, and whatever you see around you have gone through a series of complex marketing procedures.

Evolution of Marketing in the American Economy

Although marketing, in a general sense, is as old as recorded civilization, the process as it exists in America today is a very recent activity, largely a development of the past fifty years. A retrospective glance shows that the United States has passed through two phases of economic development and is now in a third phase.

First Phase: Emphasis on Agricultural Production. Down through the Civil War and the postwar years, the United States depended principally upon its agricultural capacity for economic survival. In 1820, for instance, approximately 72 percent of the total labor force was engaged in agricultural work (as contrasted with 1970, when only 4.8 percent was so employed). Originally, there was little difference between producer, middleman, and consumer. The pioneer farmer raised produce for his own consumption and traded or sold his surplus at local general stores; the pioneer manufacturer peddled his own products; the pioneer merchant performed most of the services that were later to become the work of specialized middlemen. National expansion, the development of new products, distinctive demands from market segments, and the growth of manufacturing made it possible for middlemen to play a more substantial role in the economy. They concentrated on buying, selling, storing, arranging for transportation, extending credit, and performing other services essential to distribution. Nevertheless, as long as the national economy was predominantly agrarian, the marketing picture remained fairly simple—at least by any modern standard.

Second Phase: Emphasis on Industrial Production. The full impact of the Industrial Revolution began to be felt in America at the close of the Civil War. It was found that the country did not have to depend solely upon agriculture for economic survival but that it could build factories and produce goods on a mass basis such as the world had never before witnessed. Industrialization was hastened by abundant resources of coal, iron, oil, and lumber; by the establishment of a transportation system capable of bringing all markets and sources of supply within reach of urban centers; and by the peculiar genius of Americans for always finding a better and more efficient way to do a job. Before the turn of the twentieth century, the United States had become the world's foremost industrial producer. With the challenge of World War I, the United States exceeded previous performance to such a degree that she was able to take a large hand in the rehabilitation of Europe during the 1920s. Despite the important shift of the labor force away from farms, agricultural production continued to meet the needs of a changing economy. Newly acquired knowledge about the mechanization of industry was applied to the mechanization of farming.

America's tremendous progress in increasing the efficiency of labor could not have been made without the concomitant expansion of education. The emphasis in college education shifted from classical and professional studies to the training of engineers, scientific agriculturists, industrial management specialists, and financial experts. This change was fundamental to the transition from an agrarian to an industrial economy. The process of marketing during this stage of the nation's economy became more complex, but little thought was given to increasing its efficiency. U.S. economic efforts concentrated on the task of improving productive efficiency so that more goods could be made at lower costs. The resulting technical advances gave the American worker the highest standard of living in the world.

Third Phase: Commensurate Emphasis on Distribution.   The next necessary phase of economic growth was the development of new distribution techniques. But crises overshadowed it: the Great Depression, World War II, the Korean conflict, and Vietnam.

EFFECT OF THE DEPRESSION.   Prior to 1930, little thought had been given to the much-needed development of techniques of distribution. The nation had been hypnotized by what seemed to be an endless sellers' market and had scarcely noticed the flaws in the distributive system. During the depression, however, it became apparent that production alone was not all-important, as it had seemed in the late 1920s. It was difficult to perceive major trends and changes in the economy; many thought that the nation had developed a monster of overproduction.

EFFECT OF WORLD WAR II.   Before much could be done to remedy the situation, the United States was embroiled in a second world war. Once again, all emphasis was placed upon production because the United States was pledged to become the "arsenal of democracy." The wartime stimulus to productive capacity, the postwar sellers' market with its tremendous backlog of consumer demand, and the shortages caused by governmental economic commitments and extensive postwar military preparations further delayed progress in the third phase of economic evolution: distribution.

Post-Korean Period. The marketing structure was beginning to meet the distribution needs of the economy after World War II, but it was set back at the time of the Korean conflict. Fearing shortages of goods, consumers went on buying sprees and caused temporary shortages.

During the post-Korean period, the marketing structure began to catch up with increased production facilities. With this growth, changes occurred: increase in consumer credit buying, spread of shopping centers, and increase in importance of discount houses.

Post-Vietnam Period. The changes continue. American society has become largely a credit card economy. Retail check-out counters are becoming computerized, and it can be predicted that individual items will no longer be price-marked in ways that the consumer can read but will instead be code-marked in ways that an optical scanner can read. Cash registers are becoming a thing of the past.

Necessity for a Science of Distribution. The United States has reached a stage of economic development and technical competence by means of which inadequate industrial capacity can be quickly overcome through the construction of new facilities; the nation has enough manpower, resources, and potential productive means to supply its requirements. There is no need to fear excessive production, however, if the fact that the economy must improve its methods of distribution is accepted. *The movement of products from the producer to the consumer is fully as important as production itself.* Because distribution, or marketing, is the necessary complement of production, the efficiency of marketing will have to be increased to avert a disastrous maladjustment between production and consumption.

Basic Approaches to the Study of Marketing

There are four fundamental approaches to the study of marketing: the commodity approach, the institutional approach, the functional approach, and the systems or managerial approach. None of these approaches can be used exclusively of the others. In the solution of a particular problem, any two can be combined advantageously; in a study of the whole subject, all four are necessary because only by combining them can a true and complete picture of marketing in American society be obtained.

The Commodity Approach. The commodity approach concerns the distribution of individual products and the gathering of full information about each. The brief discussion of wheat marketing earlier in this chapter exemplifies the approach, but only partially; a thorough study of the marketing of wheat would entail examining not only the channels of distribution but prices, brands, advertising, and all other aspects of the marketing process as well. Chapter 24 includes examples of the marketing of specific commodities. However, to present a complete picture of marketing through the commodity approach alone would be an endless task because it would require examination of all the thousands of products distributed in the commercial world. Through its classification of types of commodities, the commodity approach provides an immensely useful tool for the description of marketing. It separates all commodities into two basic groups—industrial goods and consumer goods—each with its subdivisions. All products belong to one of these groups; some may fall into both classifications, depending upon their use.

INDUSTRIAL GOODS.   Industrial goods are those ". . . bought for motives other than personal or household satisfaction."[1] They include land and buildings for business purposes, equipment (installation and accessory), maintenance, repair and operating supplies, raw materials, and fabricated materials.

---

[1] Irving J. Shapiro, *Marketing Terms: Definitions, Explanations and/or Aspects* (S-M-C Publishing Co., 1973), p. 82. See Appendix A for partial text of this publication.

Raw materials are "products of nature which enter into the physical product being made, and which have been processed only enough for their convenience in distribution. . . ."[2]

Fabricated materials and *parts* consist of "raw material which has been processed into a stable form which requires only dimensional changes to permit incorporation into a product. Example: lumber, leather, cloth."[3]

Supplies are "materials of relatively short life used up during manufacturing and which do not physically enter the final product."[4] Examples are fuel, lubricants, stationery, typewriter ribbons, and cleaning materials.

Equipment consists of goods not incorporated into the final product which are of relatively long life, taking two forms: major installations and accessory equipment. Major installations include items such as boilers, dynamos, power lathes, and bank vaults. Accessory equipment includes items such as typewriters, desks, desk-top calculators, filing cases, and small tools.

CONSUMER GOODS.   Consumer goods are those (1) ". . . bought for personal or household satisfactions, (2) ". . . used directly in satisfying human wants."[5]

Convenience goods are a type of item that the consumer wants to buy with a minimum of effort at the most convenient, accessible place.[6] Examples are tobacco, soap, newspapers, packaged confections, and many drug and grocery products.

Shopping goods are the kind of item for which reasonable alternatives exist and which the buyer wants to purchase only after making price, style, and quality comparisons in a number of outlets.[7] Examples are millinery, dress goods, shoes, costume jewelry, furniture, and residential real estate (if not bought for speculation).

Specialty goods are consumer goods that a significant proportion of buyers demand and for which they are willing to make a spe-

[2] Shapiro, *Marketing Terms*, p. 139.
[3] Ibid., p. 61.
[4] Ibid., p. 117.
[5] Ibid., p. 38.
[6] Ibid., p. 40.
[7] Ibid., p. 153.

cial purchasing effort. Examples are leading makes of watches and specific brands of fancy groceries.[8]

The Institutional Approach. Whereas the commodity approach analyzes marketing in terms of the goods marketed, the institutional approach views it from the standpoint of the agencies that do the marketing. It analyzes each wholesale and retail institution of the marketing mechanism. Almost invariably, it places emphasis upon *middlemen:* the individuals or business organizations that specialize in performing the functions and services involved in the purchase and sale of goods as they flow from producer to consumer. The common classification of middlemen according to (1) whether or not they take title to the goods they handle and (2) their position in the marketing channel is useful in showing the scope of marketing.

MERCHANT MIDDLEMEN AND AGENTS. On the basis of whether or not title to the goods is taken, there are two categories: *merchant middlemen*, who take title, and *agents* or *functional middlemen*, who do not take title.

WHOLESALING AND RETAILING MIDDLEMEN. On the basis of position in the marketing channel, there are again two categories: *wholesaling middlemen*, who operate between the producer and one or more of the groups, which include other wholesaling middlemen, industrial consumers, and retailers; and *retailing middlemen*, who specialize in selling to the ultimate consumer. Wholesaling and retailing middlemen may themselves be either merchants or agents.

The Functional Approach. Instead of describing marketing in terms of the commodities sold or the institutions transacting the business, the functional approach analyzes the economic services involved in the flow of goods from producer to consumer. These are divided into the following three major groups.

FUNCTIONS OF EXCHANGE. This group includes buying and selling. *Buying* (or *assembling*) in marketing is the process of concentrating or controlling goods or services with a transfer in title. *Selling* (or *distributing*) is the process of assisting and/or persuad-

[8] Ibid., p. 158.

ing a prospective customer to purchase a commodity or a service that has commercial significance to the seller.[9]

FUNCTIONS OF PHYSICAL SUPPLY. *Transportation* is the physical transfer of commodities from the place of production to the place of consumption or to and from any intermediary points. *Storage* is the function of holding and preserving goods from the time of production to the time of final sale.

FACILITATING FUNCTIONS. Financing, risk taking, market information, and standardization and grading facilitate marketing. *Financing* embraces the monetary operations used to control or modify the direction of the flow of goods and services. *Risk taking* is the assumption of financial responsibility for loss through such factors as physical deterioration, obsolescence, theft, damage, waste, changes in supply or demand, or changes in price. *Market information* includes gathering and interpreting facts, estimating the value and prices to be paid for a product, and identifying the type of consumers who will purchase it. *Standardization* refers to the determination of basic specifications to which manufactured goods must conform and of classes into which the products of agriculture and of extractive industries must be sorted.

COMMENT. Generally, all three groups of functions may be performed in the marketing of any commodity or service. However, in present-day industry, many of these functions fall within the purview of marketing management and are included in the various elements of the marketing plan.

Systems or Managerial Approach. The systems approach regards the various elements of a marketing program as being interrelated rather than independent. Decisions about elements in the marketing program are made on the basis of this concept.

If, for example, a traffic manager wants to save money on transportation, he may decide that the purchasing department should order thousands of pounds of raw material at a time. But if there is insufficient warehouse space to store such a large supply, or if a tremendous amount of employee overtime is required to handle

---

[9] Some writers on marketing include assembling and distributing under functions of exchange. Assembling may occur without purchasing (title exchange), however, and so, too, may distributing.

the shipment, then all savings in transportation costs may be wiped out through loss or increased costs. When transportation and warehousing are considered as interactive and integrated, the firm is utilizing the systems approach.

In the systems approach, the firm also becomes thoroughly committed to the marketing concept, which holds that all efforts of the firm should be built around what the consumer wants and needs. Everything else is secondary.

An Integrated View of Marketing

Whereas each of the four basic approaches to the study of marketing provides an understanding of special aspects, none provides an overall picture of the process. To gain such a picture, it is necessary to bear in mind the larger patterns in the flow of goods from producer to consumer.

Concentration, Dispersion, Assorting, and Equalization.   One aid to an integrated view is to see the marketing process as composed of three recurring movements or stages. The first is *concentration,* or the physical bringing together of goods at some central point. In the example of wheat marketing, concentration begins with the local buyers, who bring together the products of their own areas, and it continues as the terminal market brings together the wheat of the various local areas. A second movement in the flow of goods is *dispersion,* or distribution of the previously concentrated goods. In the example, the dealer at the terminal market disperses the wheat to the miller, the cereal manufacturer, or the exporter, who in turn concentrates and disperses his product toward the ultimate consumer. In the interplay of concentration and dispersion, there must be a balancing of supply and demand; this is known as *equalization.* Prior to *equalization,* there is a mental process of *assorting,* which is the determination of variety and quantity of merchandise that will be required to fill a future need.

Channels of Distribution.   Another aid to an integrated view is consideration of the distribution channels. A channel of distribution is the sequence of markets through which a commodity passes under the guidance of middlemen from production to the point of consumption. There are four major channels.

FROM PRODUCER TO CONSUMER. This is the channel frequently used by the producer of industrial goods who sells directly to the concern needing his product. Occasionally, as in the distribution of Fuller brushes, it has been adapted for the distribution of goods to the ultimate consumer.

FROM PRODUCER TO ONE MIDDLEMAN TO CONSUMER. This channel is typical of the marketing carried on by mail-order houses, department stores, and chain stores. Usually, the sole middleman is the retailer who buys his goods directly from the manufacturer. This channel is also used when producers sell to the consumer through manufacturers' agents or other types of agent middlemen.

FROM PRODUCER TO WHOLESALER TO RETAILER TO CONSUMER. This has been called the *normal* channel of distribution for consumer goods. Although it is declining in importance, it is still the most commonly used channel of distribution for manufactured articles.

FROM PRODUCER THROUGH AGENT MIDDLEMAN TO WHOLESALER TO RETAILER TO CONSUMER. This channel is often used for the distribution of goods that are sold to the ultimate consumer by small independent retailing establishments. Where it is used, the producer is also generally small scale.

REVIEW QUESTIONS

1. Define and illustrate each of the major approaches to the study of marketing.
2. In what ways are concentration and dispersion similar to and different from buying and selling?
3. List the eight major marketing functions.
4. Trace the marketing channel from manufacturer to consumer for a product of your own selection.
5. List the types of ultimate consumer goods.
6. What is the marketing concept?

2

THE NATURE OF CONSUMPTION

Consumption is the use of goods and services for the satisfaction
of human wants. During consumption, the utility of goods and
services is ordinarily destroyed or impaired. For example, we consume clothes by wearing them until they no longer meet our
specifications and their value to us has been destroyed or lessened.
Consumption is not identical with mere purchase of goods because
some goods are bought for resale. Hence, the middleman does not
consume the goods in which he deals. Furthermore, consumers buy
goods in anticipation of future needs and do not consume them
immediately.

Basic Types of Consumption

Basically, there are two types of consumer and two types of
market for goods.[1] The *industrial* (or *business*) *market* is com-

---

[1] The term *market* is used in this chapter in its broadest sense to mean all the
potential buyers of merchandise; it does not here refer to a physical location or
marketplace.

posed of all the commercial and production enterprises that consume raw materials, fabricating parts, operating supplies, and equipment in activities carried on to make a profit. The *consumer* (or *ultimate consumer*) *market* is composed of the general public, who as individuals or as groups consume goods with the intention of satisfying their personal desires. The purchasing motives of the two types of consumer are thus completely different.

The Industrial Market

Scope of the Industrial Market. The industrial market includes the following groups of purchasers.

PRODUCERS. These business organizations (whether manufacturers or extractors) specializing in the production of goods require raw materials, operating supplies, and equipment; some require fabricated parts.

SERVICE ORGANIZATIONS. Service organizations need many materials for industrial consumption. A barbershop, for instance, consumes barber chairs, scissors, hair preparations, and many other products.

INSTITUTIONS. Publicly and privately owned institutions, such as hospitals, need certain products for consumption: food for patrons, office equipment, and medical supplies. Although some institutions do not operate for the purpose of profit making, they are members of the industrial market, and their purchasing has characteristics similar to those of other members.

GOVERNMENT. Government, which needs many products not only for the institutions it runs but also for its own operation, is another non-profit-making part of the business market. A city hall requires operating supplies and equipment; a state capital requires the same on a larger and more complex scale; and the federal government is probably the largest single consumer of industrial goods in the American economy.

MIDDLEMEN. As previously indicated, wholesalers and retailers are not consumers of the goods they handle for resale, but they are consumers of the office supplies, fixtures, and other commodities used in running their businesses.

Characteristics of the Industrial Market. The industrial market has characteristics that set it apart from the consumer market.

LIMITED NUMBER OF PURCHASERS. Whereas the consumer market includes everybody, the industrial market is restricted to the types of organizations listed in the preceding section.

LARGE TOTAL VALUE OF PURCHASES. Although prices of identical products are usually lower for the industrial than for the consumer market, and although industrial buyers are smaller in number, total industrial sales measured in dollars are larger than consumer sales.

LARGE-SCALE PURCHASES. Since the dollar value of products sold to the industrial markets equals or exceeds that of products sold to ultimate consumers, it is clear that the usual purchaser of industrial goods spends a fairly high amount annually. Inasmuch as his requirements are greater than those of the average consumer, he will be able to take advantage of unit savings on price, transportation, handling, and the like; his purchase at a single time will probably consist of many units.

PURCHASES ON A PERFORMANCE BASIS. Buying for the industrial market is normally buying to help a business make a profit. Consequently, the industrial buyer takes great pains to purchase the best quality at the best price. He compares one product with another in terms of performance. He considers technical points carefully; he may have his own laboratory check the products offered him. In some cases, he will buy according to specifications, awarding his contract to the seller who can supply the commodity at the lowest price.

DIFFUSION OF BUYING RESPONSIBILITY. As salesmen catering to the industrial market well know, there is no one individual in a plant of any considerable size who makes all purchasing decisions. Even where there is a purchasing agent, his principal function is likely to be placing orders for goods that have been specified by other members of the plant. The superintendent of maintenance may be responsible for choosing the products that keep the floors clean, the chief engineer may determine the choice of fuel, and the board of directors may decide upon major purchases. In many instances, a group of people within the buying organization will be responsible for decisions. The group is some-times called the *buying* (or *purchasing*) *committee*.

DEPENDENCE OF THE MARKET UPON GENERAL ECONOMIC PROS-PERITY. Industrial demand is a derived demand. All purchasing, whether for industrial or personal use, depends upon the economic well-being of the ultimate consumer. All industry exists to supply the ultimate consumer, directly or indirectly; and unless he is financially able to purchase, even companies catering exclusively to industry will find that demand for their own products has dis-appeared. Industrial machinery is purchased only to satisfy con-sumer wants indirectly. This means that during times of economic depression, the derived demand for industrial goods will contract more than the demand for consumer goods. People will still buy necessities such as food, but they will pay lower prices for them. However, they will buy fewer luxuries, and the manufacturer of luxuries who has been thinking of purchasing and equipping a new factory may hesitate because there is insufficient sale of his prod-ucts to justify such ventures. As industrial expansion contracts, so does the industrial market—and much more rapidly than the con-sumer market.

SPECIAL FACTORS INFLUENCING INDUSTRIAL BUYING. As we have stated, the industrial consumer usually buys products on the basis of performance, but there are some situations in which other factors become more important. For example, the mill operator whose plant has had to shut down temporarily because of breakage of a machine part will be interested in the speed with which de-livery of a new part can be made, assuming that different manu-facturers offer parts that work equally well. Even if the price of one manufacturer is considerably higher than that of another, the mill operator will choose the source that provides immediate delivery in order to avoid unnecessary delays in his own operations. More-over, there are situations in which reciprocity is the buying deter-minant. Some industrial consumers make a practice of ordering from firms that buy from them, even though this policy may entail certain disadvantages with regard to price or quality.

The Consumer Market

Scope of the Consumer Market. The domestic consumer market is composed of the entire population of the United States. It includes some 204.8 million individuals in fifty states. To describe all elements of the domestic consumer market would be difficult. However, study of several major factors in consumer buying should provide a practical understanding of the consumer market that will be valuable from a sales viewpoint.

A sales manager generally begins his analysis of his consumer market with a geographic description. He computes company sales for each sales region of the United States, and may even prepare a statement of sales volume by size of city and by total rural versus total urban sales. But his geographical analysis is only the start for sound marketing. Using modern research techniques, the sales manager may gather statistics about the sex, age, and national origins of his customers and prospects; he may want to know in what kinds of homes they live; he may want to know their economic status as indicated by income figures, rentals, or possession of luxuries.

Characteristics of the Consumer Market. This market has characteristics as definite as those of the industrial market.

LARGE NUMBER OF PURCHASERS. Each of the 204.8 million persons in the United States is a consumer. Even so, a good share of the actual purchasing is done by a relatively small number of consumers. The needs of an infant, for instance, are taken care of by an "agent," probably his mother. Various studies indicate that the woman of the family makes more of the purchases than the man.[2] Families with high incomes buy more than those with lower incomes.

GEOGRAPHIC CONCENTRATION OF PURCHASERS. Much of the American consumer market is concentrated geographically: about 5.6 percent in metropolitan New York City; 23.5 percent in ten metropolitan areas (New York, Los Angeles-Long Beach, Chicago,

---

[2] It has been discovered, however, that many purchasing decisions are joint decisions, with various members of the family participating.

Philadelphia, Detroit, San Francisco-Oakland, Washington, D.C.-
Maryland-Virginia, Boston, Pittsburgh, St. Louis-Illinois); about
54.5 percent in ten states (New York, California, Pennsylvania,
Illinois, Ohio, Texas, Michigan, New Jersey, Massachusetts, and
Florida).

GEOGRAPHIC SHIFTING OF PURCHASERS. Many population
shifts are taking place in the United States: from the East to the
West and Southwest, and from rural to urban to suburban areas.

SMALL-SCALE PURCHASES. The typical consumer usually buys
for current needs. Although he may have a large family and a big
house, there is still the problem of storage. This, added to innovations in food preparation and packaging, accelerates the trend toward frequent small purchases.

FREQUENCY OF PURCHASE. The smaller his purchase, the
more often the consumer must buy.

PURCHASE ON OTHER THAN A PERFORMANCE BASIS.[3] The
typical consumer is not a skilled buyer. He is influenced by all
kinds of factors other than quality, such as advertising and sales
talk. His untrained purchasing is done on a trial-and-error basis.
There is much evidence to show that he does not always get what
he pays for, that price is not necessarily related to quality.

SPECIAL FACTORS INFLUENCING CONSUMER BUYING. Many
factors help to determine the degree to which a particular segment
of the public is a market for any product or service. One important
factor is the number of social classes represented in the group. A
market may also be segmented in such a way that only a small
group can be considered an active market for a particular product.

Occupation. The occupation of the consumer will affect his
needs in various ways. People engaged in physical labor, for example, need working clothes that are different from those needed by
professional or white-collar workers. They also require food with
higher caloric content.

Income. In general, the higher the income, the more money
available for spending on consumer wants; but even the family
with the lowest income requires a minimum expenditure for food,

[3] See discussion of advertising appeals (page 200). These are sometimes described as *emotional buying* motives.

shelter, and clothing. The relationship of consumer requirements to income was first stated in *Engel's law:* As income increases, a smaller percentage is spent for food; approximately the same percentage, for clothing; usually the same percentage, for light, heat, and rent; and a larger percentage, for health and recreation.

Engel's law was formulated in Germany in the nineteenth century. Subsequent studies have revealed diversions from this law and have also substantiated some of its conclusions. Studies in the United States have shown that although a smaller percentage is spent for food as the income increases, a larger percentage is spent for clothing and miscellaneous items.

Nationality and Religion. The nature of consumer requirements, particularly for food and clothing, varies with national origin. Requirements also vary with religion.

Sex. Women do more buying than men, and the increased employment of women has augmented their buying power. It has been estimated that 70 percent of consumer products, on a dollar basis, are purchased by women. So aware are retailers of the importance of women buyers that one of the leading types of retail institutions, the department store, caters primarily to them.

Age. The consumer's age has a considerable effect upon the nature and extent of his needs. Medical advances in the past half century are responsible for a proportionate increase in the number of older people; the pill and ecological concerns have meant a decline in the proportion of children in the U.S. economy. Witness the catering to the older market (retirement communities) and the drop-off in catering to the young parents' market (Johnson & Johnson now offering its baby lotion for women's skin).

Size and Number of Families. In the past, there was a general trend toward large families in the United States, but many of the newer family groups are small. This mixed pattern has resulted in demands for both large and small homes. The rising number of families has resulted in an increasing market for consumer products such as household furnishings, appliances, and clothing.

Individual Taste. Although many factors influence taste, it is essentially a matter of custom and habit. The taste of a single customer may be unpredictable, but for marketing purposes, tastes can be measured in the mass on a statistical basis. A market research study can show what percentage of consumers will want each particular variation of a product.

Geography and Climate.   Weather conditions in various sections of the country affect food, dress, and other consumption. Southern California weather calls for habits of food and dress distinct from those of northern Maine.

Fashion.   Fashion affects marketing today more than it did only a few decades ago. Improved communication and transportation have meant a shorter life for fashions. New fashions get instantaneous national exposure through television, and fast motor and rail transportation get the fashions rapidly to market. For the marketing organization, risk and costs are greatly increased by the shortened fashion cycle. These increases result from the more frequent need for markdowns to move goods that have passed the peak of demand, from the tendency of the middleman to protect himself through smaller purchases, and from the need for higher-quality salespeople to handle fashion merchandise. The handling of fashion goods by a middleman requires that he decide where he belongs in the fashion market, that is, whether he should be a style leader selling exclusive merchandise or a style follower selling mass products at lower prices. His choice of location and of store architecture is governed by this decision.

Availability of Goods.   The commodity supply influences the consumer's purchasing pattern. If retailers are temporarily out of stock, consumers must accept substitutes or postpone or forgo purchases. Commodity shortages in national emergencies may create abnormal demands that stem from long-deferred opportunities to buy.

Price.   Generally, as price decreases, demand for a commodity increases. This holds true, however, only if the commodity is one for which the demand is relatively elastic.

Consumers' Cooperatives

A *cooperative* is an association of individuals (producers, middlemen, or consumers) who have banded together for the purpose of doing business at reduced costs. Profit for the organization itself is never its motive. It divides all surplus earnings among its members. In the *consumers' cooperative,* a group of consumers set up their own retail stores.

Characteristics of Consumers' Cooperatives. The following characteristics, in the main, will be found wherever a consumers' cooperative is examined. They may even be termed the *principles of cooperation.*

OPEN AND UNLIMITED MEMBERSHIP. Anyone may join the 'group. The most a person will be required to do is to pay membership fees.

DEMOCRATIC CONTROL. Each member is entitled to only one vote in deciding the policies and procedures to be followed by the cooperative.

LIMITED RATE OF INTEREST ON CAPITAL. Like all business enterprises, the cooperative needs funds to function. These may be obtained by borrowing, but a limited and less-than-current interest rate will be paid for the use of such funds.

SALE OF GOODS AT CURRENT MARKET PRICES. Cooperatives offer no reduced prices. Members and nonmembers alike must pay current market prices at their stores.

CASH PAYMENT. Only cash sales are made; no credit is extended to purchasers.

PATRONAGE DIVIDENDS. The cooperative does not distribute its excess funds in the way that business usually does. If the cooperative has an undivided surplus at the end of its fiscal period, it passes these savings (never termed "profits") back to its members in the proportion that each has made purchases from the store during the period.

SUBMISSION TO MEMBERS OF PROPERLY KEPT ACCOUNTS. Like any other business organization, the cooperative keeps books. Fiscal reports are submitted to its membership, showing income, expenses, and the current financial standing of the organization.

POLITICAL AND RELIGIOUS NEUTRALITY. The principles of consumer cooperation prohibit affiliation with any political or religious group.

EDUCATIONAL ACTIVITY. The consumers' cooperative has taken upon itself the definite role of a public relations agency for the cooperative movement. It attempts through lectures and literature to educate both members and nonmembers in the advantages and techniques of cooperatives.

Growth of Consumers' Cooperatives. Experimental attempts at consumer cooperation have been traced back as far as 1767, and until the first half of the nineteenth century, there were spasmodic efforts to set up cooperatives. However, the participants did not realize the unique nature of their approach or see their relationship to a cooperative movement. None of the early organizations survived.

THE FIRST STEP. The first true cooperative at the retail level, the *Rochdale Society of Equitable Pioneers*, was founded in 1844. This organization was formed in a small weaving community in England in a year of depression by workers who banded together to make their few shillings stretch farther in the purchase of necessities. Not only were they successful, but they set up the list of principles of cooperation that is still in use today.

CURRENT STATUS. The cooperatives are a worldwide movement, particularly strong in European countries, but important in the economies of many parts of Asia, Africa, and North and South America as well. In the United States, however, the growth of consumers' cooperatives has been surprisingly slow.

Apparent Reasons for Slow Growth in the United States. The reasons for the slow growth of consumers' cooperatives in the United States are conjectural, but can probably be found in national buying habits, the distribution structure, and the management and form of American cooperatives.

BUYING HABITS OF THE AMERICAN CONSUMER. Perhaps the principal deterrent to cooperatives is the relatively high living standard found in the American economy. Privation has not been common for extended periods of time, as it has in other countries of the world. The average consumer has therefore developed the habit of shopping around; true advocates of cooperation cannot follow such a procedure if they wish their organization to succeed. The consumer demands such services as delivery and credit, but cooperatives, when successful, decrease services to cut operating costs, and, as we have seen, offer no credit. Patronage dividends have never appealed to the average consumer; the amounts of dividends have not been substantial enough to attract a large membership.

Where cooperatives have been forced to add services, dividends have necessarily decreased.

NATURE OF THE MARKETING ORGANIZATION.   The form of the distribution structure in the United States has militated against the consumers' cooperative. Effective low-cost retailing, as evidenced by chain stores, supermarkets, and discount houses, provides severe competition for the cooperative. It should be noted also that many wholesalers have refused to do business with cooperatives for fear of antagonizing other customers.

Form of Consumers' Cooperatives.   Poor management has been characteristic of consumers' cooperatives in the United States. The members of these cooperatives are usually not well versed in business affairs, and in their effort to keep costs down, they have generally not been willing to pay salaries high enough to attract experienced, competent managers. As a result, inadequate management adds to costs. But perhaps a more basic difficulty results from their failure to start with a central organization. To a great degree, each cooperative has been operating on its own, and this has made large-scale buying impossible. To these handicaps may be added the fact that most consumers' cooperatives, although located on streets that have little traffic, do not spend much on advertising.

Outlook for Consumers' Cooperatives in the United States. The future of consumers' cooperatives in the United States does not seem bright. Economies sufficient to give them an advantage over large-scale competitors appear as only a remote possibility. In the past, federal legislation exempted their patronage dividends from corporate income taxes. Without such an advantage, the consumer cooperatives might find it more difficult to compete with profit-making businesses and still maintain their policy of selling at market prices.

1. Compare the industrial and the consumer markets in terms of characteristics.
2. Why have consumer cooperatives had only a limited success in the United States?
3. What types of purchasers constitute the industrial market?
4. List the principles of the consumer cooperative.

3

CONSUMER MOTIVATION

Buying decisions are complicated social phenomena and are not easily explained. The successful marketer must have some idea of their nature. Through understanding not only *how* the consumer behaves but *why* he behaves as he does, the marketer can make decisions that will tie in more closely with consumer needs and desires.

Need and Nature of Buying Decisions

Buying, a characteristic form of human behavior, stems from the buyer's desire to fulfill a need or to solve a problem, or both.

An important aspect of consumer motivation is the vast array of comparable products offered to the buyer in any one category. Most buyers are faced with the problem of how best to allocate a limited income for purchases. This is an overriding consideration beyond the emotional or rational elements that may have originally triggered the desire to buy.

Although active demand for a product may be stimulated and consumers may be motivated to buy, in attempting to make an actual purchase, they may find that a product is not easily obtained or is overpriced. Therefore, distribution of a product may also affect consumer motivation.

Buying decisions are extremely complex. Some motivations are learned; others are unlearned. Some are self-directed; others are primarily social in nature. Some are conscious; others are unconscious. Some are rational; some, irrational. Some are predictable; others are not. These are only a few of the dimensions in which motivations are complex.

Business Attempts to Stimulate Demand

In the competitive milieu, the individual marketing firm seeks to utilize knowledge of consumer motivations to gain market share. Through applying understanding of these motivations in the fields of product design, advertising, selling, and point-of-sale materials, the marketer hopes to stimulate buying demand.

Even today a considerable proportion of the marketer's effort is inept because motivations are so difficult to measure, understand, and apply, and yet marketers have been attempting to use such knowledge for centuries. The boot displayed outside the shoemaker's shop over a century ago was a simple reminder (based on sound psychology) that the shop sold boots.

Unlearned Behavior

Many psychologists and sociologists believe that all human beings possess certain fundamental and largely unlearned drives of a primarily physiological nature. There is no agreement among scientists in naming such drives (many, such as Freud, stress the importance of one drive over others), but most will cite hunger, sex, rest, and self-preservation. Although most social scientists agree that these drives are unlearned, none dispute that learning (or conditioning) influences the form that the drives may take.

Hunger is the drive for food, drink, and protection from the elements (shelter and clothing). In American society, satisfaction of this drive is achieved through purchase of a variety of goods and services. The choice of type of product and brand used is largely influenced by other social-psychological factors, not by the drive alone.

The biological sex drive is universal. Marketing applications of this drive take the form of communicating symbols or advertising that may be used to sell products dramatized or heightened by psychological overtones.

Rest is an all-pervasive drive resulting in desire for sleep and avoidance of physical and mental anguish. Many promotional campaigns attempt to communicate that their product produces these benefits by highlighting safety, comfort, or getting the most from the least effort.

The drive for self-preservation is also basic. Its application in marketing is indicated by advertisements emphasizing fear of the present or future. A good illustration is insurance advertising.

Learned Behavior

It is largely through learning that the basic drives are channeled and modified. Although psychologists and educators differ greatly among themselves with regard to the detailed nature of the learning process, there is one thing on which almost all agree: the *basic* form of learning. *Conditioning* (or *association*) is the key to understanding almost all learning. When a substitute stimulus can arouse the response first elicited only by the original stimulus, then conditioning, association, or learning has taken place. The means to the end are the senses of man: sight, hearing, touch, taste, and smell.[1] Psychologists have experimentally demonstrated many principles of learning of importance to the marketer. Only a few can be covered here.

Principles of Learning. A *fragmented stimulus may elicit total response.* This is known as the *law of redintegration.* In a practical marketing sense, it means that a slogan or a symbol,

---

[1] Psychologists classify the sensory receptors far more minutely than this, but such detail is not necessary here.

through repetition, may recall to the consumer the total description of a product. Examples are the slogan "It's the real thing" and the simple display of a red and white soup can.

The sum of response is greater than the total of its parts. This is the principle that when the individual does respond, his total response is more than merely the cumulative effect of many sub-stimuli or subresponses (the basic concept of Gestalt psychology). Ideally, if an advertiser gets a consumer to remember his brand as a result of advertising, he may get him to try the product. When the consumer does this, a new level of total response has been added, and the Gestalt principle is seen operating.

There is a better chance of reaction to the most recent stimulus. This is the *law of recency*. In advertising, it means simply that the advertiser who gets in the last word has the better chance of reaching the consumer effectively. For this reason, some marketing firms have placed heavy emphasis on point-of-sale displays, believing that the brand that gets in the last word right within the buying situation is the one with the best chance of being purchased.

But there are conflicting influences; neither the law of recency nor any of the other laws of learning works in isolation.

There is also a better chance of reaction to the first stimulus. The brand that the consumer tries first also tends to be in a preferred situation. If a woman, early in her married life, is reached by a specific brand promotion and buys it, it will be difficult for a competitor to convert her to another brand.

It is also true that as a result of either conditioning or learning, the individual hesitates to change because of fear of the new or unknown. Why change to a new brand when the old one is satisfactory? There is something threatening in the potential change to a new brand. The familiar brand is a part of the accepted way of things.

Too many ideas presented in conjunction repress learning. Known as *proactive* and *retroactive inhibition*, this principle simply means that if too many thoughts are presented to an individual in a short space of time, he will not learn as much as he will if he is given only a few thoughts. As applied to advertising, it signifies that to be effective, the magazine advertisement or television commercial must limit the number of ideas it tries to get across.

When conditioning is complete, response becomes virtually automatic and unthinking. Once the stimulus-response circuit has been used often enough in the human nervous system, it is largely automatic, that is, without conscious thought on the part of the individual. This process may occur for instance, in the case of brand buying, in which the choice is so automatic that the sensory receptors of the individual are almost entirely closed to the claims of any competing product. Such conditioning maximizes the problems of getting the consumer to change brands.

Learning is facilitated when an experience is pleasant or unpleasant. Purchasing experiences that are definitely pleasant or unpleasant may be recalled more readily than experiences that elicit an indifferent reaction. For example, if an individual has eaten at a restaurant where the service was unusually poor, he will recall this when he is making a decision to eat out again.

Sentiment or derived feeling states are directed toward persons, objects, or situations. The sale of many consumer items is affected seasonally by Christmas, Easter, and graduation time, occasions when sentiment accelerates purchasing.

Self-Directed Behavior

Relatively few cases of buying behavior are entirely self-directed, that is, without regard for the social sphere in which the consumer lives. However, some buying behavior indicates more motivation directed toward self than toward others. Health or self-preservation is one example. A person agreeing to an operation may be purchasing a service that he needs for survival, and his relationship with others has little to do with it. Purchase of a comfortable shoe is only secondarily related to style (the latter being a social factor).

Social Behavior

A person's behavior can be greatly influenced by his relationships with others. Most marketing men are aware that man, being a social creature, seldom does anything without considering the reactions of his fellow men. Social pressure and reaction is a key element in behavior and motivation. There are at least four levels at which this social pressure is felt: cultural, social class, family, and individual.

Cultural Influence.   The drives of human beings are socially conditioned from birth. Whether an individual lives in a primitive or a highly developed culture, he cannot escape its influence. The aborigine has simple product demands, although even these are becoming more complex. The modern American culture places a premium on different kinds of values: clothing styles, entertainment, brands, formal education, and the like.

There are subcultures within a culture; for example, there are minority groups in the United States whose buying patterns may differ significantly from those of the nation as a whole. Some of these differences can be described by region; for example, southern cooking is different from northern cooking. People of the same ethnic group tend to live in the same area; this social phenomenon results in fragmented but homogeneous markets. Therefore, if advertising, selling, or any other marketing activity is to be effective, the advertiser must consider the culture and the themes, and the taboos of the subculture and adapt them to the promotion of a product or service. However, in some national advertising, there may be an attempt to find the common appeal that may stimulate every cultural level in a country.

Social Class.   To help predict certain kinds of buying behavior and indirectly to explain certain types of consumer motivation, William Lloyd Warner and his colleagues divided American society into six categories determined by a combination of ethnic grouping, income level and source, neighborhood, education, house type, and occupation. These categories may be roughly divided into the upper upper class (old landed aristocracy), the lower upper class (nouveau riche), the upper middle class (well educated, professional, or owners of businesses with high income), lower middle class (average working people with moderate education and income), upper lower class (average working people with moderate education and modest income), lower lower class (generally, those who need social and financial aid). It becomes apparent that the social class into which an individual falls has a significant effect upon his purchasing power.[2]

David Riesman developed an alternative method of social classification that is helpful in understanding buying motivation. There are three kinds of people: tradition directed (old families who have inherited wealth, power, and prestige), inner directed (independent-thinking individuals who have a definite set of goals in mind), and other directed (those attempting to move into the upper classes or striving to be accepted by their peers). Riesman's categories should not be confused with separate strata. Inner-directed people may be found within any class; tradition-directed and other-directed will usually fall somewhere within the upper or upper-middle classes.[3]

No matter how consumers are classed sociologically, certain of their buying motives reflect a striving for status. Most people, regardless of social class, want to be accepted by neighbors and associates. Many want to emulate those in the class above, to gain upward mobility. Such desire for acceptance will influence the individual's buying habits.

Studies show that income levels of blue-collar and white-collar workers are closer today than ever before. Yet the sort of neighborhood in which each lives is markedly different. The houses and property of the white-collar worker are apt to be larger and better kept. The interiors of the homes of the two groups will also reflect cultural differences.

Family.   The social pressure of the family is also frequently present as a strong motivating influence in purchasing behavior. The woman of the family often acts as buying agent for other family members. Despite her personal interests, she is constantly aware of the likes and dislikes of the other members of the family.

Social acceptance within the family is also a strong influence in buying. A man with a teen-age son is well aware of this influence when the time comes to purchase a new automobile.

Individual.   The self-image of a person may affect his moti-

[2] W. L. Warner and P. S. Lunt, *The Status System of a Modern Community* (New Haven: Yale University Press, 1942), pp. 88–91.
[3] David Riesman et al., *The Lonely Crowd* (New Haven: Yale University Press, 1950).

vation. The self-image is how the person believes the world regards him and also how he sees himself. This belief is probably not accurate. A complementary sociological factor is the image that consumers have of a product, a brand, or a store. These images convey certain meanings or implications associated with the self-image or even with basic drives. An illustration would be the specialty shop in which a woman of a certain social class may do her purchasing; another example is the drugstore, which is seen as a buying source for remedies for more serious ailments than that represented by the remedies available in a supermarket.

The symbols used by the marketing man should tie in with these images. Knowledge of symbolism in imagery is important in the fields of advertising, packaging, and trademarks.

Rational Behavior

Buying behavior is often described as an attempt to solve a problem. This implies a rational realization of the problem and a rational solution to it in the form of a purchase decision. But problem-solving behavior of this sort is rare. Ultimate consumers face many problems that *could* be solved rationally in purchasing, but rarely are. Even industrial consumers, who might be expected to be completely rational in their buying, are not always so. A large glass company faced a serious problem in gaining industrial acceptance of glass tubing because a psychological investigation showed that industrial buyers had a subconscious fear, built into them from childhood, that such tubing was breakable, despite the fact that the company promotion had indicated that it was not breakable.

The rational process in problem solving, when it does take place, is stimulated by the problem or question. This is followed by deliberation and evaluation regarding the specific step to be taken. Before a decision is made, the individual tends to weigh all positive and negative factors. The decision reached may or may not be in the same direction as the one arrived at by nonrational processes, but the overtones of all the other influences already discussed are invariably present.

Market Segmentation

Market segmentation is the dividing of the entire mixed group of people that are members of a heterogeneous market into smaller, virtually similar subgroups that are like one another in some respect. In the case of mouthwashes, for example, there are at least two rather different purposes for usage. Some consumers use mouthwash for social reasons, that is, to keep their breath fresh. Others use mouthwash for health reasons, that is, to kill germs and prevent disease. People using a mouthwash for social reasons tend to buy one brand; those using it for health reasons, another.

Reasons for Development of Segmentation. At the end of World War II, it was widely believed that the American consumer was going to have restricted product choice because of the requirements of mass production. This did not occur partly because there was a decrease in the size of the minimum producing or manufacturing unit required in many product areas. For instance, with the development of the computer it became possible—without any loss in production efficiency—to have a long run of the same basic model of a car with almost infinite minor variations—in color, interior finish, and accessories. This was made possible by having the computer specify for each car on the assembly line what specifics were to be applied to it. The same computer technology provided the necessary items at the right point in the line at the right time to achieve each variation.

The rise in *self-service* also contributed to the development of segmentation. In self-service situations, the buyer was less subject to pressures of personal selling and began to devote his attention to locating the specific product he wanted. At the same time, there was a continuing rise in discretionary buying power, which meant that the consumer became increasingly willing to spend a little bit more to locate exactly the product he wanted. This fitted very well into the marketing plans of most manufacturers, who, faced with increasing competition, found it highly desirable to protect and improve their market position by producing items that better met the needs of a specific group of consumers.

Reasons for Importance.   There are two basic reasons for the importance of segmentation. (1) The consumer gets more nearly what he wants. (2) The producer is likely to have a more profitable product mix.

When Ivory Snow was introduced, it hurt the position of Ivory Flakes by appealing to a large number of Ivory Flakes' customers. When more was known about segmentation, however, it was possible for the manufacturer to introduce Crest without materially hurting Gleem.

Some Methods of Segmenting.   There are several different methods of segmenting a market.

Purpose for Using a Product.   The electric razor is used primarily for convenience. It is fast and not messy. The blade razor is used by men who want a close shave and are willing to put up with the fuss, bother, and messiness to get it.

Geography.   People in different parts of the country may want somewhat different products. There is little opportunity to sell skis in most southern states, and suntan lotion cannot be sold during winter months in most northern states. A major food company, knowing that one section of the country likes stronger coffee than another, uses the same brand name in both regions, but offers a stronger blend in one region than in the other.

Demographics.   Markets are also frequently segmented on the basis of aspects such as sex and age. Feminine hygiene products sell to women and girls in certain age-brackets only. Sugar-coated cereals are aimed primarily at children. Most beers are aimed at the middle-middle and the lower-middle income groups.

Psychographics.   This term refers to the personality or life-style of the particular market segment. It is assumed that the market for a product can be segmented according to the individual's personality or preferred mode of living. Although there have been a number of attempts to characterize market segments in this way, the approach has not been very useful. Personality does not seem to be that closely related to buying behavior.

Brand Behavior.   This method breaks out market subgroups according to behavior such as usage rate or brand loyalty. For example, it is believed that if the company can appeal to heavy users, it will gain more in the long run. This is presumably why one well-known brand of beer claims to be right "when you're having more than one."

There is considerable skepticism about the value of this approach to segmentation. Are heavy users really that different from light users, and is enough known about how to appeal to them? Is it really useful to appeal to those who have no fixed brand preference? Why are experts sure, first, that they can be reached and, second, that they can be held?

Steps in Segmenting.   The steps in segmenting parallel those in planning the marketing of *any* product.

Defining the Segments.   This usually is done through use of marketing research. Special surveys can be designed to determine whether the market appears to be segmented; there are even several different segmentation computer programs to analyze the results of such studies.

Tailoring the Product to Meet the Segment's Needs. Once the segment and its needs have been defined, it should be possible to develop a product to fit those requirements. Marketing research, in the form of consumer product testing, should be undertaken to ensure that the product really is acceptable to the segment.

Tailoring the Package to Meet the Segment's Needs. Physically and psychologically, the package and label of the product should also meet requirements of the segment.

Pricing the Product Correctly.   If the market segment shows a preponderance of those from the higher-income groups, and if product and package are designed to stress quality, then pricing should also be appropriately higher than that of competition.

Selecting the Right Outlets for the Product.   The specific market segment very likely has some concept of what the right outlets for the particular product are. They may or may not be the kind of outlets used by manufacturers of other products in the category.

Selecting Media That Reach the Segment.   This is a most difficult step. Sometimes there *are* no specialized media that are the best choice for the particular segment. On the other hand, if the manufacturer can designate specific geographic areas as his market segment, then one option is direct mail to all homes having the same zip code. Again, if he can define his market in terms of relative income level, there is a mailing-list firm that has names and addresses from all over the country classified in this manner.

USING THE RIGHT COPY APPEALS. Armed with reasonably complete knowledge about what kinds of people make up the specific market segment and what features of the product interest them, the manufacturer should be able to use those copy appeals that will attract attention and get action from them.

Conclusion

There is no one way or source of information that best explains consumer motivation. Consumers are subject to a multiplicity of motives, and these motives may reinforce one another or conflict with one another. It would be an oversimplification to say that any one element is the major factor in buying decisions.

REVIEW QUESTIONS

1. What are the principal drives underlying unlearned behavior?
2. Discuss some principles of learning that are important in understanding consumer motivation.
3. Explain how cultural and social influences affect consumer buying habits.
4. What is market segmentation? List some products and brands (other than those mentioned in this chapter) that are segmented.

4

CONSUMERISM

Consumerism is the philosophy and program representing the consumer generally and specifically in his relationship to the marketplace and to the quality of life. A company must be concerned about consumerism not only in its marketing efforts but also in its contributions to the quality of life, for example, in relations with groups (both employees and customers) and in issues of ecology (pollution, conservation, and so forth). This is the principle of being a good corporate citizen. In a capitalistic society, this has to be accomplished within the framework of making a profit.

History of Consumerism

Before 1900. The consumer's dissatisfaction with his role in the marketplace probably dates from the time of the Industrial Revolution, when he no longer could communicate readily with the manufacturer but had to deal instead with middlemen who had little to do with the production of the goods.

The negative reaction of the consumer was probably triggered by the development of national railroads, which brought about national distribution. Particularly in the case of foods, producers were not prepared to protect the quality of their merchandise. The first public pure food measure passed the Senate in 1892, but the House let it die.

The Early 1900s. This period saw the enactment of the first real legislation protecting the consumer. It came about in an interesting way. In 1906, Upton Sinclair's *The Jungle* was published. This book, which became a best seller, was an exposé of conditions in the meat-packing industry. It eloquently described how rats and poison were getting into the hoppers for ground meat; sausage contained a little more than the consumer knew or wanted. Meat sales fell drastically, and the packers were alarmed. As a result of public demand and President Roosevelt's support, the Pure Food and Drug Act was passed in 1906. This law banned transportation of adulterated, contaminated, filthy, or decomposed foods across state borders.

The Federal Trade Commission Act became law in 1914. It prohibited interstate advertising that was false or misleading and, hence, resulted in unfair competition.

World War I then intervened, and there was little further development in consumerism until the 1930s.

The 1930s. The onset of the depression created an atmosphere in which consumerism once again could flourish. Again, books contributed mightily to the movement. Chase and Schlink published *Your Money's Worth*, which was concerned with product quality and advertising. Another title was *100 Million Guinea Pigs*.[1] In 1929, Consumers Research had been set up to do product testing on a large scale, and Consumers Union was established six years later, with product testing as a base, but also with the broader purpose of leading the consumer into action to protect his rights.

Another war, World War II, then interrupted the development of consumerism.

The 1960s. In this period, writers again stimulated develop-

[1] For the interested student, here are complete references to these books: Stuart Chase and F. J. Schlink, *Your Money's Worth* (New York: Macmillan, 1927). Arthur Kallet and F. J. Schlink, *100 Million Guinea Pigs* (New York: Vanguard, 1933).

ment of consumerism. Vance Packard's *The Waste Makers* was highly critical of products and advertising. Rachel Carson's *Silent Spring* predicted the end of wildlife as it had been known if the chemical means of controlling insects were allowed to continue unabated. *The American Way of Death*, by Jessica Mitford, was an exposé of the ritual and costs of funerals and burial.

But perhaps the greatest stimulus of all was a book by Ralph Nader, *Unsafe at Any Speed*. It attacked the basic safety of automobiles and with the unwitting cooperation of General Motors (which settled out of court a suit by Nader charging them with harassment) made Nader a national figure.[2]

In 1962, President Kennedy listed the four basic consumer rights: to have safe products, to be heard, to choose, and to be informed. Shortly thereafter, a presidential assistant for consumer affairs was appointed.

In the decade since then, there has been more government activity protecting consumers than in all the preceding years.

Areas of Concern to the Consumer

Every aspect of marketing today is subject to consumer challenge.

Product. It has been charged that the consumer is given little role in product planning and that the social implications of the product are not considered. Criticism is leveled against planned obsolescence, that is, designing a product so that it will wear out or go out of style before necessary. Products such as snowmobiles are criticized because of the damage they do to the environment.

Product development also often seems to leave much to be desired. (A liquid dentifrice was put on the market before it was discovered that it eroded tooth enamel.)

The manufacture of products today seems to be at a particularly low quality level. Roofs leak. Mowers don't mow. Cars leave the factory with all kinds of defects.

[2] Vance Packard, *The Waste Makers* (New York: McKay, 1962). Rachel L. Carson, *Silent Spring* (Boston: Houghton Mifflin, 1962). Jessica Mitford, *The American Way of Death* (New York: Simon and Schuster, 1963). Ralph Nader, *Unsafe at Any Speed* (New York: Grossman, 1965).

Packaging and Labeling. There have been many charges in this field. One is that there are too many varying package sizes, particularly in the lines carried by supermarkets; this makes it difficult or impossible to compare prices. Another complaint is that some private brand packages are designed to look like national brand competitors.

There has been considerable debate about packages that are ecologically undesirable, particularly nonreturnable bottles and cans.

Labels have been criticized for not being sufficiently informative. Why should food labels not list nutritional information such as calories, the presence of sugar, the presence of saturated fats? Why should not labels always carry the name and address of the manufacturer?

Pricing. Much pricing is criticized by consumerists as being misleading. Sometimes prepricing (i.e., the manufacturer lists the price on the label) is deliberately too high so that the retailer can cross it out and show what *appears* to be a discount price. The cents-off label is particularly offensive to the consumerists because there is usually no easy way of telling what the regular price has been and whether the store-marked price includes the cents-off deduction.

Advertising. Advertising is the marketing function criticized most often. In a recent survey, fully one-half of those questioned said that they did not believe what they saw and heard in advertising.

Criticism is leveled at the *weasel*, a statement about a product or its benefits that is true but that lacks meaning or is irrelevant to the purchasing decision. An oven cleanser advertised that it "has 33 percent more power." More than what? Often, a product will claim that it contains more of ingredient X than its competitors. What is the value of ingredient X?

Television advertising, in particular, has been charged with being misleading. For example, a soup company put marbles in a plate of soup to bring the solids to the surface for a more appealing photographic appearance. Today, the FTC is clamping down on such practices.

There has been considerable negative reaction, too, toward

child-directed advertising. Many people think that it is overdone, that such advertisements tend to make children pressure parents to purchase products.

Promotion and Personal Selling. The retailer, too, has been charged with misleading and deceptive practices. One target of criticism is the *bait-and-switch ad:* An item is advertised at a very low price, but when the customer tries to purchase it, the retailer tells him that it is not a very good product and that he would be well advised to purchase a higher-priced item. Some retailers make it difficult for the customer seeking the price special advertised that week or day. It is often in an out-of-the-way location, or there is no shelf stock.

Personal selling has been especially attacked. Too many people have been approached by the unscrupulous door-to-door salesman who pretends that he is conducting a survey and then attempts a sale once inside the door. Another offender is the door-to-door salesman who uses the approach that his prospect has been especially selected or will reap benefits from helping the salesman find other prospects.

Personal selling has also been criticized because it is so often high pressure. Too often, the salesman attempts to push the purchaser into a decision before he has had a chance to consider all the points and alternatives. Many states now have legislation that provides for a cooling-off period of several days after the purchaser has signed a sales contract so that he can change his mind if he decides that he has made a mistake.

Services and Servicing. Numerous studies have shown that it is difficult for the consumer to get a fair deal from many kinds of service establishments. The auto-repair shop is high on this list. Many consumers have protested the way the telephone company charges for phantom work. A person moving into a new home has to pay so-called installation charges even if he is willing to leave all telephones exactly where the previous homeowner had them. Nearly everyone has had the frustrating experience of waiting for a repairman or deliveryman. When he says he will be there—if he commits himself at all—may or may not bear any relationship to the time of his arrival.

Consumerism in Other Countries

The consumerism movement is probably going on in developed societies all over the world. Certainly it is not limited to the United States. It is occurring, for example, in the Soviet Union. Two Soviet consumer advocates studied everything from rental contracts to dry cleaning, in terms of relationships between buyer and seller.

They reported that an apartment renter is fined—and rightly so —if he is late with the rent. But if a light goes out, and he puts in a call for an electrician, the electrician may or may not show up in a reasonable time, if he shows up at all.

As in the United States, these researchers report, the service establishment is often unwilling to guarantee that the repairman or deliveryman will arrive at any specific hour. The consumer must take off the whole day from work, and even then, the serviceman may not appear.[3]

The Response of Industry

For the most part, industry is responding well to all these criticisms. There are exceptions; one industrialist maintained that "we know more about the needs of the consumer than any government will ever know."

The minimal response a company can make is simply to react to complaints and inquiries from consumers. Some companies, for instance, are offering toll-free calls to customers who have either complaints or inquiries.

A more positive reaction is a leadership approach. In this case, the company assigns its own consumer advocate a major role in corporate affairs. He participates in all corporate decisions that have consumer implications and not only responds to the consumer as problems develop but actively leads the company toward innovation in consumer affairs.

[3] "Echoes of Nader Heard in Moscow," New York Times, 7 November 1971.

1. Define consumerism.
2. Which president of the United States was the first to acknowledge the rights of consumers? What were those rights?
3. Which marketing function has received the greatest amount of attack by consumerists? Why do you think this has happened?
4. List some additional criticisms of the various marketing functions that have been made by consumerists.

5

MARKETING MANAGEMENT

The concept of marketing management is relatively recent. This approach to marketing, evolving slowly up to the time of World War II, soon afterward became a necessity for a firm's survival. Originally, production and sales were considered the two major functions of a business. However, with the rise in discretionary income, and as the population increased and consumers became more knowledgeable and discriminating, business realized that it had to pay greater attention to the consumer and his requirements and demands if it was to survive in an increasingly competitive economy. There were other pressures, too. Automation was rapidly increasing production to the point where overproduction could become a serious problem unless new products were developed or existing products were tailored more to consumer demand. Improved marketing techniques (better marketing research and changes in retailing methods such as increased self-service, giant supermarkets, and discount centers) were both a cause and an effect of the change to an emphasis on marketing management. As a result of all these factors, the philosophy of managerial policy changed. It became consumer-oriented and more profit-conscious than ever before. Some writers feel that this was the start of a marketing revolution comparable to the Industrial Revolution.

Marketing Team

The growing importance of marketing in business operations has made it imperative to reorganize the marketing structure of businesses. Today, a large corporation usually has a vice-president in charge of marketing at the senior executive level, equal in rank to major executives of the business. Marketing operations are integrated at the top level with the other chief functions of the business and are often given more consideration in vital decisions than production, finance, or other functions.

The staff of the marketing vice-president is composed of managers of sales, product planning, advertising and sales promotion, merchandising, and marketing research. Each manager has an appropriate staff to carry out the specialized activities of the particular function.

Integration is again the key word; the entire marketing team and its effort must be coordinated to achieve effective marketing. The marketing research manager and his staff must furnish marketing intelligence with which basic marketing decisions on strategy and tactics can be made. Once the basic marketing plan has been determined, the product planning department must develop products required to implement the plan. Advertising and sales promotion, usually involving close cooperation with advertising agencies, must be tied in with the basic plan, as must merchandising. For example, the merchandising manager must make sure that the product is distributed in the number and kinds of stores specified in the plan. The sales manager and his staff of salesmen must make certain that they call on the right types of outlets, with the proper frequency, using the most effective appeals; in addition, they must see that the product or products get adequate shelf space and displays.

With the ever-increasing emphasis on consumer orientation and on a profitable volume of sales, it is the responsibility of the marketing team to adapt the business to the heterogeneous factors found in the marketplace.

The Marketing Plan

Elements of the Marketing Plan. If marketing success is to be achieved, the company cannot afford the risk of making decisions without some overall plan. The competitiveness of the market does not permit such a luxury. The firm without a basic marketing plan (which is, of course, constantly modified by pressures of consumer and economic change) is in serious danger of failing in its sales efforts.

It is the responsibility of the marketing vice-president to see that a marketing plan for the overall product line of the company is developed and that marketing plans for each specific product within the line are also developed. Further, it is his responsibility to relate these overall plans to production and financial objectives of the company.

The marketing plan, which includes both overall strategy and specific tactics, is put together as a result of cooperative effort among the several branches of the marketing team.

The sales forecast, put together by the marketing research team, is usually the starting point. Even this cannot be constructed without aid from the other marketing specialists. The forecaster must know plans for the product line so that he can make forecasts for each segment of it. He must have some idea of the advertising budgets because his forecasts will depend in part upon advertising pressure used. Thus, even the basic starting point of the forecast must include some elementary knowledge of what the rest of the marketing team has in mind for the year.

Once the forecast has been distributed to the remainder of the group, each member establishes his objectives and implements them with the necessary detail. The *product mix* (i.e., the proportion of each of the various products to be included in a commodity line or lines during the year) must be programmed by the product planning group. If styling is a factor, there must be predecisions about colors, finishes, and materials to be used; the number of each style must also be planned. Sufficient detail concerning changes, innovations, and new products must be provided by the product planning group so that the remaining marketing team members can put together their segments of the plan.

Decisions on product line immediately trigger a second problem: the pricing mix or strategy. Depending upon the financial objectives of the company and the marketing situation, the product line must be balanced so that the desired profit will be obtained under stringent competitive conditions. Decisions must be made about the range of prices within product line and related gross margins. Considerations of discount structures and whether or not the company should have a second line of products at a lower price as well as its top line must be decided upon.

The advertising group must also plan its efforts; most often it will do this in close cooperation with its advertising agency. The *media mix* (i.e., the kinds of advertising media) to be used must be planned, and tactics to be employed (timing and scheduling of the various advertising efforts) will also be determined. The second major portion of the advertising campaign, the advertising appeal, is also a necessary element of the plan. (This very important area is discussed at length in Chapter 17.) In marketing parlance, the advertising appeal is sometimes termed the *copy platform*. Other aspects of advertising such as cooperative advertising and advertising to the trade must also be reviewed.

The merchandising group, aided by the thinking of other members of the marketing team, will outline its goals for marketing channels required to make this a successful marketing effort. It will draw up a plan showing the nature and number of wholesaling middlemen and retailers required in each sales region. Requirements may well vary by product and even by price line within a product group. The objective will be to select a distribution mix that will assure proper physical distribution of the right goods at the right time at the right place at minimal cost.

It may be the responsibility of either the merchandising or the sales promotion group to recommend techniques to be used in securing wholesale and retail distribution, as well as ways to improve nonadvertising stimulation of consumer purchases such as packaging, displays, appeals to be used in selling to middlemen, and couponing.

The sales manager must also contribute his part of the plan if the whole is to be an integrated program. He must set up sales quotas for each product by region, which are determined largely by sales forecasts he has received. He must decide the amount of sales effort to be expended in terms of manpower needed to achieve these goals and must show the degree to which his present sales staff can handle the load. If new personnel is required, his plan will show the number and qualifications of staff members needed and will indicate methods and costs of recruiting, selecting, and training. In addition, he must make decisions regarding sales incentives to stimulate the sales force to reach the predetermined goals.

Integrating the Marketing Plan. When all elements of the marketing plan are delivered to the marketing vice-president, it is his responsibility (or one that he delegates to some portion of his marketing team) to put it together into a coordinated marketing plan. Although it depends on the nature of the product line, a separate marketing plan is usually drawn up for each product (but not for such specifics as varieties within a product). Once the marketing plan for each product has been put together, there is usually also an *overall* summary marketing plan for the entire company line.

At the time of putting together the marketing plan for a particular product, integration of all elements in the plan is crucial. It may be only then that discordant portions of the plan become evident, requiring further discussion between the marketing vice-president and members of his team. Once the plan is in finished shape, it is normally organized around four major elements: (1) the goals, (2) the marketing program, (3) the marketing organization, (4) the marketing budget.

The goals state the aimed-for sales, costs, and anticipated profits. Sales will be determined largely by forecasts; costs, largely by consideration of the elements in the planned program; and profits, by subtracting costs from sales. The marketing program includes a statement of the specific strategy and tactics required to achieve these goals. The marketing organization includes a statement of the detailed organizational team, inside and outside the firm, needed to execute the program during the period. The marketing budget reviews detailed costs of all operations needed to carry out the program. It will normally break costs into major categories by nature of marketing effort: advertising, merchandising or sales promotion, salesmen, and the like. The details of each set of costs will be indicated.

Executing the Marketing Plan. The marketing plan, once approved, becomes the blueprint for marketing strategy and, to a lesser degree, tactics for the ensuing year. (Some marketing vice-presidents actually have skeleton five-year plans as well so that they have some concept of their long-range problems.) If the planning has been sufficiently sound, there is usually little reason to make major strategy changes as the year progresses.

However, even though the marketing plan represents the best thinking of a marketing team, it is not to be regarded as sacrosanct and inflexible. Sometimes there are major changes in marketing conditions that could not have been anticipated, such as war or crop failure, which will mean that the very tenets on which the plan was predicated have not held true. In such cases, the basic strategy of the plan must be modified.

More common is the change of lesser magnitude in the marketplace. A new brand may enter the market without warning, necessitating strategic changes geared to meet the new condition. An economic recession may hit a particular region. A competitive brand may raise its level of advertising expenditures markedly, and the company competing may be faced with a decision about raising its own advertising expenditures. A small competitor may be bought by a large corporation, and company strategy may have to be modified to meet this threat. New distribution channels may show signs of strengthening consumer importance in the particular product field; this would mean consideration of modifying the company's distribution mix.

It must not be forgotten that markets fall within a cultural and social framework which may be affected by political or legal change. Changes in a company's position within an industry must be considered, as must the industry's position within the economy. All specific as well as general elements of an economy are complicated and interacting, and marketing management attempts to quantify as many of these variables as possible. From this information, appropriate mathematical models may be constructed (through the use of the computer) so that the effects of any significant change in the economy may be measured in advance.

This chapter cannot attempt to describe all the problems facing marketing management as it executes the marketing plan. However, the important point to be kept in mind is: No marketing plan remains fixed. The marketing economy is dynamic and variable. The marketing plan must be sufficiently flexible to adjust to variations in the economy.

REVIEW QUESTIONS

1. What are the steps in formulating an effective marketing plan?
2. Describe briefly the major elements of the completed marketing plan.
3. Discuss the factors that may necessitate a change in the marketing plan.

6

METHODS OF DECISION MAKING

To keep pace with the growing complexity of marketing, management has begun to use sophisticated methods in its decision making. These methods are derived from the behavioral and mathematical sciences. Their application has become more useful because tedious and repetitive computations have been transferred to the computer.

Management Science

The quantitative techniques currently employed as aids in decision making are derived from a field known as *operations research* (O.R.). Originally, this field dealt with the application of scientific methods, coupled with probability theory, to various kinds of business problems. With the development of the computer and with the increasing diversity of problems encountered in business, operations research has become known as *management science*. This term has come to mean a procedure that defines business problems and their alternative solutions and constructs appropriate mathematical models with related controls that may be applied to the problem or series of problems. Management is then in a position to select the most appropriate solution. A *team approach* is characteristic. Usually the team is composed of a group of experts in several areas, who aid in the definition of problems, suggest alternative solutions with the aid of operational models, and help to make the final decision that is optimal in light of the goals and constraints of the organization.

Sometimes, problems are peculiar to a single department or division of a corporation. At other times, the solution of a problem may affect many departments or divisions and will require the *systems approach*. This approach attempts to measure the effect of a decision on all the direct and indirect operations of a company. For example, a systems evaluation may be required when a company acquires subsidiaries operating in different fields. Management must evaluate the effect of such acquisitions on all activities of the subsidiary companies as well as resolve the problems arising from the need to integrate the acquisition with operations of the parent company.

Marketing research is the formal method by which much of the information required to construct operational models used in decision making is collected. The marketing research department is responsible both for the collection of data and for the tabulation and analysis of such data as they are related to market problems. From the analysis, management science specialists construct operational or mathematical models that will help in the solution of the diverse problems currently facing business.

Procedure in Reaching a Decision

Generally, decision making involves two kinds of decisions: programmed and nonprogrammed. Programmed decisions usually deal with routine business problems for which policies have been set, such as ordering office supplies, paying telephone bills, scheduling employee vacations, and recruiting salesmen. Nonprogrammed decisions involve nonroutine matters and formerly were solved on the basis of the executive's experience, judgment, intuition, or a combination of these factors. The nonprogrammed decision poses the greatest difficulty for management. For example, reaching decisions about such questions as the simplification or expansion of a product line, the value of a proposed acquisition or merger, the changing of distribution and warehousing systems, the measuring of changes in market share for a branded product, or the implementing of marketing plans with appropriate strategy usually requires an organized and well-ordered problem approach and the services of specialists in marketing research, mathematics, the behavioral sciences, and data processing who may work as a team.

The best procedure to follow in seeking a solution to a problem is a detailed series of sequential steps that serve to clarify thinking and may suggest an operational solution. The steps described in the following paragraphs provide an organized program for reviewing and evaluating a problem.

Define the problem.   Describe the problem that management is considering, indicating the limits (sometimes called *parameters*) within which this problem falls. This can be a most difficult step, but once a problem is properly defined in light of the objectives or goals of a company, it may be considered partially solved.

Construct a model.   A *model* is a shorthand way of describing a problem in line with what is actually happening in the business situation. It is anything that is used to represent something else. For example, the model for a particular problem may be a map representing a section of a city, or it may be a numbering system used as a method by which activities are tabulated and summarized. Models may be implicit or explicit. Many people carry in their minds models of problems that, in reality, are series of seeming relationships which lend themselves to a solution. These are *implicit* models and may reflect many of the intellectual and emotional biases that characterize subjective thought. Conversely, business uses the *explicit* model form that may be called a *mathematical,* or *symbolic,* model. Such a model, used to represent objects or events in a defined marketing problem, usually lends itself to an analytical operation that may lead to an acceptable solution.

Determine alternative solutions.   All reasonable solutions to the problem should be sought, and a model of each should be prepared. The number of alternative solutions will depend upon the problem objective. Once the model related to the problem and the models of alternative solutions are constructed, good business practice requires that the solutions be tested within the restraints of the system.

Evaluate the solutions.   Management is now in a position to judge these solutions with reference to the objectives of the corporation and the variables and restraints that characterize each solution. These alternative solutions are always given in terms of probabilities so that management's judgment may be abetted in making the appropriate decision. Marketing management then must choose the model that seems to provide the optimal solution to the problem.

Establish control procedures.   Once an operational model has been chosen, controls should be established to permit management to check on the effectiveness of the solution. For example, if a selected model is used to make a short-range forecast broken down on a month-by-month basis, management is then able to compare actual monthly sales with the forecasted monthly sales. When actual sales go below or above the preset mathematical control limits, the predictive model employed should be reviewed and revised if necessary.

Apply the solution.   The operational model with its control limits is now applied to the current problem. As data are collected, management will learn whether the chosen model has helped to solve the problem. Often, the operational model may be applied, but significant changes may take place in the market that may render the current solution obsolete. Therefore, management must go through the entire selection process again to overcome these unanticipated market changes. Much of the tedious arithmetic calculation can be expedited by the use of the computer. Changes may take the form of adding or deleting variables from the mathematical model, with subsequent changes in the computed relationships.

Business problems often must be dealt with in an aura of uncertainty. Frequently, decisions are based upon models that have been derived from fragmentary information or random variables (i.e., variables whose value is determined by random or chance process). As a result, some solutions with their appended probabilities may be misleading. As a general rule, therefore, many business executives treat much of the data used in an operational model as random.

Qualitative information also may create difficulties in constructing a symbolic model. Many of these kinds of data cannot easily be quantified, yet it may have a significant effect on what is happening in the marketplace. For example, such activities as advertising, public relations, and buying patterns may be difficult to quantify in constructing an operational model because they reflect peer and reference group stimuli.

Some business problems may be solved without recourse to mathematical models. Management may use a graphic method to portray all the relationships in a business problem that must be reviewed before the problem can be solved. The flow chart technique requires comprehensive knowledge of all the elements of a problem and of the kinds of information that are required to derive a solution. Once these steps, with their restraints, are placed in proper sequence in a diagram, a solution may be evident.

Examples of Mathematical Models Used in Decision Making

It is impossible, within the limits of this book, to describe all the various models that may be employed by marketing management in making decisions. However, certain techniques that have become well known and are widely used in business will be discussed briefly.

Linear Programming. Generally, this technique is applied to *allocation* problems, which are concerned with optimal use of scarce resources. For example, allocation problems may be encountered in the determination of a company's product mix. Problems of blending ingredients, production scheduling, inventory planning, and advertising mix also fall into this area.

In employing linear programming, a specific numerical goal must be set. This goal may be maximum return on investment, reduction of costs of an activity, or some such objective that can be represented as a linear function. If the activity is not linear, this technique may not be used. Every activity involved in the problem must be defined, and the assumption is made that there is one relationship between the activities as defined.

It is then possible to construct a mathematical model that attempts to determine the optimum allocation of these limited resources when there are alternate uses for them.

Most linear program problems are solved by using a computer that has been properly programmed.

Game Theory. This theory deals with systems in which two or more decision makers are in competition with each other. The objective is to select an optimum strategy with which to counter competitive activity. The goal of all game theory is to devise simple rules for making the decisions so that a player using the rules, or *strategies*, will win most often in repeated situations. Game theory has been applied to allocation of advertising expenditures, competitive bidding strategies, and relatively complex managerial problems.

Queuing Theory. This theory is a formal attempt to deal with the *waiting line*, that is, the problem of randomly fluctuating demand for service, for example, at supermarket check-out counters, airline ticket counters, tollbooths on freeways, or in any other situations where queues are apt to form. This type of model becomes a framework into which are placed historical data composed of the number of customers to be served and the number of service counters required. First, estimates of the solution are obtained; then, the best combination of costs and service demand is included in the solution.

PERT/CPM. Many business problems that require going through a series of steps before an objective can be achieved may be controlled by a method known as *Program Evaluation and Review Technique* (PERT) or *Critical Path Method* (CPM). The Navy Special Projects Office utilized some 2,000 contractors in the development of the Polaris system. Their diverse activities had to be coordinated closely to ensure the timely and successful completion of the Polaris. To achieve this coordination, PERT was developed. About the same time, the CPM management control technique was being developed by industry to meet similar problems. Although superficially different, both PERT and CPM proceeded from the basic concept of using a network as a model for an actual project. In marketing, this method may be employed in organizing market plans, distribution plans, advertising campaigns, new product development, or construction of new outlets.

Once the particular project has been defined in terms of individual activities, each of which may possess special characteristics and can impose time restraints on subsequent activities, the use of PERT can be extremely valuable. After the network has been assembled and the estimates of time have been provided for each step, it is possible to compute the *critical path*. This path is the longest time path through the network and is used for monitoring and controlling the project.

Most computers have PERT programs that make it relatively easy for management to apply network analysis to problems in which a series of steps and elements must be coordinated. A typical PERT program will list the sequence of events, estimate the time of each event, incorporate these findings into a network of activities and time, and permit the computation of the critical path for control purposes.

A simple example from the field of marketing research will suffice. Once the study has been authorized, it will be scheduled to cover a stated time period. Some phases can be worked on concurrently, but most are independent, and little or nothing else can be simultaneously scheduled. Sample design (determining who will be questioned) and questionnaire development can be handled concurrently. This part of the critical path is the length of time needed for the longer process. Field instructions cannot be prepared until finalization of the questionnaire; the next step (field interviewing) cannot start before this step is finished. Except for the data processing program, the remaining steps are all completely successive: preparation of the completed questionnaires for processing, data processing, analysis, and physical preparation and duplication of the report.

A related type of network analysis is now being used by business firms. This newer procedure is known as the *precedence diagram method*.

Markoff Process. This process is a method of evaluating the movement of some variable (e.g., the sale of branded shoes) to predict the future movement or market share of that variable. This process is used by marketing men to evaluate and predict the sales and market share of competitors' products if there has been no significant change in the competitors' strategy. Moreover, this process will indicate what the brand share of the market is now and how it may change in light of current market activity. It is an important method for maintaining a continuing picture of the trends and countertrends in the marketplace.

Usually, data used in the markoff process are obtained through marketing research. For example, to learn the future position of a branded television or radio set, data are collected by a retail audit of a representative group of stores. In this audit, information on how different brands are selling on a month-to-month basis is noted. These data are then incorporated into the markoff process to measure market share, brand loyalty, and brand switching by consumers.

Bayesian Statistical Method.   As previously noted, marketing decisions are often made in an aura of uncertainty. Often management is faced with reaching a decision when some of the data are in qualitative form, making it difficult to arrive at an appropriate quantitative decision. For example, many marketing problems are related to the effects of pricing and promotional strategy, package design, product guarantees and quality, and new product development. This information is generally found in qualitative form.

There are many techniques for turning qualitative data into quantitative material, but the *Bayesian probability approach* is the most orderly and consistent method. It is derived from an elementary theorem of probability formulated in the eighteenth century. Without prior knowledge of distribution of a statistical series, a parameter (i.e., an arbitrary constant or variable in a mathematical operation) may be computed based upon judgment, experience, or fragmentary evidence. A probability statement may also be made about the subjectively derived parameter.

In cases where no data are available, marketing management uses prior judgment coupled with the Bayesian method as a basis for making quantified estimates. In some situations, there may be fragmentary quantitative data that must be reviewed and then assigned a subjective probability through application of Bayesian techniques. With this probability estimate, the expected value of the parameter to be included in the decision model may be calculated.

In large companies, marketing management may be required to make a number of decisions that are related to a specific course of action. To assure optimization of these decisions and to learn how they may be related to subsequent decisions, it may be necessary to use the Bayesian method if the data are incomplete.

A marketing manager may find it difficult to arrive at a decision because of a seeming lack of data. However, after careful search, he may uncover sources of data that will bear on the final decision. It is never certain that the cost of obtaining new data will be outweighed by the subsequent decision derived from them. The Bayesian method provides the manager with a method for evaluating the new information and helps him decide whether the cost of collection of these data would be worthwhile.

Other Methods.   Many other methods may be employed in helping the marketing manager reach a decision, including techniques of information retrieval, applications of communications theory, factor analysis, theory of statistical inference, techniques of experimental decision, and input-output theory, sometimes used in intra-industry analysis.

Often there are very complicated problems which result in mathematical models that are too complex to solve. To deal with these problems, researchers may use *simulation.* This technique attempts to show in simple mathematical form the relationships that are amenable to an analytic solution of such a problem. In using simulation, however, it is necessary to simplify relationships; and because of the many assumptions that must be made in the simplification process, the derived models may be difficult to apply to the solution of the real problem. Simulation should be the last resort of management. Generally, it cannot be used to derive optimal solutions but may provide a basis for comparing several alternative solutions if the derived models are accurate enough to be applied to the problem.

A Word of Caution

Despite widespread use of the computer and of quantitative techniques in decision making, the solution of marketing problems continues to depend upon executive creativity, ingenuity, and analytical ability. No matter how sophisticated the mathematical techniques, the uses to which the analyses and comparisons are put are determined primarily by the knowledge and abilities of management. However, quantitative methods do provide additional bases for increasing the correctness of the final decisions.

There is no such thing as a static market; hence, there can be no such thing as total current information about a market. The best that the marketing strategists can do is to employ the available data and make the best decisions possible. If their planning rests upon current data that are wisely employed, there should be little need for marketing executives to face successive market emergencies.

The steady outpouring of data, important to the profitable operation of business and produced by private and public agencies, threatens to outdistance the ability to deal with it. Each technical advance produces a corresponding increase in the quantity of material that must be digested. Business faces the problem of keeping abreast of this enormous explosion of knowledge and new techniques of operation. Whether change is exploited profitably or is merely a bench mark of the obsolescence of a business depends on the ability of management to assimilate and utilize the reported results from research.

REVIEW QUESTIONS

1. For what reasons are nonprogrammed decisions more complex than programmed decisions?
2. List the sequential steps that should be used in an effort to arrive at an operational solution to a marketing problem.
3. Define operations research (management science). How is the systems aproach related to this?
4. Define each of the following terms: (a) linear programming, (b) game theory, (c) queuing theory, (d) markoff analysis, (e) Bayesian statistical method.

7

THE OVERALL MARKETING PICTURE

Marketing in the U.S. economy is vast, complex, and dynamic. Before examining the nature of its complexities, the student should have clearly in mind a broad concept of the flow of goods from producer to consumer. This chapter provides an overview of the entire process and gives a basic description of the types of producers and middlemen involved.

The Producer

Although production is not in itself a part of the marketing process, the producer does take the initial step in the process when he disposes of his goods. Basically, there are three categories of producers: manufacturers, farmers, and nonagricultural extractors of natural resources. These represent, respectively, production by man alone, production by man and nature in combination, and production by nature alone. Each category serves it own types of customers.

Manufacturers. This category includes primarily those establishments (known as *plants*, *factories*, and *mills*) that transform raw or fabricated substances into new products and that characteristically use power-driven machines, assembly lines, packaging equipment, and the like. It does not, however, include firms engaged in the erection of buildings or other fixed structures.

The materials processed by manufacturing establishments include products of agriculture, forestry, fishing, mining, and quarrying. The final product of a manufacturing establishment may be *finished* in the sense that it is ready for utilization or consumption, or it may be *semifinished* to become a raw material for an establishment engaged in further manufacturing. For example, the product of the copper smelter is the raw material used in electrolytic refineries; refined copper is the raw material used by copper wire mills; and copper wire is in effect a raw material used by electrical equipment manufacturers.

The materials used by manufacturing establishments may be obtained directly from producers, through customary trade channels, or without recourse to the market at all (in the latter case, by transference from one establishment to another under the same ownership). Manufacturing production is usually carried on for the wholesale market, for interplant transfer, for individual users upon order, and sometimes for direct sale to the domestic consumer.

In 1967, there were approximately 311,000 manufacturing establishments in the United States. The total dollar value added by American manufacturers was $262.132 million and the average value per establishment was more than $670,000. Despite this average, many manufacturing concerns are decidedly small scale. This means that they do an annual volume of less than $250,000, or employ fewer than fifty people.

To ensure proper perspective, it must be remembered that shipment of goods to manufacturers' branches and to manufacturers' own retail stores involves no change of title and that the goods so shipped are redistributed to other types of customers. It is pertinent to mention, furthermore, that 9 percent of manufacturers' sales are negotiated through agents, brokers, and the like.

Farmers.   According to the latest figures, there were approximately 2.9 million farms in the United States in 1970, with an average income per farm of $5,451.[1] Thus, farming, too, individually is a small-scale business.

Most farm products are sold through some sort of wholesaling middleman, with merchant middlemen taking precedence over agent middlemen. Farmers who live on the outskirts of large cities may sell directly to local retailers or local truckers, the latter usually reselling the merchandise in one of the wholesale markets. A small percentage of the fruit and other produce grown in this country is sold directly to the ultimate consumer through the medium of roadside stands, public markets, and door-to-door selling.

Other Extractive Producers. Although agriculture is technically an extractive industry, it differs from the other extractive industries in marketing methods. The others include producers who extract their products from the land (mine operators, oilwell operators), from the forest (producers of lumber and allied products), and from the sea (fisheries). They, too, are small scale in nature, and their production is typically small scale.

Most raw materials produced in these industries are sold to manufacturers or other processors; only a very small percentage of the fish and prepared lumber is sold directly to ultimate consumers.

The Wholesaling Middleman

The wholesaling middleman engages primarily in two kinds of activities: (1) selling merchandise to retailers; to industrial, commercial, institutional, and professional users; or to other wholesalers; and (2) acting as agent in buying merchandise for, or selling merchandise to, such persons or companies. This field is much broader than the usual conception of wholesale or jobber because it includes manufacturer-owned and manufacturer-operated sales outlets, agents and brokers negotiating sales (or purchases) for others, and assemblers of farm products.

According to the Census of Business in 1967, wholesale business

---

[1] U.S. Bureau of the Census, *Statistical Abstract of the United States: 1971* (Washington, D.C.: U.S. Government Printing Office, 1972), pp. 586, 599.

establishments were defined to include only recognizable business places whose annual sales were in excess of $5,000. An organization engaged in more than one type of activity was classified on the basis of its major source of receipts.

Size.   In 1967, the average wholesale establishment had an average sales volume of $1.475 million.[2] Wholesaling, then, is a much larger scale operation than manufacturing, and it is not surprising that many wholesaling middlemen help finance the manufacturers whom they represent.

Number.   In 1967, there was a total of 311,464 wholesale establishments. This, interestingly enough, is smaller than the number of manufacturers.

Location.   The number of wholesaling establishments tends to be in direct proportion to the size of the population in any area, as may be deduced from the table below.

According to the 1967 report of sales by wholesalers, the concentration of wholesale activity is still characteristic of the U.S. economy. One hundred counties accounted for 74 percent of the nation's wholesale sales in 1967.

About 54 percent of the wholesale business establishments were

Percent of Sales and Population in Various Areas

Location	Percent of Sales by Establishments Located in Each Area	Percent of Total Population
Middle Atlantic	25.6	18.4
East North Central	21.4	20.0
West North Central	9.4	8.0
Pacific	12.7	12.9
South Atlantic	11.4	14.9
West South Central	8.0	9.6
New England	4.9	5.7
East South Central	4.1	6.5
Mountain	2.5	4.0

Sources: 1967 Census of Business; U.S. Bureau of the Census, *Statistical Abstract of the United States: 1970* (Washington, D.C.: U.S. Government Printing Office, 1970).

[2] This is the 1967 estimate, based on a total volume of $459.476 billion.

located in these metropolitan trading areas, and they provided employment for 67 percent of all wholesale trade employees.[3]

Types.   Wholesaling distribution is handled not only by merchant middlemen and agent middlemen but also by producers' sales branches. The following table shows the relative importance of the various types of wholesaling middlemen in terms of sales in 1967.

Percent of Sales by Middlemen

Type of Middleman	Percent of Total Sales
Merchant wholesalers	44.8
Manufacturers' sales branches and offices	34.3
Agents and brokers	13.5
Petroleum bulk stations, terminals	5.3
Assemblers (mainly of farm products)	2.1

SOURCE: 1967 Census of Business.

Customers.   Although the industrial user was the major customer of the wholesaling middleman in the past, the figures reported in 1967, given in the following table, show that the retailer has become the most important customer.

Percent of Sale to Various Types of Customers

Type of Customer	Percent of Total Sales
Industrial, commercial, federal government, etc.	38.5
Retailers	39.4
Wholesalers	14.5
Export	5.9
Consumers and farmers	1.6

SOURCE: 1967 Census of Business.

[3] SOURCE: U.S. Bureau of the Census, *Statistical Abstract of the United States: 1970* (Washington, D.C.: U.S. Government Printing Office, 1970).

The Retailing Middleman

The retailer is the middleman who completes the marketing process by selling to the ultimate consumer.

Size.   The average retailer in 1967 did a volume of business amounting to approximately $176,000 per year.[4] This is about 12 percent of the average volume done by the wholesaler; the comparison further indicates the small size of the typical retail business in the United States.

Number.   During 1967, there was a total of 1,763,324 retail establishments, and these had 9,380,616 employees. Therefore, it may be said that the average retail establishment has fewer than 5 employees.

Location.   Retail sales within each geographic area are in almost direct proportion to the size of the population, as the following table indicates.

Percent of Retail Sales and of Population, by Census Area

Location	Percent of Total Retail Sales, by Census Area	Percent of Total Population
East North Central	21.0	20.0
Middle Atlantic	19.0	18.4
Pacific	14.2	12.9
South Atlantic	13.2	14.9
West North Central	8.4	8.0
West South Central	8.7	9.6
New England	6.1	5.7
East South Central	5.1	6.5
Mountain	4.3	4.0

SOURCES: 1967 Census of Business; U.S. Bureau of the Census, *Statistical Abstract of the United States: 1970* (Washington, D.C.: U.S. Government Printing Office, 1972), pp. 12, 743.

Customers.   The customer of the retail dealer is the ultimate

[4] Based upon a volume of $310.214 billion.

consumer, as opposed to the business or industrial consumer or the middleman.

1. Who are the principal customers of the manufacturer?
2. List the main types of wholesaling middlemen, indicating the relative importance of each.
3. What is the difference between wholesaling middlemen and retailing middlemen?
4. Give some examples of agent retailing middlemen.
5. In which geographic sections is the proportion of wholesale sales higher than would normally be expected from an analysis of the retail sales figures? How do you explain this exception to the rule?

8

THE WHOLESALE DISTRIBUTION STRUCTURE FOR MANUFACTURED GOODS

A *wholesaler* is "a business mainly concerned with selling to those who buy for resale or industrial use . . . for purposes other than personal or household use."[1] The producer who sells directly to industry or retailers is technically a wholesaler; the nature of his activities will be discussed in Chapter 11 under the topic of "direct marketing."

Types of Wholesale Organizations

As we have seen, there are two basic types of wholesaling: by a merchant middleman, who takes title to the goods, and by an agent middleman, who does not take title. These basic types may be subdivided in many ways, none of which is necessarily exclusive of the others: (1) by the areas they serve, (2) by the nature and variety of the merchandise they handle, (3) by the kind of services they offer, and (4) by the types of consumers they serve. The U.S. Department of Commerce adopts a somewhat different classi-

[1] Irving J. Shapiro, *Marketing Terms: Definitions, Explanations and/or Aspects* (S-M-C Publishing Company, 1973), p. 183.

fication, but based upon a similar scheme: its census categories include (1) service and limited-function wholesalers, (2) manufacturers' sales branches, (3) bulk tank stations, (4) agents and brokers, and (5) assemblers.

The Merchant Wholesaler of Consumer Goods

Functions. For both producer and retailer, the wholesaler of consumer goods typically performs functions of exchange, physical supply, and facilitating.

SERVICES TO THE PRODUCER (MANUFACTURER). As has been previously pointed out, the typical producer in the American economy operates on a small-scale basis and needs a variety of services. The wholesaler is able to offer him the following services.

Distribution. Because the wholesaler specializes in distribution, he can relieve producers of a great deal of the responsibility and expense of selling.

Evaluation of demand trends. Success in wholesaling depends in some measure on the ability of a wholesaler to know what goods retailers and consumers will buy; consequently, he develops an acute sensitivity to market conditions. He is able to suggest new products that the producer can successfully offer for sale, and he can give advice about packaging, size of units, or quantity of goods.

Transportation. Through large purchases, the wholesaler can obtain lower freight rates than the producer can when the latter makes small shipments directly to retail customers. Economies in packaging, billing, and accounting also result from these larger shipments.

Storage. The wholesaler has facilities to store goods during peak production; he thus has a reserve supply from which he can fill orders during periods of low production.

Financial aid. Financial support is offered by the wholesaler in many indirect ways. Through quantity purchases by the wholesaler, the producer can obtain quick income. The producer's sales expenses are less than they would be without the help of the wholesaler; thus, his financial burdens are lessened to that extent.

The producer is saved the cost of extending credit to many retailers, and in some cases, the wholesaler may actually finance the producer through loans.

Reduction of risk. Wholesale buying and selling reduce the producer's risk. For example, the wholesaler may purchase commodities outright and in this way reduce the producer's financial risk by assuming responsibility for losses resulting from destruction, deterioration, style changes, theft, fire, price changes, and uncollectible accounts.

Services to the Retailer. The wholesaler offers the retailer the following services.

Buying. This is the major service of the wholesaler. He acts as purchasing agent for the retailers because he knows their needs intimately. He has a staff of trained buyers who know products, markets, and prices. He assembles a variety of goods from many different sources and stocks these in advance of demand. These activities greatly facilitate the retailer's purchases.

Transportation. Most wholesalers have their own trucking facilities, which offer the retailer the advantage of flexible transportation. Moreover, transportation from producer to wholesaler usually costs less per unit than when retailers buy directly from the producer because the wholesaler buys in such large quantities that he can take advantage of carload shipping. Ordinarily, this saving more than offsets the charges for wholesale delivery service to retailers.

Storage. The wholesaler stores a large and varied stock of goods near the point of retail demand. The retailer is thus relieved of the need of carrying a large stock of commodities because he can obtain quick delivery from the wholesaler's stock.

Financial aid. The wholesaler's extension of credit to the retailer is significant because the retailer, being typically small scale, needs credit to operate.

Risk taking. The presence of the wholesaler in the market structure enables the retailer to make smaller purchases, thus passing back to the wholesaler the risks both of large stocks and of price fluctuation.

Market information. The wholesaler gives information to the retailer on such aspects of distribution as demand, merchandising, selling methods, store layout, and advertising.

Types of Merchant Wholesalers of Consumer Goods, by Area Covered. On this basis there are three types of wholesalers: national, regional, and local.

NATIONAL WHOLESALER. This wholesaler distributes on a nationwide basis with a nationwide sales force. He operates through branch warehouses, and his stocks, whether general or limited to a narrow line of specialties, are larger than those of regional wholesalers. Because of the volume of their business, national wholesalers can offer retailers the advantage of their large-scale and specialized purchasing economies, and they can extend liberal amounts of credit. The names of national wholesalers usually carry prestige, but their type is declining in importance. One reason for this decline is their lack of close personal contact with retailers. Because of the great scope of their territory, they seldom know the requirements of local retailers or of local wholesalers. Again, because of their scope, they cannot offer so many services as local establishments do. Finally, under many conditions, they cannot compete effectively with manufacturers who market directly to retailers.

REGIONAL WHOLESALER. This type of wholesaler distributes in two or more states but not nationally. Regional wholesalers frequently place emphasis upon private brands.[2] They have two distinct limitations: Although smaller in scope than the national wholesalers, they still lose much personal contact with their customers, and they have the additional problem of high-cost selling in markets that are distant from their headquarters.

LOCAL WHOLESALER. This wholesaler operates in a single city or a single trading area. The sales of any local wholesaler are likely to be relatively small (often less than $1 million annually), but collectively, the local wholesalers are major factors in the marketing picture, especially in the marketing of food. They have the advantage of knowing their customers personally and are able to judge credit risks more accurately than their larger-scale competitors. Because of their proximity to customers, they can provide

---

[2] In such instances, a private brand is a brand sponsored by the wholesaler.

quick delivery and at the same time have the advantage of operating at low cost. They have another advantage in that they can operate with relatively little expenditure for advertising and sales promotion. Among their major disadvantages, however, are the facts that they cannot buy goods in sufficient quantities to obtain the discounts enjoyed by regional and national competitors and that their assortment of stock may have to be limited in accordance with the less diversified needs of stores located in small trading areas.

Types of Merchant Wholesalers of Consumer Goods, by Line of Commodity Handled. On this basis there are three types of wholesalers: general merchandise, general line, and specialty (short line).

GENERAL MERCHANDISE WHOLESALER. This kind of wholesaler carries a broad variety of nonperishable, nonstyle items such as hardware, automobile equipment, electrical supplies, plumbing supplies, furniture, drugs and cosmetics, farm implements, and other hard goods. His customers include varied retail outlets such as general stores, hardware stores, drugstores, and electrical appliance shops. Because he stocks a wide variety of merchandise, his major limitation is in lack of specialization.

GENERAL-LINE WHOLESALER. This type of wholesaler carries a complete line of commodities in some single field, such as dry goods, groceries, wearing apparel, hardware, or paints. He often specializes in convenience goods, and he stocks several brands of each product. Because of the narrow range of his line, he can meet most of the demands of his customers, who operate single- or limited-line stores. The typical order received from each customer is reasonably large.

SPECIALTY WHOLESALER. The specialty wholesaler stocks a narrow range of products within a circumscribed field; for example, instead of groceries in general, he may handle only canned foods. Within his particular province, he carries a wide variety of stock. His chief customer is the specialty store. His advantages over merchandise and general-line competitors are: the fact that he has a wide number of brands to offer; the fact that he buys in large quantities and is a buying specialist, an advantage that can be handed on in savings to his retailer customers; the fact that as an expert in a narrow field, he can provide unusually reliable market information to the retailers to whom he caters. His disadvantages are the following: He can prosper only within a well-developed and concentrated market, usually only within a large urban community; his costs are high because his dealings are restricted to a single line; although he needs regular clients in order to operate effectively, he finds that many of his customers prefer to spread their purchases; and finally, he is forced to meet increased competition from specialty departments set up by general wholesalers.

Types of Merchant Wholesalers of Consumer Goods, by Amount of Service Offered. According to this classification there are two general types of merchant wholesalers: those who provide all the regular services and those who provide only a limited number.

SERVICE WHOLESALER. In distribution of consumer goods, the service wholesaler (variously known as the *full-function*, the *full-service*, or simply, the *regular wholesaler*) is the most common; he extends to the producer and the retailer most of the services listed on pages 67–68. He maintains his own sales force and makes some 90 percent of his total sales to retailers. His stock is likely to contain between 2,000 and 250,000 different items assembled from a wide variety of sources.

LIMITED-FUNCTION WHOLESALER. Limited-function (or *limited-service*) wholesalers perform only a part of the regular services. Such establishments fall into at least five distinct categories.

Cash-and-carry wholesaler. This wholesaler maintains a warehouse, usually operated by one man; sells only on a cash basis; and requires customers to transport their purchases. He has the following advantages over other kinds of wholesalers: He can usually offer lower prices because of lower expenses and thus appeal to small retailers who are trying to compete with large retailers; and furthermore, he can conduct his business with a minimum of advertising and sales effort. The cash-and-carry wholesaler is able to offer large and readily available stocks to his customers, although these are necessarily limited to commodities that can be easily transported and that can be handled by one individual. He has the following disadvantages: He cannot give expert market advice to the retailer because he lacks the specialist's knowledge of distribution, and he does not pay the costs of transportation, which must be paid by the customer.

Drop shipper (or desk jobber). This wholesaler obtains orders from retailers and sends the orders directly to producers. He maintains an office but has no warehouse because he stores no goods. His advantages are: He can offer quick and relatively inexpensive delivery because the commodities go directly from producer to retailer without the intervening costs of shipment to a warehouse (since he takes title to the commodities, he assumes responsibility for their delivery and thus performs part of the function of risk taking); moreover, unlike his cash-and-carry competitor, he can offer credit to customers. The disadvantages of the drop shipper are as follows: He must purchase and sell in carload lots; his retail customers must be willing to accept merchandise in original containers and to assume the cost of unpacking and any necessary repacking; he must contend with the resentment of manufacturers who feel that he is making a profit without offering them any particular advantages; and he will find his business particularly difficult to manage if he combines it with service wholesaling because then his customers will expect drop-shipment prices on goods that are regularly handled and stored by the full-function wholesaler.

Wagon (or truck) wholesaler. This wholesaler carries his stock in a truck and sells only from it. Because of his unusual techniques of combining storage with transportation, he can provide immediate delivery of small lots. He successfully handles advertised perishable commodities such as groceries and tobacco products; he assumes the risk for such commodities, relieves the retailer from the possibility of loss through spoilage, and at the same time minimizes the risk by having a fast turnover for his stock. He need offer no credit unless he finds it profitable to do so in special cases. The wagon wholesaler operates under the following disadvantages: His line of goods must be extremely limited; his truck may be idle much of the time, for many manufacturers will hesitate to distribute through him because they cannot always find him when they need him or because they regard him per se as a poor businessman and a poor credit risk; his sales cost and, therefore, his prices are sometimes high because of his outmoded business methods.

Mail-order wholesaler. This wholesaler receives and fills orders by mail. He deals most often in staple items such as automobile equipment, clothing and furnishings, drugs and drug sundries, and machinery. Such products can be ordered by specification or brand. The mail-order wholesaler may sell specialties and novelties that are not readily available from other wholesalers. For obvious reasons, he avoids perishable or style goods. His disadvantages include a high cost of doing business chiefly because of the expense of the catalog (his sales volume may not be sufficiently large to absorb this cost) and the reluctance of retailers to order by mail (it is easier for many retailers to order directly from a salesman or by telephone).

Retailer-wholesaler warehouse. This warehouse is owned and operated by a retailers' cooperative or by a wholesaler who sponsors a voluntary chain of retail stores.

Rack jobber. With the growth of supermarket merchandising, a new form of middleman, the rack jobber, has evolved. The rack jobber specializes in products such as housewares, cosmetics, and drugs. He supplies stock, sets up displays, and is paid only for that stock which his customer actually sells.

The Merchant Wholesaler of Industrial Goods

Functions. Like his counterpart in the consumer field, the industrial wholesaler performs services both for the producers whose goods he handles and for his business and industrial customers. He assists the producers in selling, in matters of transportation and storage, and in financing and risk-taking. He helps industrial consumers by making efficient and economical buying possible and by anticipating their needs. He calls on his specialized knowledge in searching for the best sources of supply. The industrial wholesaler provides rapid transportation at low unit cost, an advantage which his customers would not have if they ordered directly from manufacturers. He makes it unnecessary for industrial consumers to carry large stocks of commodities, since he has storage facilities. In addition, he frequently helps to finance his customers by extending credit, and he provides information on prices and goods.

Types of Establishment. Merchant wholesalers of industrial goods may be considered in three broad groups.

THE MILL-SUPPLY WHOLESALER. The mill-supply wholesaler (frequently referred to as the mill-supply house) markets to all types of industrial consumers. He typically offers a broad line of merchandise and a large selection (ranging from 20,000 to 30,000 items)[3] of staple commodities such as equipment, accessories, and standard parts and supplies. His greatest advantage is that he can guarantee quick delivery of materials that are needed suddenly, for he maintains stocks close to his market. He acts as purchasing agent for his customers, buying in large enough quantities to obtain maximum discounts both from manufacturers and from transportation companies. Like most other wholesalers, the mill-supply wholesaler extends credit to his customers and provides information such as technical data concerning merchandise.

SINGLE-LINE WHOLESALER. This type of industrial wholesaler concentrates upon one family of commodities, such as electrical goods, steel, paper, or chemicals. He offers an intensive coverage of his line and serves as purchasing specialist for his customers. Like the mill-supply wholesaler, he carries a large stock near the point of demand and can furnish quick transportation. He, too, extends credit and is a source of information for the small-scale industrial consumer.

WHOLESALER SPECIALIZING IN CUSTOMER TYPES. An industrial wholesaler may limit his line to fit the precise needs of a particular class of customer, such as the dental profession, the oil industry, or agriculture. He has a full stock of items needed by his restricted clientele but does not handle additional lines, such as electrical, steel, paper, or chemical goods. More than other wholesalers, he is an expert purchasing agent. Like the others, he locates his warehouse near his customers so that he can provide fast delivery, he extends credit, and he is a source of technical information concerning the products in which he specializes.

---

[3] A specialty mill-supply house, such as an electronics parts wholesaler, typically handles 5,000 to 6,000 items. A large general-type mill-supply house may handle as many as 65,000 items.

The Agent Middleman

The agent middleman in wholesaling does not take title to goods. There are several types: the broker, the commission merchant, the manufacturers' agent, the selling agent, and the resident buyer. They normally handle consumer goods, industrial goods, or both.

Broker. The broker specializes in particular commodities, usually for sale to wholesalers. He has virtually no freedom in arranging terms of sale and has no permanent relationship with the principals. He facilitates selling or buying for clients whom he represents.

A broker's selling services may be an advantage to manufacturers whose production is small, seasonal, or not worth the investment in a sales force; to those whose market is scattered or distant from the point of production; to those wishing to introduce a new product (the manufacturer uses his own sales force once the product has been introduced by the broker); and to all his clients who have need of market information and advice about buying or selling.

Brokers cannot be used effectively unless the product is highly standardized and available from many sources. Further, brokers may display favoritism in selecting products to be sold and may not have the same vital interest in completing the sale as the producer's own sales force has.

Commission Man. The commission man, or commission *merchant*, operates primarily in produce markets. His main function is to find potential buyers and to secure the best possible price. He sells without giving advance notice to the owner, and his dealings need no confirmation by the owner. The commission man stores goods in warehouses and makes deliveries to purchasers; he may supply credit at his own risk; and because he knows the nature of the goods and the sources of supply and demand intimately, he may provide marketing information to both seller and buyer. He collects proceeds of the sale and deducts costs and commission before remitting the remainder to the principal.

Manufacturers' Agent (or Representative). The manufacturers' agent works under long-term agreements with one or more manufacturers to market portions of their output in a limited territory and in accordance with terms dictated by the manufacturers. Although he may represent several organizations producing non-competing products, he handles a limited line of goods. Because his line is restricted, he offers specialty selling superior to that of the typical wholesaler. Like the commission merchant, he often stores goods and makes deliveries. Like most wholesalers, he is a source of information and advice, particularly to the producer, whom he is likely to advise on styling and design. Because he has an established clientele, he is useful in introducing new products; he is useful also if he covers areas of sparse demand to which it would not be profitable for a producer to send salesmen. Because he is paid commission only on the items he sells, he may be useful when a manufacturer's output is too small or has a unit value too low to warrant employment of salesmen.

Selling Agent.   The selling agent is a middleman who, under a long-term contract, handles the entire output of a particular producer with almost complete freedom in arranging prices and sales conditions. He rarely carries any extended amount of stock because the manufacturer he represents usually delivers directly to buyers from his own stock. The selling agent's strongest point is the kind of representation he offers: He maintains a competent sales force, supplies showrooms, and may even take charge of advertising. He is useful in still other ways: Frequently, he helps finance the producer by endorsing notes, guaranteeing accounts, or paying the producer even before he has collected money from sales (obviously, in performing these services, he absorbs risk); and like the manufacturers' agent, he often advises the producer on prices, styles, and designs. Selling agents are depended upon mainly by producers who have limited lines requiring broad distribution and continuous representation. There are cases in which their services are patently unsatisfactory: Sometimes a selling agent represents competing producers and is, therefore, not qualified to give any employer unbiased representation; sometimes he attempts to increase sales through price cutting, yet he must be given a free hand with regard to prices if his bargaining power is to be unhampered.

Resident Buyer and Purchasing Agent.   Two types of agent middlemen, both working under long-term contracts, represent customers rather than producers. They seek out sources of supply rather than markets. The *resident buyer* usually represents retail stores and tends to specialize in style goods; the *purchasing agent* usually represents industrial consumers. In a sense, the principal function of both is to provide clients with information on prices, qualities, grades, and styles, although they may facilitate sales by seeing that the sources will make deliveries on schedule. Because these middlemen represent the purchasers, they must be distinguished from commission merchants, who resemble them in activity but who receive their profits from sellers and who may therefore be tempted to recommend poor bargains.

Miscellaneous Agent Middlemen.   Three miscellaneous types of middlemen are important in the distribution of manufactured goods. First, there is the *auction firm*, which operates on the wholesale level to facilitate transfer of goods. Second, there is the *import-and-export* agent, located in the United States but handling foreign goods for domestic sale or domestic goods for foreign sale. Third, there is the *factor*, found particularly in the textile field, who specializes in financing producers by purchasing accounts receivable and in supplying sales and market information. (There are other types of agent middlemen who specialize in the collection and dissemination of information about the marketing of manufactured goods, such as advertising agencies and market research agencies.)

REVIEW QUESTIONS

1. What services does the merchant wholesaler of consumer goods perform for the producer?
2. List and define the types of merchant wholesalers of consumer goods, by area covered.
3. List and define the types of merchant wholesalers of consumer goods, by line of commodity handled.
4. List and define the types of merchant wholesalers of industrial goods.
5. List and define the types of agent middlemen.

9

THE WHOLESALE DISTRIBUTION STRUCTURE FOR AGRICULTURAL GOODS

Although the American economy is no longer predominantly agrarian and agriculture now supports only 4.8 percent of American families, it still largely supplies the population with two of the few absolute necessities of life: food and clothing. Characteristics peculiar to this vast agricultural enterprise affect the marketing structure and necessitate marketing practices differing considerably from those applicable to other kinds of goods.

Factors Affecting Farm Marketing

Characteristics of Agricultural Production. Farming, as we have seen, is generally a *small-scale* business. Unlike many other types of production, it is not geographically concentrated; in 1970, there were 2.924 million farms in the United States, scattered throughout the country. Changing and often unpredictable weather causes farming conditions to vary continually and limits the farmer's control over the quality and quantity of his output. Farming also differs from other types of production in that it is simultaneously *specialized* and *diversified*. The owner of a farm may specialize in the raising of one or more commodities, but at the same time, he may raise subsidiary products that require a completely different type of marketing. For example, the farmer who specializes in growing corn may raise hogs secondarily. If so, a major part of his corn may be sold commercially as grain, and a sizable part may be reserved for feeding hogs that are to be sold as meat products. He may grow other crops that are partly for his household consumption and partly for market consumption, and in addition, he may raise chickens and cows. His marketing problem, consequently, is more complicated than that of a manufacturer who chooses a location favorable for marketing, adjusts the quantity and quality of his output to fit current demand, and specializes in a line of goods that can be sold through a single marketing channel.

Characteristics of Agricultural Products.   Besides the weather and seasonal problems, farmers have to contend with the *bulkiness* and *high perishability* of their products. These two characteristics create special difficulties in marketing.

Characteristics of the Consumption of Agricultural Products. Although farm products are grown in rural regions, most consumption is concentrated in urban regions, often many miles from the source. A small percentage of farm products is used in the area where they are grown. This means that farm products must be distributed all over the United States through many kinds of middlemen and that raw or processed farm goods are costly to the ultimate consumer regardless of the profit to the producer. The demand is constant, although the quantity and quality of production are unpredictable. The consumer demand will not change (except for so-called luxury items) because of shortages or surpluses, nor can the volume of demand be regulated by manipulation of prices.

Total Effect of These Characteristics upon the Agricultural Market.   In the distribution of agricultural commodities from producer to ultimate consumer, there may be as many as three distinct types of wholesale market used: (1) a local wholesale or *growers' market*, (2) a central or *terminal market*, (3) a secondary central or *secondary terminal market*. These three types of wholesale market are necessary because of small-scale and somewhat specialized agricultural production and small-scale but generalized ultimate-consumer demand. Specialized production requires local concentration, which occurs at the growers' market. Similar products must then be gathered from numerous growers' markets over an area of many miles, and here the two types of terminal market are utilized.

Because of variations in the quality of the products, they must be graded and standardized. This is done by the wholesaling middlemen, who also supply transportation from farmers to consumers and storage to care for consumers' steady demand.

The Local Wholesale Market

The local growers' market (sometimes called the *country shipping point*) is the first place of concentration. It is situated near a local production area, and it is operated by wholesaling middlemen who specialize in handling farm commodities.

Functions. This market performs the following marketing functions: (1) *grading* and *standardizing*; (2) *buying*; (3) *selling* to other middlemen; (4) *financing* the farmer by extending him credit throughout the year; (5) *risking* by taking physical possession of goods, thus accepting the risks involved in possible deterioration, price changes, and the like; (6) *supplying market information* not only to the local operators in the market but also to central and terminal markets if they exist; (7) *storage* of commodities it has purchased; and (8) *transportation* of commodities.

Types of Middlemen in the Local Wholesale Market. Four different types of middlemen are customers in the growers' market. First, there are *local buyers*, either merchant or agent, traveling or resident, who pay cash to the farmer for his produce. Second, there are *representatives of the central market*, who purchase largely from the local buyers instead of from the farmers. Third, there are *local retailers*, who purchase directly from the farmers for resale to ultimate consumers. Although local retailers buy only in small quantities, they are regular customers. Fourth, there are *representatives of cooperative associations* (this type is discussed on page 84).

Additional Facts about the Local Wholesale Market. Each local growers' market specializes in one product or group of products; separate markets exist for cattle, cotton, apples, citrus fruits, wheat, and so on. The kinds of middlemen buying in such a market vary with the product. In a few cases, such as tobacco marketing, the local market is identical with the central market.

The Central Wholesale Market

The central wholesale market has many names, including *primary central market* and *terminal market*. Here the products from a number of local farm markets are concentrated and then dispersed to other regions. The central market for very perishable products is situated in the production area; for less perishable products, it may be situated out of the area. But it is always a center of transportation. The central market is less specialized than the local market because it tends to assemble many varieties of products within a broad related field. If it handles wheat, for instance, it handles rye and other grains; and if it handles citrus fruits, it deals in other fruits.

Functions.   Like the local market, the central wholesale market performs all marketing functions, but on a larger scale and with better facilities. Its functions of exchange are, of course, outstanding. It buys from the local markets or sometimes directly from large producers situated in accessible areas, and it sells to middlemen or sometimes directly to large industrial consumers. So important are these functions that two distinctive types of facilities have been developed for performing them: the *auction* and the *commodity exchange*.[1]

The functions of physical supply also are important. The transportation provided usually means free delivery from the seller to

[1] The *auction* handles largely farm products of high perishability, title to which must be transferred rapidly if the marketing process is to be completed before deterioration occurs. The sellers in the auction are usually middlemen of the central market; the buyers are industrial consumers, large-scale retailers, speculators, and representatives of the secondary central market. The *commodity exchange* is concerned with relatively durable products. Its functions, although similar to those of the auction, are of a more extensive nature. It provides a trading place operating under standard rules, and as explained on pp. 251–252, it offers a method of reducing risk. Both the auction and the commodity exchange perform functions other than those of buying and selling.

the carrier and the making of arrangements for further delivery to the purchaser; large storage facilities are available in or around the central market; and special protection is given to perishable commodities. Financing is one of the central wholesale market's functions. The middleman frequently requires cash in order to carry on his business, and this is provided in the form of negotiable warehouse receipts whereby the middleman who stores a commodity may obtain a loan. Risk taking is another of the facilitating functions commonly performed by all operators in the central market. Finally, the products are graded. Some of the middlemen are so skilled in this task that they make a profit merely from regrading the commodities from the local wholesale markets.[2]

Types of Middlemen in the Central Wholesale Market.   The middlemen may be grouped into four main classes. Two classes, *domestic merchants* and *domestic agents*, will be described in this section. A third class is *representatives of cooperatives*. The fourth, *international middlemen* dealing in imports and exports, falls beyond the province of domestic marketing.

DOMESTIC MERCHANT.   Merchant wholesalers in central markets have various names, depending upon the type of product handled. In fruit and vegetable markets they are termed *carlot wholesalers* or *wholesale receivers* because they receive carload shipments, break these into smaller lots, and resell them to the secondary central market or to large retail producers.[3] In a market handling industrial goods, such as tobacco, they may be known simply as *dealers* or *traders*.

DOMESTIC AGENT.   As agent, this class of middleman does not take title to the merchandise that he helps distribute; rather, he specializes in bringing buyer and seller together. Two kinds of agent are usually found in the central market for agricultural goods: *brokers* and *commission merchants* (or *commission men*). The nature of their functions corresponds generally to those of brokers and commission merchants who deal in manufactured goods.

---

[2] For example, three shipments of top-grade wheat pooled with three shipments of the next grade may together meet the minimum requirements of the top grade.

[3] In practice, the carlot wholesaler may also act as an agent.

The Secondary Wholesale Market

There are two distinct forms of secondary wholesale markets in agricultural distribution: a *jobber market*, through which consumer goods are almost always distributed, and a *mill market*, through which industrial goods may be distributed. The jobber market is much more common.

Jobber Market. This market exists primarily for agricultural products that flow to the ultimate consumer without change in form. It is the market from which the small retailer makes his purchases and is frequently located in smaller cities. There is always one in a city that has a central wholesale market. The *jobbers* are merchant middlemen who buy in fairly large quantities and sell in smaller lots to individual retailers. Buying and selling are their main functions, although in a small way, they provide transportation and storage facilities. Some are cash-and-carry merchants, but the majority offer credit to their customers and therefore perform the financing function. Through the ownership of goods, they take risks. Acting as sources of information to retailers, they provide news of impending changes in prices, supply, or quality and other useful market news.

Mill Market. This market is found in the distribution of agricultural industrial products where the industries concerned are located at some distance from production centers. Many factories requiring raw cotton, for instance, are located in New England, and a concentration of wholesalers is necessary in the factory towns of that region to complete the distribution begun by local and central markets. The wholesalers of the mill market sell by sample and take title to the goods.

The Cooperative Wholesale Market

A special type of trader is found in both local and central markets, namely, the cooperative. The *agricultural cooperative*, which in many respects is analogous to a consumers' cooperative, is a group of agricultural producers who act collectively to sell their produce, occasionally combining retailing with wholesaling, and in some cases to purchase farm supplies as well.[4] Such a group may also be known as a *farmers' cooperative* or a *producers' cooperative*.

Types of Cooperatives.   Cooperatives may be grouped into those operating only in local growers' markets and those operating in central, or terminal, markets. The latter usually operate locally as well.

LOCAL MARKET COOPERATIVE.   This is an immediate outlet for the individual farmer and is the type of cooperative to which he can belong personally. It deals in such commodities as dairy products, grains, and citrus or other fruits.[5]

TERMINAL MARKET COOPERATIVE.   This type of wholesaling middleman is situated in the central market and handles such commodities as livestock and fruits and vegetables. It represents local farmers and remits its savings to them.

Cooperative Methods of Handling Farm Products.   Cooperatives may act either as merchants or as agents.

MERCHANT COOPERATIVE.   This type of organization purchases goods outright from each producer, paying him the market price. At the end of its fiscal period, it returns to him patronage dividends in proportion to the value of the commodities that he has sold to the organization.

AGENT COOPERATIVE.   This type of organization receives the commodities of the individual farmer and pools them with similar commodities of other farmers. Often it makes no attempt at grading and merely pays its members the average price that it is able to secure for each commodity. When it grades commodities, it pools each grade separately and pays each farmer according to the quality of his products. In either case, pooling has its advantages: It eliminates the necessity for marketing each producer's output

---

[4] Individual mention should be made of the *bargaining association*, important in the marketing of milk, whereby producers band together in order to obtain higher wholesale prices through collective bargaining power.

[5] A local cooperative may be independent, or it may be associated with other locals in one of two possible forms. There is the *federated association*, in which local groups retain independence except for the allocation of minor responsibilities to a central authority; control is exercised from the bottom up. There is also the *centralized association*, in which a central organization manages the local groups; control of major policies and decisions is from the top down.

separately; it simplifies storing and shipping and makes these functions more economical; and it aids orderly marketing. In other words, it helps balance the quantity of each product with its current demand, thus encouraging price stabilization.

Advantages of the Farm Cooperative.   In principle, the efficiently administered cooperative offers many advantages to the farmer who belongs to it: (1) It returns to the farmer, in the form of patronage dividends, the middleman's normal share of the marketing profits. (2) It increases his bargaining power because he does not negotiate sales prices, leaving it to the cooperative, which may well be the most powerful middleman in a particular market. (3) It fosters price stabilization by reducing the number of small lots being offered for sale competitively. (4) It reduces marketing costs. Studies have shown that the agricultural cooperative can effect many economies in marketing not only through careful management and the mass handling and grading of commodities but also through education of its members. It can teach them which varieties and grades are most in demand and how to improve the quality of their products. (5) It encourages orderly marketing by attempting to hold back the farmer's goods when prices are low and to sell them when prices are high. This aids price stabilization. (6) It maintains a larger and more efficient sales organization than independent farmers could dream of supporting. One producers' cooperative, Sunkist Growers, Inc. (formerly the California Fruit Growers' Exchange), for example, has been unusually successful in bringing oranges to the consumer through its skillful promotion of the Sunkist orange. (7) Through lobbying and other means, the farm cooperative obtains legislative and administrative governmental aid for farmers. Parity prices are a case in point, and so are many of the activities of the Department of Agriculture in behalf of the farmer.

Disadvantages of the Farm Cooperative.   The typical producers' cooperative has many shortcomings in actual practice: (1) Most such cooperatives practice poor business methods. Inefficient management and slipshod bookkeeping and office procedures are prevalent because of unwillingness to spend the money needed to buy business skill. (2) The typical cooperative lacks the strength of permanent and stable membership. Many farmers join in times of adversity but withdraw and market through their own channels when prices are inflated. (3) Many members complain about the system of pooling, partly because it delays the profits that they could gain immediately by selling their goods themselves and partly because it deprives them of the opportunity of negotiating their own prices. Although the cooperative through its superior bargaining power can obtain higher prices, it is sometimes difficult for the farmer to believe this if he does not personally take part in the negotiations. The farmer's complaint appears justifiable when there is pooling without grading because then the marginal farmer gains from the efforts of others who contribute outstanding products to the pool. (4) Like other business organizations, the cooperative is forced to depend upon employees who lack the deep interest in efficient and profitable marketing that private owners would have. Often, in practice, it depends upon employees who feel that they are insufficiently compensated for their efforts. (5) The farm cooperative's drive for orderly marketing has not been so successful in practice as it has in principle because individual members resent attempts to control their production.

Government Control of the Farm Market.   The first attempt by the government to deal with the problem of farm surpluses was through the Agricultural Marketing Act of 1929 which created the Federal Farm Board and made the initial effort to control farm prices by storing surpluses. The act also encouraged the formation of farm cooperatives to aid in orderly marketing of agricultural products and to make loans to farmers at low interest rates. This was followed by a series of Agricultural Adjustment Acts beginning in 1933. These acts attempted to restrict production of agricultural commodities and to increase farm income. The 1933 act was declared unconstitutional in 1936, but subsequent acts accomplished the same purpose through constitutionally acceptable methods.

The Soil Conservation and Domestic Allotment Act of 1936 and the Agricultural Adjustment Act of 1938 had several objectives. Two of the most important were the establishment of parity prices along with marketing quotas and the provision for loans by the Commodity Credit Corporation to farmers to enable them to store surpluses. Another restriction on agricultural competition resulted from the Agricultural Marketing Agreements Act of 1948, which became the basis for controlling the marketing of fruits, vegetables, and fluid milk.

The Agricultural Act of 1949 established an adjusted parity price for agricultural commodities. The farmers received between 75 and 90 percent of the base parity figure, depending upon the supply of agricultural products. There are some seventeen crops covered by this support program. In addition, the Department of Agriculture is permitted to make direct purchases of perishable farm products that cannot be stored easily. This act also permitted soil-bank payments to farmers for removing from production portions of land normally used for farming.

Recent Trends

The volume of food products marketed for domestic consumption has increased by more than two-fifths since World War II. Export markets for these products have also grown. The increase in output of services performed by the food marketing industries has been greater than the growth in physical volume because of added marketing services per unit of product handled. This growth has been associated with major changes in the structure of the food marketing industries, particularly the trend to fewer but larger establishments. Changes in ownership by purchase or merger have furthered this movement, and a surviving company often concentrated its operations in its most efficient plants (frequently its largest plants).

Technological developments in equipment, improved transportation, and economies of scale that only relatively large plants can exploit all have had a part in improving efficiency of the marketing system. Consumers and farmers as well as marketing firms have benefited from this improved efficiency. However, the competitive structure of the market for farm and food products has changed. The trend is toward fewer and larger food marketing establishments, and in many food marketing industries, there are now fewer buyers and sellers.

1. Through what markets are farm products generally distributed? State the difference in distribution structure between consumer goods and industrial goods.
2. How is the agricultural market affected by the following: the characteristics of agricultural production, the characteristics of agricultural products, the characteristics of the consumption of agricultural products?
3. What types of middlemen are there in the local wholesale market?
4. How does the central wholesaler market differ from the local wholesale market?
5. What types of cooperatives are there in the wholesale distribution of agricultural goods? Indicate their advantages and disadvantages.

10

THE RETAILING STRUCTURE

Retailing includes "that business activity mainly concerned with selling to consumers."[1]

The Importance and Nature of Retailing

Importance. The three feet of counter between salesclerk and customer is the point at which distribution ends and consumption begins. Retail trading is the last link in the long chain of activity between production and distribution, and probably the most important one. All business is dependent upon it. A decline in retail sales means fewer sales for the wholesaler, and this, in turn, means fewer sales for the producer.

Changing Picture of the American Retail Structure. Retailing is fundamental and is the most ancient form of commerce, but it is not static. A major landmark in the evolution of American retailing can be set at the time of the Civil War, with the coming of the Industrial Revolution to America. Another may be set at

---

[1] Shapiro, *Marketing Terms*, p. 142.

about 1900, with the growth of mass distribution. But retailing visibly takes on new aspects with each decade.

RETAILING BEFORE 1865.   America depended largely on trading posts, general stores, itinerant peddlers, and urban stores with limited lines of goods for its retailing. Trading posts were established in earliest colonial times and were the retailing institution of frontier society. Traders moved west with the frontier, buying and selling raw materials, unprocessed commodities, and manufactured articles among settlers, Indians, and pioneers. Some operated independently, but others (notably the Hudson's Bay Company) were virtually corporate chains. As towns developed, the trading post was replaced by the independent general store, which still performs a minor function in the American retailing structure.

RETAILING FROM 1865 TO 1900.   With the Industrial Revolution, there came a period characterized by small-scale establishments, each handling one commodity. Grocery stores, for example, took over much of the general-store trade insofar as food was concerned. Stores catering to the demands of women, with their increasing interest in style and variety of clothing, developed into the first women's specialty shops. Only a few large-scale establishments, such as department stores and mail-order houses, were established during this period.

RETAILING SINCE 1900.   Mass distribution on the retailing level has grown rapidly since the turn of the twentieth century, although the bulk of retailing is still handled by small-scale dealers. Between 1900 and 1920, the department store and the mail-order house developed tremendously and perhaps reached their peak of importance as far as total national distribution was concerned. In the 1920s and 1930s, particularly during the depression, corporate chain stores rose rapidly, and following them came the voluntary or contract chains formed by independent dealers. The first supermarkets were established by independents; by the middle 1940s, the chains had converted so many units that the supermarket was a significant factor in the distribution of consumer goods. With the growth of suburban shopping areas after World War II, the self-contained shopping center appeared, and this later developed into the roofed-over mall. At the same time, the discount house also evolved. This type of limited-service retailer, selling below usual market prices, has grown considerably, although many ran into financial difficulties later as they increased services but were unable to raise prices significantly to cover these services.

Small-Scale Retailing

An arbitrary but common method of classifying retail establishments is based on the dollar volume of their annual sales. A *small-scale* concern is generally defined as one with annual sales below $100,000. However, some marketing experts set the minimal sales limit for a large-scale concern at $500,000 or even higher. The small-scale establishment is usually identical with what is commonly called the *independent small-scale retailer*. It not only falls within the volume limitation but also is unconnected in ownership and management with any other retail establishment. By the $500,000 limit figure, the retailing portion of the American economy is generally small scale. Large-scale retailers were outnumbered by small-scale retailers eleven to one in 1967. The latter accounted for about 57 percent of the nation's retail dollar sales.

In terms of the variety of stores operated, small-scale retailing falls into four main categories: the general store, the single-line or limited-line store, the specialty shop, and the consumers' cooperative. Since individual stores may vary in an unlimited number of ways, the lines of demarcation between the first three types are not rigid. The description of each type given here is therefore to be regarded as generally representative. The advantages and disadvantages of each are to be considered suggestive rather than comprehensive (the student will be able to think of others) and should be understood as relative to many factors. Low prices, for instance, are an advantage or a disadvantage, depending upon whether they are compensated for by wide sales; and the friendly atmosphere so essential to the rural store might be detrimental economically to a store that counts upon speed and efficiency of sales.

General Store. This type of store carries a variety of nonrelated items of merchandise and is not departmentalized. Its main characteristic is its varied stock, emphasizing groceries and dry goods, with a display of cutlery, shoes, and other articles. Necessarily, such a store has a limited selection of merchandise within any one classification; it will not, for example, have many styles of shoes. Today there are few general stores; they are found mainly in rural areas, particularly in the South.

ADVANTAGES.   The varied stock of the general store encourages impulse buying; a customer going in for a pound of sugar may go out with a new shirt and pocketknife as well. Normally, the owner manages the store, and his personal interest and participation are decided advantages. Sometimes the store is situated on the lower floor of his dwelling, and he and his family act as clerks; low overhead and easy availability of part-time help mean low out-of-pocket costs. Because of its friendly atmosphere, its personal relationship with customers, and above all, its convenient location, the general store in some respects has an advantage over more distant competitors that may carry a superior selection of merchandise. If the customer is not too demanding, the stock is broad enough to satisfy his basic needs.

DISADVANTAGES.   The general store is not well adapted to urban areas, where it would be in close competition with other retail outlets. The limitation of its stock is its major shortcoming. Furthermore, since no one item moves quickly, its merchandise tends to be shopworn and out of date. The owner is unable to do either specialized or large-scale buying; hence, he cannot purchase goods as cheaply or sell them as cheaply as many of his competitors. Being chief salesclerk, chief buyer, and bookkeeper as well, the owner usually exercises inefficient control over his store. In such circumstances, poor management is associated with, although not necessarily inherent in, the general store. Another major disadvantage of general-store merchandising in rural areas is the need for extension of credit to customers who may not be able to pay until after the harvest; this forces the proprietor to buy on a hand-to-mouth basis and possibly to borrow from a bank in order to purchase more inventory.

OUTLOOK.   General stores are still found in small towns and farm areas. A type of general store may also be found in certain quarters of large cities; a Mexican neighborhood may have its general store where Spanish is spoken and where the stock is adapted to neighborhood tastes and needs. General stores today play a much smaller role than they played in earlier periods of American retailing. Yet there is evidence that a revival may take place in small villages. As residents travel more and more to large cities for their shopping goods, local specialty shops may decrease in number, and local stores now handling convenience goods may take over a part of the shopping goods trade and become modified general stores.

Single-Line or Limited-Line Store. The typical independent store emphasizes a reasonably good variety within a single or a limited line of merchandise. Examples include gasoline stations, automobile accessory stores, grocery stores, furniture stores, jewelry stores, and eating and drinking establishments. Their merchandise is departmentalized, but they may carry sidelines. Drugstores, for instance, often sell clocks, books, toys, and a diversity of other goods.

CLASSIFICATION.   Such stores may be classified either by location or by the kinds of services offered.

In cities, some operate in neighborhood areas, tending to specialize in convenience goods, such as drugs or groceries. Others are concentrated in shopping districts, perhaps near office buildings, theaters, or transportation terminals; among these are stores dealing in shopping goods (women's dresses, jewelry, and the like) as well as stores handling convenience goods. In small towns, single- or limited-line stores operate in competition with general stores and chain stores and often handle the bulk of local trade.

Classified by services, there are cash-and-carry stores and those that offer credit, deliver, take telephone orders, and the like. Few of the latter attempt to offer all possible services, but most offer two or three.

ADVANTAGES.   The advantages of the single-line store are similar to those of the general store. The wide assortment of merchandise within a limited line encourages impulse buying. A friendly atmosphere and a personal relationship with customers are normally present. The building housing the neighborhood store may also contain the family residence of the owner and thus ensure low out-of-pocket operating costs. Neighborhood locations and the offering of special services make many single- or limited-line stores convenient for the customer; furthermore, store hours may be adjusted to neighborhood demands. If the store is large enough to have employees, an added advantage is the close relationship between owner and worker.

DISADVANTAGES. A distinct disadvantage is the small size of the trading area. The proprietor may have to depend upon circulars or "shoppers" for his advertising; he cannot make use of one of the best advertising mediums of the retailer: the newspaper. The single-line retailer who does more than $100,000 business a year is rare; thus, he is unable to do large-scale buying. For the convenience of his customers, he is forced to stock many slow-moving items. Usually, he must perform all the functions of managing, purchasing, selling, and accounting; he cannot specialize, nor can he normally afford to hire people who are specialists; and as with the general store, the frequent result is poor management.

Specialty Shop.   This retail store makes its appeal on the basis of a restricted class of shopping goods. Unlike the single-line store, it deals with only a portion of a larger line. A men's haberdashery, for example, may handle shirts, underwear, handkerchiefs, jewelry, and other small items of dress but probably not the suits and coats of a single-line clothing store. A store that sells electrical household appliances will handle radios, refrigerators, deep freezers, toasters, television sets, electric mixers, air conditioners, and many other items but probably no nonelectrical appliances. In the specialty shop, the customer will expect to find items of dress or appliances that may not be stocked by less specialized dealers.

ADVANTAGES. The handling of a restricted line of merchandise leads to a number of concrete advantages. The store can cater to discriminating customers because of the large assortment of items within the field of specialization. It can purchase what is most likely to appeal to its special clientele and thus secure a rapid turnover. Unlike the less specialized store, it can do larger-scale buying in its small range. The proprietor can develop a knowledge of the product and of vendors that will allow him to purchase carefully. In addition, he can provide effective sales training for his clerks at low cost. Because the specialty shop emphasizes service and quality of goods rather than cheapness, he may have less worry than other small-scale retailers over price competition.

DISADVANTAGES. The risk of a specialty retailer is great because his inventory is concentrated on a restricted line and frequently on a line of style goods. Style goods involve extraordinary risk, and their sales, more than those of other types of merchandise, are likely to be seasonal. If sales are seasonal, the retailer must expect a high overhead because seasonal goods require more space than goods with year-round demand. Furthermore, in a shop with no sidelines, there is relatively little impulse buying, a fact that may result in a small volume of sales per customer.

OUTLOOK. The small independent specialty shop is an important part of the distribution picture in secondary urban shopping areas, suburbs, and small communities. Although the departmentalized type will probably be more prominent during the next few years, it is possible that there will also be some growth in the nondepartmentalized shops because of the growth of self-contained shopping units in suburban areas. This has resulted from the increased concentration of population in suburban areas, as the most recent census indicates.

Consumers' Cooperatives. In many places throughout the country, consumers have banded together to form cooperatives to increase their purchasing power. In reality, many cooperatives are small-scale retailers. The cooperative form of marketing has made little progress in the United States. The reasons are the cooperatives' inability to pay for high-caliber employees; the difficulty in obtaining prices equal to those obtained by chain stores, supermarkets, or discount houses; and the difficulty in providing important services such as credit, delivery, and telephone ordering.

The consumers' cooperative in the United States is more of an ideology than a practical marketing operation. Its members are people who are emotionally involved with the cooperative movement and who patronize these stores through loyalty. It is doubtful that this movement will ever make significant headway because it cannot attain the operational efficiency and widespread acceptance of the large number of retailers who use price as a means of attracting customers.

Large-Scale Retailing

Despite the proportionately high sales volume and the large number of small-scale retail outlets, large-scale retailing has made marked inroads into the field of marketing since 1900. The growth of the chain type of organization specifically illustrates this fact; although in 1967, chain stores constituted less than 12.5 percent of the total number of retail outlets, they did more than 40 percent of the retail business. The following economic changes have encouraged the development of large-scale retailing.

Increased concentration of the population. As people have moved from rural to urban or suburban areas, they have provided a new market for large stores.

Improved communication. Rapid development in communication has made it possible for large stores to use advertising media covering larger geographic areas, and the advertising has stimulated consumer demand.

Improved transportation. This has enabled customers to travel to central stores with greater convenience.

Higher living standards. As living standards have been raised, people have wanted a greater variety of goods. Large-scale establishments have prospered because they could meet this demand.

Mass production. The manufacture of consumer goods on a mass scale has stimulated mass distribution.

Increased variety of goods. As the number of manufactured consumer products increases and the demand grows, the retail distributor who can carry a large stock has an advantage over the one with limited capacity.

Department Store. The department store is a retail establishment that handles a wide variety of lines, such as women's ready-to-wear and accessories, men's and boys' wear, piece goods, small wears, and household furnishings. For purposes of merchandising, publicity, store operation, and control, it is organized into separate departments. The large variety of available goods and departmentalization are its chief characteristics. A store must have at least twenty-five employees to be classified as a department store. As a rule, the department store is located in a downtown or central-city district; however, with the decentralization of urban population, department stores have grown up in secondary shopping areas. Usually, the department store occupies more than one floor of a building, and it caters primarily to women.

CLASSIFICATION. On the basis of ownership, department stores can be separated into two general types: the *independent store* and the *chain store*. The independent store is controlled by its own management; only in the case of voluntary groups is there any sharing of control with other managements. The chain department store, by definition, is one that is under common ownership with other stores. It may take one of two forms. In one, all the stores of the chain are centrally owned and operated; in the other, all are centrally owned, but they are operated under individual managements.

MAJOR DIVISIONS OF ORGANIZATION. The four major activities of the department store are *merchandising, publicity* (or *promotion*), *store operation* (or *management*), and *control* (or *finance*). Merchandising includes all buying and selling. It is usually under the direction of a merchandising manager aided by special assistants who direct the work of the several merchandising divisions, which in turn are composed of selling departments. A publicity division is responsible for every form of nonpersonal public promotion of goods, services, or ideas. Specifically, its activities include advertising and display plus such miscellaneous types of publicity as announcements of special events. A store operation division handles the day-to-day management of the store. Among its specific responsibilities are maintenance and purchasing of supplies and equipment, and personnel. The control division is in charge of the organization's budgetary and other financial operations.

SPECIAL FEATURES OF DEPARTMENT STORE OPERATION. The following special features of the department store are fairly common: the basement store, the leased department, and the branch store. The basement store is a separate section set aside for the sale of budget merchandise. It may account for 10 to 20 percent of the total sales. A leased department is one operated as a concession by an individual or a chain, for example, restaurants, beauty salons, and the millinery, optometry, jewelry, women's shoes, and confectionary departments. Because leased departments are managed in accordance with the uniform policies and regulations of the department store, the customer generally assumes that they are an intrinsic part of the store. The branch store has developed as the result of population movements from city centers to suburban areas; many department stores have met the demand for nearby shopping facilities by establishing branch stores with inventories that may or may not be similar to that of the parent store, depending upon the needs and tastes of the community.

ADVANTAGES.   From the customer's point of view, one advantage of the department store is the convenience of finding a broad variety of merchandise under a single roof. This fact, plus the maintenance of many customer services, has led one New York department store to boast that within its walls it can provide goods or services suitable to any event from birth to death. An important advantage, from the dealer's point of view, is the reputation for reliability that a department store enjoys. Moreover, the department store has a distinct reputation for being willing to experiment; it could have been predicted that department stores would be the first to promote television shopping, the first to offer interior decorating advice to customers, and the first to employ shoppers' aides to help customers select merchandise. Since the department store offers so many goods and requires such a large sales volume, it can do a great deal of advertising and can draw patronage from a broad trading area. Because of the volume of goods it sells within a year, it uses large-scale and specialized purchasing. It is able to use specialists in its entire operation, whether in advertising, control, display, or other activities. The department store can also integrate retailing with wholesaling and sometimes with production. Where possible, it circumvents the wholesaling middleman by buying directly from the producer.

DISADVANTAGES.   One major problem of the department store is its high fixed cost, caused by such factors as the expense of its downtown location and its numerous customer services. The downtown location brings special problems; for instance, congestion, parking difficulties, and inner-city decay and crime may keep customers away. Certain wastes result from departmentalization; for instance, since the sales personnel of one department is trained only in a given line, it is difficult to shift these salespersons to another department when special occasion demands. Specialization of activity within the store makes for a certain inflexibility that brings about complex management problems. The department store is so large and specialized that its clerks can have little personal acquaintance with the customers (in this respect it is at a distinct disadvantage when compared with the small independent store). Because of the lack of personal relationship, the store suffers from abuses of the many liberal services that are offered. It is not unusual for customers to demand delivery of dollar purchases; and it is not uncommon for customers to return merchandise that they have spoiled. But a department store will rarely refuse to exchange merchandise or refund the purchase price.

OUTLOOK. With the problems of decay and crime in the inner cities, downtown department stores are having very real sales problems. In those cities where there has been urban development, the department stores have done well. The future of the downtown department store hangs on what the cities do to rebuild their cores. The future of the suburban department store, on the other hand, is in no doubt. As suburbs continue to grow and prosper, so do the suburban department stores.

Many of the existing limited-line stores and specialty shops may well become variety stores and take over that part of the department store trade that is now devoted to notions, household appliances, and various other inexpensive items. Independent department stores, in turn, may well become departmentalized specialty shops.[2]

Departmentalized Specialty Store. This type of store makes its appeal on the basis of a restricted class of shopping or specialty goods and is organized in departments. It may specialize

___

[2] Note the evolution that has taken place in the retail structure of the past hundred years. The apothecary's shop of a century ago has been in many cases replaced by a variety store that maintains a prescription department; the corner cigar store of even thirty years ago now carries haberdashery and sporting goods as well as cigars and tobacco; more than 90 percent of the supermarkets in the United States carry nonfood items, sometimes including electrical household appliances, garden furniture, certain forms of clothing, and patent medicines. Such changes indicate that the role of the department store will also be modified as the conditions that fostered its development become modified.

in clothing and accessories or home furnishings or dry goods, but unlike the existing form of department store, it does not typically handle all three. In actual practice, however, the line of distinction between the two types of organization is sometimes hard to discover; and from the marketing standpoint, most of the characteristics, advantages, and disadvantages are the same for both.

Mail-Order House.   The mail-order house receives its orders and delivers its goods by mail and is usually dependent for its sales upon a catalog. Various types of retailers do a portion of their business by mail-order methods, and conversely, some establishments that originally limited their operations to mail have now opened retail stores. In fact, about two-thirds of the sales of the major mail-order houses are over the counter.

The catalog is a feature of mail-order marketing, and it represents a sizable investment (currently for a full-line house, about $2.25 per copy, including distribution). Certain methods of organization used by the mail-order house are so typically identified with it that they may be called characteristics. Branch warehouses, for instance, are frequently established in various parts of the country. These enable the mail-order house to compete effectively with local retailers both in costs to the purchaser (because delivery is chargeable to the customer) and in speed of delivery. Orders are filled on a systematic basis, and the entire functioning of the organization is on a specialized, departmentalized system. The mail-order house tends to emphasize unbranded and private brand merchandise; it does so by contracting with manufacturers for large lots of merchandise to be purchased at low cost. It follows definite policies in its dealings with patrons, offering guarantees on goods and facilitating the return of goods by having a liberal adjustment policy.

CLASSIFICATION.   There are two varieties of mail-order house: the *full-line house*, which closely resembles the department store in the variety of its stock, and the *specialty house*, which offers only one or a few lines of merchandise (such as sporting goods, shirts, or books) to be purchased at low cost.

ADVANTAGES.   The low prices offered by the mail-order house are one of the many advantages provided to the consumer; these are made possible through the decreased cost of operations resulting from low rental locations and absence of sales personnel. Other advantages are the ease with which the consumer can shop at home and the variety of lines and assortment of goods that may be offered. Such advantages are particularly attractive to consumers in an outlying area where shopping in ordinary retail establishments may be difficult. These advantages are augmented by the speed with which products are delivered from the mail-order house. Most of these firms fill orders within twenty-four hours after receipt. The reputation for honesty and reliability that the retail mail-order house has established is a strong point in its favor.

DISADVANTAGES. From the consumer's viewpoint, there are definite inconveniences in buying by mail. The average consumer simply does not like to write letters or even to fill out order blanks and insert them in addressed envelopes. It is more difficult to make credit arrangements with a mail-order house than with a neighborhood dealer. Purchasing by description is frequently unsatisfactory, particularly for style items, seasonal commodities, or types of goods where examination before purchase is desirable. If the consumer does not consider the goods acceptable, he has the task of repacking and shipping them back. There is also a psychological disadvantage in having the customer pay the cost of delivery. Where distances are greater or where articles are bulky, the gross price of articles bought by mail may represent no saving.

From the retailer's viewpoint, there are obvious difficulties in selling by mail commodities that are perishable or that require installation or servicing. The mail-order house must make commitments in advance. Months before it is prepared to sell an item, it must send a description and a price to the printer of the catalog. This creates problems in handling style goods and, if prices change, any kind of merchandise. Finally, in small communities, there is the hostile rivalry of local dealers, who compete with mail-order houses by appealing to the loyalty of their fellow townsmen or by refusing to buy goods from them unless they reciprocate.

OUTLOOK. There is every indication that both the mail-order operation and the retail operation have grown considerably during recent years. Of the two, however, the retail operation has the greater potential because of the advantages of proximity and immediate availability.

Corporate Chain Store.   A chain store is composed of eleven
or more stores that are managed by a single company and sell
similar merchandise. It is usually located in an area that serves
a large number of people, and it tends to have a standardized
storefront and interior. There is no consistent policy for offering
credit or services. Most drugstore and grocery chains and some
clothing chains do not provide credit, telephone-order services, or
free deliveries. A major operating advantage is its standardization
of merchandizing procedures. All buying is done by specialists in a
central office; inventory is carefully controlled, often through electrical data processing equipment, by the central office. Because of
the large volume of their sales, chain stores normally buy directly
from manufacturers.

CLASSIFICATION.   Chain stores may be classified in various
ways: by the kinds of goods carried (such as grocery chains, variety
store chains, clothing chains, and so on), by size of the area that
they serve (local chains, regional or sectional chains, and national
chains), by the kinds of services offered (many, for instance, are
self-service stores), by the degree of central control exercised by
the management (this will vary from company to company). They
may also be classified by their functions. For instance, some chains
warehouse their items before distributing them to the store units;
but others, such as those dealing in millinery, do not. Finally, chains
may be classified by ownership: manufacturer owned, wholesaler
owned, and retailer owned.

ADVANTAGES.   A major advantage of the chain store is the
low retail price at which it can offer its goods. It buys at a lower
price than its competitors through its expert buyers and its
ability to make mass purchases at quantity discounts. Often,
a low retail price is made possible by reduced operating
costs through integration of wholesale and retail activities or
through a self-service plan that has been adopted during the past
ten years by an increasing number of grocery and other chains. In
addition, a chain may be able to sell at a smaller markup than its
local competitors and still make a profit through mass merchandising. A second advantage is the scientific method the chain uses
to select a site. Before making a decision, it carefully analyzes the
size, character, and composition of a trading area. This elimination

of guesswork, combined with the tremendous financial resources of a chain, enables it to select the finest site available. A third advantage is the ability of the chain to use newspaper advertising for its neighborhood stores; because of the number of outlets in a given area, the chain's advertising is inexpensive and is planned by experts. The virility of the chain store is largely the result of efficiency of operation, a part of which is the employment of specialists in every phase of activity. It carefully designs its program for recruitment, selection, training, placement, and supervision of personnel.

DISADVANTAGES. Despite the strong position of the chain store, its methods of operation create serious problems. One of these is the difficulty of adjusting its marketing to local conditions; the vital need for emphasizing standardization and for maintaining low operating costs makes it difficult for this type of store to adapt its merchandise to special requirements, to adjust its prices to neighborhoods, or to meet competition from local independent stores. Like other large-scale retailing institutions, the chain store lacks personal relationship with customers. Because it depends on a large volume of trade, it cannot cater to individual customers; also, many chains have adopted a policy of moving personnel from one store to another for training purposes, a policy that gives the employees little opportunity for intimate acquaintance with customers. Another disadvantage is the chain store's minimization of customer services. Since the store does not take telephone orders, extend credit, or provide free delivery, its clientele is limited to those with time and means to make their own purchases. Contrary to supposition, a study by the Federal Trade Commission (FTC) shows little difference between the losses through pilferage and deterioriation encountered by chains and independents. A noteworthy disadvantage is the public hostility that has been directed more often at the chain store than at other types of large-scale retailing.

CRITICISMS OF CHAIN STORE METHODS. The major complaints against chain stores revolve around their so-called monopoly position, their reputed tendency to resort to unfair price competition and to questionable practices in attempting to drive out local independents, and their supposed failure to contribute to local and national economic welfare. Independent dealers and wholesalers employ state and federal lobbies to represent their interests. The principal thesis of these lobbies has been that economies gained by monopolistic methods enable chains to reduce expenses and increase rates of profit as new units are acquired, but the truth of this contention has not been substantiated by the FTC or by those who have made private studies of chain store operation. Some twenty state legislatures have levied special taxes to regulate chain store profits. One form is the graduated store tax, which increases per unit with the number of stores in a given chain; another, called a *gross receipts tax,* is a graduated tax based upon the volume of business done by an entire chain in a specific year. Charges of unfair practice have become commonplace, although not always proved. Prior to the passage of unfair-trade acts and fair-trade laws, some chains did use the technique of the *loss leader,* that is, of selling certain nationally advertised goods below cost in order to attract customers. Other accusations charging that chain stores compensate for losses by raising prices on non-leader goods, that chain store brands are inferior to private brands, and that chain stores short-weight and shortchange their clientele have not been verified. Studies have shown that dishonesty by chains is no more frequent than dishonesty by independents. On the economic side, it has been held that chain stores do not carry their part of the tax burden of a community, that they are owned by nonresident groups who have no interest in the local community, and that their profits are sent to organizations which are centralized instead of being kept in the local area. It has been said that chain stores exploit their employees, giving little or no recognition to personal achievement. There is probably no way of proving or disproving all these charges, but it should be emphasized that they have not been generally substantiated.

OUTLOOK. Most chains began as single stores. Although at the outset of the twentieth century there were about 700 chains with a total of 4,500 outlets in the United States, the real development of the chain store did not take place until the 1930s. Their growth has fluctuated, but current trends indicate that they will probably play an increasingly prominent role in retail marketing.

Voluntary Chain or Retailer Cooperative. The small-scale dealer is being forced to cope with large-scale competitors to an increasing degree. Because he is rarely able to meet such competition, particularly that of the chain store, he has turned to the medium of close cooperation with other independents. The outcome is the *voluntary* (or *contract*) chain, which may be defined as an associated group of independently owned stores that assign to an organization the right to dictate some of their merchandising policies. This central organization performs functions similar to those performed by the central office of a chain; these may include buying, store design and layout, advertising, and the development of private brands. By definition, each member of such a group is independent; the major purpose of the organization is to improve the position of each member.

CLASSIFICATION. The voluntary chain may be classified on two bases: the nature of the merchandise and the relationship that the group bears to wholesaling. With regard to the nature of the merchandise, the most important type of voluntary chain is found in the grocery business; there are, however, a few large, successful organizations in the drug field and in such commodity fields as men's clothing and hardware supplies. With regard to wholesaling, there are two main types. One type is initiated by the retailers themselves and includes groups known as *retailer associations, voluntary associations,* or *retailer cooperatives.* The retailer cooperatives usually set up the wholesaling function with which all members deal in order to obtain quantity discounts. Cooperative savings are retained over a period of time (usually one year) and then are passed back to the retailers in proportion to the amount of merchandise each has purchased. The advantage is that the so-called savings are tax-exempt. The *wholesale-sponsored* chain organizes a number of retail stores and welds them together to emulate the corporate chain. Stores composing either type of cooperative chain are independently owned.

ADVANTAGES. For the average retailer, a major advantage of affiliation with a voluntary chain is the opportunity that central-organization specialists provide for improving the quality of his stock of merchandise. He is also able to benefit by large-scale buying (and consequently to offer lower prices than unaffiliated competitors) and by chain advertising. If his group brings out its own branded merchandise, he will be better able to compete with the private brands of corporate chain stores; and as popular acceptance of the brand grows, he will receive increased patronage because of it.

DISADVANTAGES. A basic weakness of the voluntary association is the reluctance of many merchants to surrender independence. Some will not cooperate to the degree necessary to make their chain of outlets as effective as a corporate chain. Sometimes there will be a clash between retailers and wholesaler or among the various retailers themselves. If the group is wholesaler dominated, some will feel that important retailer problems are being overlooked by the central organization. If it is a retailer association with no strong central control, the members will often disagree about merchandise to be purchased, credit extension, and other policies. Some will be disappointed with the achievements of the association. Some will believe that they are losing privileges or services by binding themselves to one wholesale middleman instead of bargaining with competing middlemen. The competence or incompetence of their wholesaler will affect the well-being of the entire group, and there is a possibility that their organization managers will not be motivated to do their best, either because they are underpaid or because they are hindered by dissensions among members.

Supermarket. A supermarket is a large, highly departmentalized store dealing in foods and other household goods. In 1968, supermarkets represented 15.7 percent of the total number of food stores and accounted for 81.5 percent of food sales. The supermarket's characteristics are a self-service grocery department, wide aisles and excellent layouts based upon store-traffic analysis, mass displays of merchandise, private brands, price appeals, and usually ample parking space. It regularly does a minimum annual business of $1 million. The major stock consists of groceries, produce, meats, baked goods, and dairy products; but the stock may include such items as cleansers, pharmaceuticals, dietetic foods, housewares, and stationery. The supermarket may even operate a luncheonette. All departments may be under single ownership, or some may be leased to concessionaires. To meet increasing competition from supermarkets, many small independent stores have become *superettes* or *convenience stores*. Packaged merchandise is sold through self-service. Clerks are employed only for the sale of produce and meats. The superette or convenience store keeps long hours, from early morning to late at night. Some convenience stores offer neither fresh produce nor fresh meat; most offer frozen foods; some, delicatessen items.

CLASSIFICATION. Supermarkets may be classified by type of building, kind of organization, or ownership. The type of building marks the difference between the early, rapidly disappearing supermarket and the modern one. The early supermarket, located in a warehouse or factory building and emphasizing extremely low prices without any modern merchandising techniques, is now virtually extinct. The typical modern supermarket is housed in a structure especially built for its use so that optimum advantage may be taken of specialized layouts, mass displays, and other techniques. Organization is fundamentally of three kinds. There is the *public market*, which is a conglomeration of stands independently owned or leased and located in a large publicly or privately owned building. Because little emphasis is placed upon self-service or modern merchandising, the public market is not considered today a typical supermarket. There is the *concession* (or *leased-department*) supermarket, in which the dry-grocery department is usually operated by the owner and the remaining departments are usually operated by lessees. Finally, there is the *owner-operated unit*, which is the type normally found in cities. Supermarkets may be independently owned or may be parts of corporate chains. The latter account for more than 82 percent of all supermarket sales. An independent supermarket may belong to a voluntary chain.

ADVANTAGES. Supermarkets can sell many items at a relatively low price and stock a large assortment of merchandise for convenient selection by the housewife. They centralize buying and make use of large-scale advertising. They utilize one of the most effective psychological techniques for increasing the average size of sales per customer: the technique of displaying goods en masse. This practice, coupled with the fact that customers are able to handle the goods, stimulates impulse buying. Finally, supermarkets can use marketing research to select good locations.

DISADVANTAGES. The principal disadvantages of the supermarket, like those of the chain store, arise from its lack of personal relationship with customers and from its limited services. Impersonal relationship and self-service are not suited, for one thing, to the sale of shopping goods; the supermarket is therefore restricted in the type of merchandise it may carry. Again, a self-help store, located far from the homes of many of its customers and lacking telephone or delivery service, cannot satisfy those who are in a hurry; it must lose a portion of the consumer market.

OUTLOOK. The advantages of the supermarket method of merchandising outweigh the disadvantages, and the influence of grocery supermarketing will be extended to many other forms of retailing. Self-service has gradually become a characteristic of many drugstores, specialty shops, and department stores; in department stores, there is now a modified form of self-service called *self-selection*.[3]

The trend toward self-service (and/or self-selection) is an outgrowth of increasing costs of labor that have affected retail prices and therefore the purchasing power of the ultimate consumer. Self-service is a method of efficient marketing whereby merchants can minimize costs of distribution and maintain their current gross margin without passing increases on to the ultimate consumer.

Discount House. The original discount house specialized in the sale of nationally branded items at reduced prices. Sales were made on a cash basis from a limited stock. Many times selections were made from a catalog or floor sample. Products such as electrical appliances, jewelry, hardware, tools, toys, and sporting goods made up most of the inventory. As a result of competition by department stores, the larger discount houses introduced some of the usual department store services. Prices increased, and smaller discount houses where forced out of business. Discount chains were then formed, with increased inventory variety and more effective merchandising techniques. More recently, promotional department stores have been organized, selling nationally branded items and

---

[3] In this case, an individual selects several articles in which he may be interested, chooses one, and then goes to a clerk for possible alteration instructions if the commodity is a ready-to-wear item or to give final instructions for wrapping and method of payment, such as COD or charge and send.

unbranded soft lines (such as clothing, bedding, towels) at reduced prices and offering the usual department store services.

Quantity buying, as well as mass merchandising, is the key to the discount operation. This resulted from the recognition that a small percentage of products accounts for a large proportion of sales. Recent data reveal that approximately 50 to 75 percent of electrical household appliances are sold through discount stores.

Discount stores are expanding, and more stores are moving into discount operation. There are four types of discount store, according to the line of merchandise carried: the department store, the standard discount store, the discount store that has a food department, and the food discount store.

The department store type covers the usual range of merchandise offered by the discount store but also stresses fashion merchandise and caters to women. In the New York metropolitan area, Alexander's falls into this category. Two Guys is an example of the second category, which places much less emphasis on clothing. The third type is similar to the second but also has a food department; the fourth is typically a supermarket offering discount prices.

Techniques of Retailing

Along with the shifts in population, there have been substantial changes in the shopping habits of the American public. These have resulted in special kinds of operational retail techniques, many of which have become part of the more conventional retail organization.

Self-contained Shopping Center. This is composed of a group of stores designed to meet the needs of a residential area. It usually includes a supermarket, a department store, a drugstore, a variety store, and special kinds of retail outlets such as apparel and shoe stores. A large amount of parking space is available. The competition is usually controlled.

Evolving from the shopping center concept is a new dimension in the marketplace known as the planned community. The idea has taken form in towns sponsored by industrial firms. This new type of community meets consumer demands by providing community services and facilities, part of which is the shopping center. The shopping center offers entertainment, cultural, and social activities as well as serving as a place to buy merchandise.

Automatic Merchandising.   There are approximately 4.4 million vending machines in operation in the United States, accounting for $4.2 billion in sales. Cigarettes are the largest-selling item, followed by soft drinks, packaged confections, coffee, milk, prepared foods, bulk confections, ice cream, cigars, and a large variety of other merchandise.

Scrambled Merchandising.   In this form of merchandising, a retailer increases his inventory by adding a large number of unrelated lines. For example, the original pharmacy has almost disappeared, and in its place is a drugstore that may carry books, some ready-to-wear, radios, toasters, and fountain pens in addition to proprietary and ethical drugs.

Mail Order.   Some manufacturers have gone into direct-mail selling. Items sold include novelties, clothing, books, and records.

Farmers' Market.   This is a large-scale retailing operation that brings together in one place a number of concessionaires who may sell anything from food to jewelry. The principal appeal is price. There are no fancy fixtures, and purchases are strictly cash and carry.

REVIEW QUESTIONS

1. What new form of retailing institutions developed during the twentieth century? What other older forms showed their peak growth during the twentieth century?
2. How do you explain the development and growth of the retail institutions listed in your answer to the preceding question?
3. List and define the forms of small- and large-scale business.

11

TECHNIQUES OF DIRECT MARKETING

Chapters 1 to 10 described the general marketing pattern in the United States, reviewing the roles of the producer, the wholesaler and retail middlemen, and the industrial and ultimate consumers. In its route from producer to consumer, a given product need not pass through all the channels that have been described. It may be distributed directly to the retailer or directly to the industrial or ultimate consumer without the intervention of wholesaling middlemen. Direct marketing or distribution is "selling by a manufacturer to industrial users through his own salesmen, sales branches or offices, and/or warehouses."[1] The term is also applied to sales made directly from the producer to the ultimate consumer or retailer.

Evaluation of Direct Marketing

When may direct marketing be utilized successfully? What are its advantages and disadvantages in comparison with those of other established channels?

[1] Shapiro, *Marketing Terms*, p. 49.

Conditions Conducive to Direct Marketing.   Direct marketing is feasible only when there are favorable conditions relative to
the nature of the goods, the market, existing middlemen, channels of distribution, service requirements, and competition.

NATURE OF THE GOODS.   *Highly perishable goods* need to be
disposed of rapidly and, therefore, as directly as possible; rasp-
berries, for instance, are commonly sold in the immediate area
where they are grown and move directly from farmer to retailer or
from farmer to consumer. *Style items* must be marketed as quickly
as possible; therefore, such goods as women's dresses commonly
are sold directly by manufacturer to retailer. *Items of high unit
value*, such as electric turbines, are frequently marketed directly
from manufacturer to industrial consumer. *New or nongraded
goods* are frequently marketed directly, for example, when a farmer
sells his products to a retailer or to consumers.

NATURE OF THE PRODUCER.   A producing organization must
be reasonably large if it is to succeed through direct marketing. It
needs a capital investment adequate to prevent strain on corporate
finances because direct marketing is generally expensive; the producer must be prepared to absorb many or all functions ordinarily
performed by middlemen. Usually, it has to deal in more than one
product. If the expense of selling is concentrated upon a single
product, the organization will have a hard time meeting the prices
of more versatile competitors. This type of organization requires
a fairly routine production so that management may have time to
devote to the problems of direct marketing. Should production be
complex and changing, management might have to devote the
bulk of its attention to the intricacies of producing, rather than to
the problems of direct marketing, and *indirect* marketing would
be the only practical means of distribution.

NATURE OF THE MARKET.   Primarily, the market must be concentrated. If it is dispersed, with customers spread out over many
miles, direct marketing is likely to be excessively expensive. Then,
too, the market must consist of retailers who purchase in large
volume because it is clearly more profitable for a producer to service a hundred large supermarkets in one city than to service a
thousand small and widely scattered groceries that purchase the
same total volume.

NATURE OF THE EXISTING MIDDLEMEN.   In many cases, a producer favors direct marketing simply because he cannot find acceptable middlemen to handle his product; automobile companies, for instance, attach great importance to maintaining their own distributor-and-dealer organizations. They apparently feel that no other system would provide the kind of representation they desire. A producer may contend that existing middlemen are inefficient because they refuse to carry stocks large enough to serve customers properly or because they supply unsatisfactory storage facilities. He may complain that they are interested in handling competing brands and that during periods of recession, they invite depreciation of the consumer market by refusing to maintain minimum resale prices. In the light of these complaints, some producers feel justified in assuming the functions and expenses usually shouldered by independent wholesalers.

NATURE OF SERVICE REQUIREMENTS.   Certain commodities require skilled installation, servicing, or technical sales advice on the part of the retailer. These may be sold directly because the producer believes that wholesalers could not offer the proper services.

NATURE OF THE CHANNELS OF DISTRIBUTION.   The channels already set up may be unsuited to certain new types of commodities. Where no existing channel can be efficiently utilized, the producer may decide to market his goods directly rather than try to establish a special technique of indirect distribution. Or the channels may be unsuited to the distribution of standard products manufactured by new organizations. A producer who enters the marketing picture late in the history of a given commodity may find that all existing channels are filled by competitors and may be forced to distribute his output directly.

NATURE OF THE COMPETITION.   With increasing competition, many manufacturers attempt to reduce marketing costs and enlarge sales volume by marketing their products directly to large-scale buying groups, such as chain stores and department stores. Similarly, many small retailing groups are becoming parts of cooperative undertakings and seek to eliminate middlemen by bargaining directly with manufacturers.

Advantages of Direct Marketing.   Direct marketing may provide several potential advantages.

FASTER MARKETING.   In the case of extremely perishable goods or style goods, as previously noted, speed of distribution can be increased by direct marketing. A department store buyer can make his selection of fashion items directly in the manufacturer's showroom without waiting for the middleman.

REDUCTION OF SALES COSTS. If the market is concentrated, if the volume of unit purchase is high, and if other conditions previously enumerated are favorable, the organization that adopts direct marketing will more than likely find its sales costs reduced.

SPECIALIZED AND INTENSIVE SELLING. Because the salesmen will be employees or agents of the producer, their techniques can be adapted to the particular commodities at hand and thus be far superior to the techniques of less specialized middlemen. Moreover, selling can be greatly intensified through supervision and direct compensation.

CONTROLLED PRICES. Because a cut price makes the consumer question the value of a product, producers do not like to have middlemen offer their products at below a given minimum price. Unless producers can legally enforce resale price maintenance contracts with all wholesalers, they find it difficult to restrain middlemen from price cutting. However, if they have their own sales forces, as they do in direct marketing, they can be virtually certain that their products will not be sold to retailers at less than standard prices. The retailers, of course, may still cut prices to ultimate consumers.

BETTER CONTROL OF SERVICING. In direct marketing, servicing is under the immediate control and supervision of the producer. Complaints and requests for service go straight to him and can be given prompt and efficient attention.

CLOSER CONTACTS WITH CONSUMERS. The producer who depends upon traditional marketing channels has little or no immediate contact with the final user of his commodities; he must rely upon the reports of middlemen when he attempts to gauge users' reactions. Under direct marketing, however, a producer maintains continued contact with purchasers, notes their reactions, and carries his story directly to them.

NO PRIVATE BRAND COMPETITION. Middlemen may concentrate on selling private brands of their own, or they may handle many brands without favoritism. When the producer eliminates the middlemen through direct marketing, he may be sure that his own sales force is offering only his brand to the customers.

Disadvantages of Direct Marketing.   Even when many of the conditions favoring it are present, direct marketing may be undesirable. The disadvantages and hazards may outweigh any corresponding advantages.

INCREASED INVESTMENT IN INVENTORY AND PLANT.   A producer who markets directly must perform functions ordinarily carried out by middlemen. One of these functions is warehousing. Anticipating future demand, the middleman purchases stock from the producer and stores it near the point of sale, regardless of the location of the producer. Thus, he enables the producer to operate on smaller margins than would otherwise be possible. Producers who market directly must assume the functions of physical supply; they must allow for possible future demand by adding to their inventories.

INCREASED COSTS OF SALES AND OFFICE PERSONNEL.   With direct marketing, costs of sales personnel are increased. Salesmen are needed to make the selling contacts normally performed by middlemen. Because the producing organization must acquire additional storage space and enlarge its credit facilities, more clerical personnel are needed to perform all the added routine office operations.

ASSUMPTION OF OTHER FUNCTIONS OF MIDDLEMEN.   In direct marketing, the risks and other facilitating functions ordinarily assumed by the middleman must be shouldered solely by the producer. Also, he must study reactions to his product and gain information essential to the successful standardization of his merchandise; he must cater to the demands of each customer individually; and he must do all the advertising and promotional work. These added responsibilities cause the producer's cost burden to rise considerably.

Direct Marketing to Business Firms

Direct marketing takes various forms, depending upon whether the sale is being made to a business organization or to ultimate consumers. Direct marketing to the business firm may be either to the industrial consumer or to the retailer. The techniques are approximately the same for both.

Direct Marketing by Personal Solicitation. In this case, the producer's salesman calls personally upon the business firms that are prospects. This method accounts for about 70 percent of sales to industrial consumers and also for many sales to large retailers such as chain stores, department stores, and supermarkets, but it is rarely used in selling to small retail stores.[2] The producer who adopts this form must be sure to meet four requirements: (1) He should have a product that is of high unit value or one that is ordered in large quantities by the average customer. (2) He should have specialized skill in either the sale or the installation of his product. (3) He should have adequate capital to maintain services in the chief market areas. (4) His market should be geographically concentrated.

The advantages and disadvantages for such a producer are the same as those listed on pages 113–116.

Direct Marketing by Mail. In marketing by mail, the producer generally provides his customers with catalogs or at least with continuous announcements describing the available items and giving their prices. Orders are received by mail, and the merchandise is delivered by mail. The producer who adopts this form must be certain that his product meets the following requirements. (1) It should be relatively small so that it will be reasonably portable. (2) It should be relatively inexpensive because the purchaser is more likely to buy a commodity that he has not been able to examine first if its price is low. (3) It should be an item relatively difficult to obtain through standard marketing outlets; if it is locally obtainable, few buyers will trouble to order by mail unless special inducements are offered. (4) It should not be particularly perishable or fragile. (5) It should be a commodity that is easily described by advertising because buyers want to know what they are getting.

ADVANTAGES OF MAIL-ORDER MARKETING.   First, this method

---

[2] Retail stores frequently send buyers to the premises of the producer and thus establish, in effect, another form of direct marketing.

reaches customers in scattered areas; it may well be the best method for a manufacturer whose customers are not concentrated. Second, because it is inexpensive, it can sometimes be used by a producer who has insufficient capital to distribute through the commonly accepted marketing channels. Third, it may provide an outlet for commodities that middlemen are not willing to stock. Fourth, it has the important advantage of flexibility; the producer who wants to test the marketability of a new product can do so by mail without a large initial investment and a large initial stock.

DISADVANTAGES OF MAIL-ORDER MARKETING. The chief disadvantages of this form of direct selling are the barriers that confront the potential customer and, in many cases, restrain him from making purchases. One such barrier is the trouble of searching through a catalog, filling out an order blank, and mailing an order. It is much simpler for the business buyer to tell a salesman exactly what he wants, or to walk into a wholesaler's display room, or merely to pick up his telephone and give his order. Another disadvantage is that business buyers must purchase cautiously, and there is no opportunity for the purchaser to examine the goods in advance. The disrepute into which some mail-order marketing has fallen is another restraining force. Many fly-by-night organizations have sold inferior products by mail, and prospective customers are wary of them. It is also difficult to give special information or instructions before purchases are made or at the time of delivery. No amount of printed information can quite replace the information a salesman can give personally, especially if the goods are technical or mechanical in nature.

Direct Marketing by Integration. *Integration* is absorption of the functions of one operator in the distribution channel by a business organization not normally connected with those functions. Through integration, the producer may assume the functions of the typical industrial market wholesaler. This type of activity accounts for some 12 percent of all sales to industrial consumers. The producer engaged in integrated marketing establishes *branch warehouses*, that is, warehouses used mainly to stock, sell, and deliver his products. To succeed, the producer must meet the following minimum requirements: (1) He must be sure that his product has a high unit value or will have a large average sale.

Preferably, it will be a product that requires specialized selling or installation skill. (2) He must have enough capital to maintain the physical facilities and the staff of employees that are required. (3) He must be certain that the market area covered by each branch is sufficiently concentrated to warrant the opening of the branch. An example of a firm that meets all these qualifications is Johns-Manville, which manufactures building supplies. This firm has another qualification: It carries a broad line of merchandise.

Direct Marketing to Ultimate Consumers

Direct marketing to ultimate consumers takes three distinct forms, which are analogous to those used in selling to business and industry. Marketing through personal solicitation usually means some variety of door-to-door selling by the producer's own sales force.[3] The other forms are marketing by mail and marketing by integration.

Direct Marketing by House-to-House Selling or Personal Solicitation. To be successful, the producer should ordinarily be sure that his product is one that has basic appeal to most families and should concentrate his selling activities upon small groups or small areas. Unlike producers who sell directly to business organizations, he need not have a large capital or necessarily deal in articles of high unit value or quantity demand.

ADVANTAGES OF HOUSE-TO-HOUSE SELLING.   This form of marketing is useful when the producer wishes to introduce a new product or to avoid the competition of established brands. It is particularly useful when he has articles that require demonstra-

---

[3] There are many individual types of door-to-door selling. Truck selling, in which the producer moves his stock along the street, is a once-familiar but now dying example and one that is especially suited for perishable food commodities like fruits and vegetables, dairy products, and baked goods. Another is the call-and-delivery technique used by such service organizations as laundries and dry-cleaning establishments, which operate upon regular routes. A third is that in which the prospective customer who answers an advertisement is called upon by a demonstrator and/or a salesman. Lastly, there is the direct sales approach used by canvassers and others, as in selling cosmetics.

tion under home conditions; it is widely successful, for instance, in selling vacuum cleaners. Like mail-order marketing, it is sometimes used when middlemen cannot be found to stock the product. Always the producer will have the advantages of controlling his own sales force and of adjusting his techniques to the requirements of the individual commodity.

DISADVANTAGES OF HOUSE-TO-HOUSE SELLING. The housewife often resents the intrusion of a salesman. Frequently, she is distrustful of his product because she knows from experience that much unscrupulous high-pressure salesmanship goes on at the door. Even when she is interested, sales negotiations may be prolonged through the presence of other members of the family, interruptions, and the like. These disadvantages the producer must accept in stride. He will have further problems in continually supervising his sales force because there is usually a high employee turnover to add to the expense of his operations.

Direct Marketing by Mail. All requirements, advantages, and disadvantages outlined in the discussion of mail-order selling to business firms apply here.

Direct Marketing by Integration. Farmers may erect roadside stands or may establish places of business in public markets. Manufacturers may sell directly to the consumer through their own retail outlets. A large manufacturer such as Firestone may operate a chain of retail stores, and a small manufacturer such as a local bakery may operate a single outlet. Some factories make all or part of their sales at the factory door.

DIRECT MARKETING OF AGRICULTURAL PRODUCTS. The farmer who engages in direct marketing through his own retail establishment must meet certain qualifications: (1) He must be located close to his prospective customers; otherwise he cannot both produce and retail his goods. (2) He must have sufficient time to devote to his retail activities. (3) He must have specialized knowledge of such marketing. (4) He must have sufficient capital to support his investment in personnel and equipment.

The technique of direct marketing through stands or concessions in public markets offers advantages to the agricultural producer who is able to cope with its problems. He will obtain higher prices for his products than he could get from a middleman. He will have an outlet for his products at times when normal marketing channels are glutted.

However, the technique has formidable disadvantages. It takes considerable time, and just at the moment when the farmer can least afford it: when farm production requires his attention. It forces the farmer to sell in small quantities, and the retail sales are often insufficient to dispose of his total harvest. It compels the farmer to be concerned with the problems of grading, packing, transportation, and sometimes, extending credit. A major disadvantage is that the farmer cannot sell all year round and hence loses contact with his market; he may be forced to build a new clientele at the beginning of each harvesting season.

DIRECT MARKETING THROUGH PRODUCERS' RETAIL STORES. The producer who maintains one or more stores in order to market his own products faces a difficult and involved process. First, he must either produce a variety of merchandise sufficient to stock most of the inventory required by his clientele or find inexpensive supplies of private label merchandise. Second, he needs a large capitalization. The cost of distributing products to the ultimate consumer is at least as great as the cost of production, and this means that the producer's financial requisites will be doubled. Third, if his retail operation is on a chain basis, he will definitely need specialized and trained personnel.

Where it works, this form of marketing offers many advantages to the producer: (1) If his goods are perishable or subject to changing styles, he can sell them quickly by maintaining his own retail outlets. This probably accounts for the growth of local chains of dairy stores. (2) He has close contact with his customers, so he can use his outlets to test, under actual selling conditions, the customers' reactions to new products, price changes, and advertising displays. (3) He controls the selling process and sets prices as he deems fit. (4) In addition, he can obtain retail distribution for products that ordinary retailers would not stock.

The disadvantages are many: (1) The complexity of this form of marketing causes increases in the cost of distribution. (2) Some retailers refuse to stock the producer's goods if he competes with them through his own outlets; consequently, there may be fewer sales than traditional channels would provide. (3) The producer will seldom be able to own enough stores to serve the wide area that is covered by the ordinary channels used by competitors.

DIRECT MARKETING AT THE FACTORY DOOR. Many factories sell directly to consumers. If they are small-scale bakeries, custom tailor shops, furniture factories, or the like, the factory door may be their only outlet. If they are large-scale manufacturers, they will have other outlets, and factory-door selling is likely to be a mere service and perhaps an annoyance.

One advantage of factory-door marketing is its basic appeal to consumers who believe that the factory-to-you technique gives them a special price (as indeed it may). Another is the appeal to consumers who want fresh goods, a significant factor where the goods are perishable. The factory-door technique may allow the producer to move seconds that might not be accepted by middle-men. Finally, this marketing process costs relatively little.

The disadvantages, apart from the annoyance to large-scale producers, are that sales may be smaller than they would be if made by salesmen and that a large volume of business can rarely be expected.

Direct Marketing to Retailers

With the increasing size of chain store operations and individual retail stores, there is a growing trend for large retailing establishments to buy directly from the manufacturer. These large retailers can afford to buy in carload lots and therefore receive an additional quantity discount. Although this activity eliminates the wholesaler as a separate middleman, it does not eliminate the wholesaling functions. Part of the saving obtained by buying directly from the manufacturer is used to pay for storage, transportation, and merchandising control.

REVIEW QUESTIONS

1. What conditions are conducive to the development of direct marketing?
2. What are the alternative methods that may be followed in marketing directly to the business consumer?

3. What are the methods that may be used in marketing directly to the ultimate consumer?
4. Under what circumstances may marketing to or through a middleman be considered direct marketing?
5. What personal examples of direct purchasing can you give?

12

GOVERNMENT EFFECTS ON MARKETING

Government regulations and controls have had extensive effects on marketing. They are an important segment of the student's knowledge if he is to acquire a comprehensive understanding of the marketing structure.

Many problems arising out of government intervention are the result of lack of understanding of the theory of imperfect competition that characterizes much of American business. Moreover, the continually changing economic conditions prevent the development of valid guidelines enabling the government's relation to business to be put into proper perspective. Many concepts (e.g., productivity, restraint of trade, value added) are difficult to pinpoint factually and thus result in additional problems of interpretation.

The Relationship of Government to Marketing

There are three points of view regarding the proper relationship of government to marketing: laissez-faire, middle of the road, and control and operation.

Laissez-Faire. The classical economic doctrine opposes governmental regulation of business. This doctrine maintains that government and business are, and should remain, two independent entities. Neither should encroach upon the functions of the other. This view dominated the economic thinking of America until the Civil War; after that, its influence declined while the other two doctrines emerged.

Middle of the Road. This view asserts that business (including even monopolies) should remain free of governmental regulation insofar as such freedom is conducive to the public welfare. Natural monopolies, such as railroads, are condoned but must be regulated wherever necessary for the public welfare. Thus, in the public interest, the government may regulate the rates and profits of railroads, light and power companies, and other public utilities.

Control and Operation. Other forms of the political state hold that the government should own and/or operate the means of production and should control all, or nearly all, forms of economic activity.

Government regulations in the field of marketing have had three objectives: (1) *To maintain competition.* Competition is an outstanding characteristic of the American economy, and extensive legislation has been enacted to preserve and support it. (2) *To aid special interests.* One federal law, for example, assures the farmer parity prices; another law apportions a certain percentage of government contracts to small business. (3) *To regulate economic activities affecting the public welfare.* Such activities as interstate communication and transportation are vital to the continued existence of the state and essential to the public welfare; they are regulated by means of legislative acts, executive directives, recommendations of special investigatory bodies and committees, and in some cases, public ownership.

Marketing Functions Affected by Government Regulation

Government regulations affect virtually all phases of distribution: (1) exchange, or buying and selling; (2) physical supply, including transportation and storage; (3) facilitating functions, including standardization, risking, market information, and financing; and (4) pricing.

In addition, many general business practices are affected by government regulation.

Legislation Affecting General Business Practice

Two kinds of legislation affect general business practices: long-range business-practice legislation and discriminatory legislation.

Long-Range Business Practice Legislation. The principal regulator in this field is the federal government, although some states have comparable legislation.

ILLEGAL NATURE OF MONOPOLY. Much federal legislation has been enacted to outlaw monopoly. The earliest antimonopoly law was the *Sherman Antitrust Act* (1890), which prohibited combinations, contracts, or understandings that would tend to stifle competition. The *Clayton Act* (1914) put additional teeth into the law by prohibiting monopoly-breaking tie-in contracts between purchasers and pricing discrimination. The *Robinson-Patman Act* (1936)[1] outlawed price discrimination in selling so that large-scale purchasers could no longer obtain unfair price advantages. In addition to this basic legislation, a number of federal laws have been passed to prevent monopoly in the farm market.

PROHIBITION OF UNFAIR TRADING. The *Produce Agency Act* (1927) and the *Perishable Agricultural Commodities Act* (1930) prohibited unfair-trade practices in central markets selling fruits and vegetables. Even before these laws, however, the federal government had taken steps to improve business practices.[2] The *Webb-Pomerene Act* (1918) permitted American business competing in the export field to operate certain types of combinations and monopolies. The *Capper-Volstead Act* (1922) exempted cooperatives from provisions of the Sherman Act. The *Agricultural Marketing Act* (1929) directed the federal government to exercise

[1] The Robinson-Patman Act is also discussed on pages 132 and 191.
[2] The Federal Trade Commission Act will be discussed on pages 128, 132, and 136.

only a limited control over marketing agreements of certain groups that restrict production, fix prices, and engage in other monopolistic practices. The net result of these exceptions is that, in practice, the federal government gives farm cooperatives a limited monopolistic position.

Discriminatory Legislation. Many federal, state, and local laws aid one industry at the expense of another.

INTERNATIONAL DISCRIMINATION. The federal government has provided tariff protection for many industries; tariff barriers have been raised against foreign wheat, cotton, other agricultural products, and a variety of manufactured goods. This policy has been severely criticized on the ground that American producers who cannot compete effectively in some fields should concentrate on those in which they maintain superiority.

Other forms of international trade discrimination are practiced by the federal government in connection with the banning of certain imports. For example, the reason given for prohibiting the importation of Argentine beef is that its use here would spread hoof-and-mouth disease; the real reason for the ban appears to be that Argentine beef could undersell domestically produced beef in a free, competitive market.

NATIONAL DISCRIMINATION. The dairy industry's campaign against colored margarine illustrates the operation of national discriminatory laws. This industry succeeded in having federal legislation passed to prohibit the coloring of margarine prior to sale and to impose a tax of ten cents per pound. When the consequent rise in the price of margarine discouraged its purchase, the butter producer was able to maintain high prices on his product. The discriminative intent of this law to penalize an industry in competition with the dairy interests was obvious. It has since been repealed, and margarine now outsells butter.

STATE DISCRIMINATION. State laws may discriminate in the following ways: (1) by placing heavy taxes on products competing with a state's major industries, (2) by heavily taxing businesses incorporated in other states, (3) by restricting the shipment of products "to prevent spreading of animal and plant disease," (4) by imposing fees and regulations designed to hamper interstate trucking, (5) by instituting restrictive controls over marketing practices.

Typical examples of discriminatory state legislation may be cited. Most states levy fees on interstate truckers and set up rigid limits on truck width, length, weight, and load maximums. The requirements of the various states often conflict with one another. Many levies and requirements originated in the depression years to protect local industries and trucking interests and have never been removed. Some states ban shipments of food from other states "to prevent the spread of plant disease." Others place a heavy tax on margarine sold within the state to eliminate this source of competition. One state even makes it mandatory to color cream imported across its lines; clearly, the purpose is to keep the price high in order to protect an inefficient dairy industry. Some states frankly admit motives of this kind for numerous discriminatory barriers that adversely affect the economic progress of the nation.

LOCAL DISCRIMINATION. The power to license a business may be misused for discriminative purposes. Discrimination is particularly deplorable where party politics governs issuance of licenses. Another common form of local discrimination is exemplified in Pennsylvania communities that prohibit the retail sale of more than four quart bottles (or twelve small bottles) of beer to a customer for consumption away from the premises. It is legal to drink more than that amount of beer on the premises. The reason for this odd restriction is to ensure that large orders for beer will be placed only with distributors.

Government Regulation of Buying and Selling

Government regulation of exchange affects both buying and selling because they are simply two sides of the same procedure. The exchange functions regulated may be grouped under three headings: advertising and promotion, branding and the use of trademarks, and retailing.

Advertising and Promotion. Various laws and government

regulations controlling advertising and promotion have been enacted to safeguard the public welfare.

LAWS ON FALSE AND MISLEADING ADVERTISING. The *Federal Trade Commission Act* of 1914, applicable to interstate commerce, was the first federal law directed against this practice. It did not go far enough because it applied only to false and misleading advertising that resulted in unfair competition. In 1938, the *Wheeler-Lea Act* was passed, making all fraudulent advertising illegal in interstate commerce. The *Printer's Ink Model Act* (1965), which has been passed by many states, outlaws the interstate use of false, misleading, or deceptive advertising. In general, consumers now have reasonably adequate legal protection against unfair advertising.

In recent years, the FTC, responding to consumer pressures, have applied much more rigid standards of what is acceptable advertising. For example, television commercials must not use dummy products or photographic techniques that make the product look different from what it looks like in its actual state, and advertisers must be prepared to substantiate their claims.

REQUIREMENT OF HONEST DESCRIPTION. This is a requirement of common law that refers to the sanctity of a contract. A buyer may sue the seller if he can prove that the latter misrepresented the goods at the time of sale. A similar provision in the cold-storage laws of most states requires that foods kept under refrigeration must be designated as "cold storage" when sold.

BINDING CHARACTER OF ORAL STATEMENT. Although no federal legislation covers this point, nearly two-thirds of the states have laws obligating the seller to live up to his oral statements in selling. These laws are known as *uniform sales laws*.

The FTC has ruled that in personal selling, the buyer has three days in which to change his mind after he signs the sales contract. This is an attempt to minimize the effects of high-pressure sales tactics, which are so much resented by consumers.

USE OF THE MAILS TO DEFRAUD. Fraud in selling by mail is covered only by postal regulations, but these are far-reaching. The U.S. Postal Service has the right to refuse to accept mail from or deliver mail to a company convicted of fraud. Very few business organizations could operate without mail service.

Brands and the Use of Trademarks. Laws regulating branding and trademarks are designed either to protect the owner of a product or to protect the consumer.

PROTECTION OF OWNER. Laws in effect prior to 1938 prohibited the misuse of a registered trademark, brand, or brand name. The *Lanham Act* of 1946 provided that the user of a properly registered trademark becomes its owner after five years of uncontested use.

PROTECTION OF CONSUMER. The first national law against misbranding was the *Pure Food and Drug Act* (1906), which barred misbranded foods and drugs from interstate commerce. The provisions of this law were extended to cosmetics by the *Food, Drug and Cosmetic Act* (1938). In the meantime, other products were being protected by the gradual enactment of branding and trademark legislation, including a law (applicable to most products in interstate commerce) making it illegal to misbrand a commodity when misbranding would result in unfair competition.

Retailing. Many state laws and municipal ordinances have been passed to regulate retail business. The following are the most common examples.

REGULATION OF HOUSE-TO-HOUSE CANVASSERS. Peddlers usually are licensed by municipalities. In many places, they are required to pay special fees.

HEALTH AND FIRE REGULATIONS. State and municipal governments set up health standards for retail businesses, particularly food stores and restaurants. Local fire regulations must be observed by public places, including all retailing establishments.

RESTRICTIVE ORDINANCES. Local zoning ordinances sometimes exclude retail stores from specified areas, such as residential districts.

LICENSE REQUIREMENTS. Local or state governments may require retailers to obtain licenses authorizing them to do business or to sell certain products, such as milk, ice cream, beer, and drugs.

SALES TAXES. Many states levy sales taxes on retail transactions. A few tax wholesale transactions. Some municipalities in states that have no sales taxes have imposed similar taxes of their own.

Four states have so-called anti-chain-store taxes on retail chains. Frequently, the state tax rate paid by a chain depends upon the sales volume or the number of its retail outlets. The purpose of such discriminatory taxation is to help the small independent storekeeper to compete against large-scale retailing enterprises. Taxation of this kind penalizes chain stores for their efficiency.

Government Regulation of Transportation

Federal and state governments have regulated transportation in two ways: by establishing controls over private carriers and by owning or operating transportation facilities.

Control over Private Carriers. Various governmental controls regulate the rates and operations of private carriers.

REGULATION OF RATES. The *Interstate Commerce Commission Act* (1887) gave the Interstate Commerce Commission (ICC) authority over both freight and passenger rates of interstate carriers. In addition, the public utilities commissions of most states control the rate structures of intrastate carriers.

REGULATION OF SERVICE AND FACILITIES. Legislation authorizing government agencies to regulate transportation rates also granted them the supervision of schedules, routes, and stops of carriers. Both the state public utilities commissions and the ICC, for example, have the authority to order a railroad to obtain new equipment.

STATE REGULATION OF TRUCKING EQUIPMENT. Trucking companies operating within a state must obtain a license, which may not be granted unless an examination of the trucks indicates that they are safe to operate on the state's highways. In addition, there are usually requirements concerning width, length, weight, and load maximums. Controls of this kind are often discriminatory in nature.

LAWS REGULATING SPECIAL ASPECTS OF TRANSPORTATION. Two examples of special regulations may be cited: (1) A federal law stipulates that cattle being shipped in interstate commerce must be removed from the car and fed and watered at specified intervals. (2) Another federal law sets up regulations for the interstate transportation of explosives.

　Government Ownership or Operation of Facilities.　This discussion refers, not to facilities operated exclusively by government agencies for their own use, but only to facilities that provide public transportation for a fee. Two examples for such regulation are: (1) the U.S. Postal Service utilizes government-owned facilities for local pickups and deliveries, although it makes use of privately owned carriers for shipments between post offices. (2) Some municipalities own and operate passenger transit lines. New York City, for instance, owns and operates all its subways; Philadelphia owns its subways but leases them to a private company.

Government Regulation of Storage

　Control of Private Storage.　The *United States Warehouse Act* (1916) provided for the federal licensing of warehouses that store farm commodities. The act authorized these warehouses to offer negotiable warehouse receipts. By passing uniform laws regulating the use of the receipts, most of the states have helped to make them readily negotiable.

　Government Ownership or Operation of Storage Facilities. Three kinds of warehouses are owned and operated by the government: (1) *Municipal warehouses* are found mainly in a few port cities. They are commodity or dock warehouses, municipally owned and operated and made available for public use on a fee-paying basis. (2) *Customs warehouses* are owned, operated, or otherwise controlled by the federal government and are used for the temporary storage of imported goods in case of a tax dispute between the importers and government appraisers. (3) *Internal revenue warehouses* (*bonded warehouses*) are maintained for the convenience of merchants who owe federal taxes on stored commodities but wish to postpone tax payments until they are ready to market the commodities.

Government Regulation of Pricing

The federal government has been more active than state and local governments in regulation of pricing. Many federal regulations have controlled specific policies and techniques of pricing; others have set up more direct controls over price levels, particularly during emergency periods.

Government Efforts to Regulate Policies and Techniques of Pricing. The *Federal Trade Commission Act* (1914) set up an administrative commission to prevent unfair methods of competition, such as illegal price-discrimination agreements. The *Clayton Act* (1914) broadened the scope of federal controls by outlawing price-discrimination agreements whereby favored distributors gained an unfair competitive advantage. Finally, the *Robinson-Patman Act* (1936) limited quantity discounts to the cost savings resulting from large-scale transactions. To control price discrimination in intrastate commerce, many states have passed their own statutes forbidding this practice.

Government Efforts to Regulate Price Levels. To control the price level of a broad range of commodities in the public interest, federal and state governments have enacted numerous laws to support farm prices, to regulate the resale prices of manufactured goods, and to stabilize prices during periods of national emergency.

SUPPORT OF FARM PRICES. The severe agricultural depression during the period from 1920 to 1929 led to widespread agitation for raising and stabilizing the prices of agricultural products. The *Grain Futures Act* (1922), which regulated trading on the commodity exchange, and measures such as the *Capper-Volstead Act* (1922) and the *Cooperative Marketing Act* (1926), which helped the farmer to bargain effectively with distributors, did not solve problems of agricultural surpluses and sharply reduced farm income. In 1929, the *Agricultural Marketing Act* set up the Federal Farm Board, which was authorized to use a revolving fund of $500 million to support farm prices. Farmers borrowed money at low interest rates from the board to buy surplus commodities and keep them off the market until prices could rise to a profitable level. But since no control was exercised over production, surpluses increased; and instead of improving, the farm crisis became graver. Consequently, the government enacted the *Agricultural Adjustment Acts* of 1933, 1938, and 1941, which instituted various measures to control production, thus raising farm prices and restoring the farmer's purchasing power.

The first of these laws imposed processing taxes on production in excess of prescribed quotas. It was voided by the U.S. Supreme Court mainly on the ground that Congress has no constitutional power to regulate and control agricultural production. The other two laws provided for the determination of agricultural parity prices that would restore the farmer's purchasing power to the level prevailing at a designated time. Parity prices were to be maintained by government action, including subsidies, financial aid, and the purchase of farm commodities. The *Agricultural Act* of 1965 provided a shift away from support prices above world market prices. Average price-supporting loans bolstered the incomes of farmers who cooperated in limiting output; the government made direct payments equaling the difference between loan rates and support rates. The *Agricultural Act* of 1970, covering the 1971 to 1973 crop years, provided a cropland set-aside program for some farm products and established payment limitations per producer. In 1973, a new four-year farm bill was passed to encourage full agricultural production and help reduce food prices. Government-supported *target prices* significantly under average market prices were established by the bill.

SUPPORT OF RESALE PRICES OF MANUFACTURED GOODS. Two kinds of legislation have been utilized to support the retail prices of manufactured products: *fair-trade* and *unfair-trade acts*.

Fair-trade acts permit manufacturers to set minimum resale prices for their products and to contract with wholesalers and retailers for strict adherence to price schedules. Resale price maintenance has been most frequently applied to drugs, cosmetics, mattresses, power tools, stereo equipment, cameras, books, cigars, liquor, and a few grocery products. The practice was legalized in interstate commerce by the *Miller-Tydings Act* (1937). Fair trading hit its high point in the early 1950s, when forty-five states had laws permitting it. Since that time, eleven states have outlawed it, and the courts or legislatures of twenty other states have limited it.

Unfair-trade acts (or loss-limitation acts), which prohibit sales below cost, are in effect in approximately two-thirds of the states. The middleman is not permitted to sell a commodity at less than the wholesale cost plus the average cost of distributing that commodity. This type of law is difficult to enforce; adequate enforcement would require examination of the books of every retailer whose pricing policies were brought into question.

BASING POINT PRICING. A ruling by the U.S. Supreme Court has made it illegal for manufacturers to use basing point prices. By means of this pricing technique, a manufacturer offers his merchandise at a single price to all buyers within a designated sales area, disregarding differences in transportation costs. (See discussion of this procedure in Chapter 16.)

STABILIZATION OF PRICES DURING EMERGENCIES. During World War II, the federal government tried to keep prices down to the lowest possible level because it feared that restricted production of consumer goods might cause a runaway inflation. In April 1941, an executive order of the president created the Office of Price Administration, which obtained authority to control commodity prices and residential rents under the *Emergency Price Control Act* of 1942. It not only regulated prices but also rationed commodities. Throughout the emergency period, it attempted to protect the consumer from excessive prices that would normally result from a scarcity of goods. During the Korean War, this responsibility was assigned to the Office of Price Stabilization.

Plagued with galloping inflation in the early 1970s, President Nixon took action. In Phase 1 of his program, he froze nearly all pay and price increases (except unprocessed farm products). In Phase 2, starting in late 1971 and extending until early 1973, he lifted the freezes but restricted wage hikes to 5.5 percent annually and price rises to 2.5 percent. Phase 3 removed these lids, with the Cost of Living Council policing to keep wages and prices within reason. By June, 1973, however, prices (particularly of food) had risen so rapidly that Nixon temporarily froze prices, but not wages.

Government Encouragement of Standardization

Government agencies have encouraged the increased standardization of merchandise through regulation of the following marketing factors: product specifications, containers, quantity statements, and labeling accuracy.

Product Specifications. The federal government has attempted to protect purchasers by setting minimum standards for various products. It has banned the marketing of certain harmful goods and has set up grade standards for trading on commodity exchanges. It has also helped producers within an industry to reduce the number of unnecessary variations in product specifications.

MARKETING OF HARMFUL PRODUCTS. The *Pure Food and Drug Act* (1906) was the first law to ban the marketing of harmful products. It forbade the transportation of adulterated, contaminated, filthy, or decomposed foods or drugs across state borders. In 1934, an amendment to this act extended product inspection, on a voluntary basis, to seafoods. In 1938, the law was superseded by the *Food, Drug and Cosmetic Act*, which also regulated cosmetics. Many foods, such as milk, must meet minimum state and local standards.

GRADE STANDARDS ON COMMODITY EXCHANGES. Three federal acts defining the trading grades for cotton and grain are: the *Cotton Futures Act* (1914), the *Grain Standards Act* (1916), and the *Cotton Standards Act* (1923). The *Commodity Exchange Act* (1936) combined provisions of these three laws. These laws are described on pages 140 and 141.

PROMOTION OF INDUSTRY-WIDE AGREEMENTS. The federal government, through its National Bureau of Standards, arranged many agreements among industries to limit excessive diversity in the specifications for products of the same type. These agreements have greatly reduced the variety of forms, shapes, and sizes of such products as paintbrushes and sheet steel.

Containers. Both federal and local governments have enacted laws to regulate use of containers. The *Standard Barrel Act* (1915) prohibited shipment in interstate commerce of barrels with false bottoms. Numerous state and municipal laws forbid use of fraudulent containers. In addition to industry-wide agreements, several federal laws contain provisions to reduce the variety of containers used in interstate commerce. Among these laws (in addition to the Standard Barrel Act) is the *Standard Baskets and Containers Act* (1928). The federal government has been particularly interested in standardizing containers for farm commodities.

Quantity Statements.   Local bureaus of weights and measures usually enforce laws that help the consumer to obtain the correct weight and measure. The *Grain Standards Act* (1916) and the *Cotton Standards Act* (1916) set federal standards of weights and measures for transactions on commodity exchanges.

Labeling Accuracy.   The federal government has enacted several laws to regulate labeling. Mislabeling of foods and drugs was outlawed in interstate commerce by the *Pure Food and Drug Act* (1906) and the *Food, Drug and Cosmetic Act* (1938). The *Federal Trade Commission Act* (1914) prohibited in interstate commerce product mislabeling that tended to result in unfair competition.

Distributors of foods, drugs, cosmetics, and wools in interstate commerce must now state the ingredients on the label. The 1938 act required that this information be shown on labels for drugs and cosmetics; the *Wool Products Labeling Act* (1939), which became effective in 1941, required that labels for woolen garments state the percentages of virgin wool, reprocessed wool, and reused wool.

In 1951, the *Labeling Act* prohibited the use of false advertising or misleading names (such as "lapin" for "rabbit") for fur products.

In 1966, the *Fair Labeling Act* provided compulsory authority for federal regulation of industry's packaging and labeling.

Government Control of Risking

A primary function of insurance companies and commodity exchanges is to reduce business risks. Legislation has been passed to regulate this function.

Regulation of Insurance. Federal controls apply to activities of insurance companies in interstate commerce. The aim is to protect policyholders, and the principal concern is with the financial structure of the companies. State legislation has also been enacted along similar lines. Insurance companies are required to meet minimum financial standards. In some states, the laws require them to offer certain standard insurance policies and also to limit their offerings to conditions and terms approved by the state department of insurance.

Regulation of Commodity Exchanges. The *Cotton Futures Act* (1916), the *Grain Futures Act* (1922), and the *Commodity Exchange Act* (1936) have regulated the functions of commodity exchanges.

LIMITATION OF TRADING TO APPROVED MARKETS. For trading in commodities, markets are required to meet standards established by the Department of Agriculture.

REGISTRATION OF BROKERS. This requirement facilitates the work of inspecting the practices of brokers on the commodity exchanges.

USE OF STANDARD, SPECIFIED GRADES IN TRADING. Trading could not readily be carried on without standardization and specification of grades.

PROHIBITION OF FALSE AND MISLEADING REPORTS. This requirement is designed to prevent abuses such as the manipulation of commodity prices. Thus, it is illegal for traders to issue misleading reports in order to raise the prices of commodities owned by their customers.

LIMITATION OF PRICE CHANGES FOR A TRADING DAY. In order to prevent extreme price movements and panic on the exchanges, a maximum price drop or advance must be set for each commodity. Trading ceases as soon as there is a maximum drop in price.

GOVERNMENT INSPECTION OF RECORDS. Provision for government inspection of trading records not only discourages illegal manipulations but also increases the likelihood that the exchanges will obey all specifications for their operations.

Government Regulation of Market Information

The few laws that have regulated dissemination of market information have dealt mainly with the activities of traders on the commodity exchanges. However, under common law, purchasers of market information do have some protection because the seller who gives false information may be prosecuted for obtaining money under false pretenses.

Government Control of Financing

The government has done little to regulate financing of marketing operations. Such efforts have dealt mainly with legal interest rates and rediscount rates, control of credit terms, and use of negotiable documents in title transfers or in credit transactions.

Control of Maximum Interest Rate.   Various state governments have set a maximum legal rate of interest. A higher rate is permitted for installment purchases and loans (including so-called small loans) on which repayments are made over a long period of time.

Control of Credit Terms.   The federal government has regulated margin requirements for the purchase of commodities on the commodity exchange. It has also controlled credit terms and installment purchases. Government agencies such as the Federal Reserve Board have determined periodically the amount of margin requirements on equity purchases, and they have established time limits within which purchasers must complete payment for merchandise and/or home purchases on the installment plan.

Recent federal legislation gives the consumer greater protection when he is offered credit. The *Truth in Lending Act,* passed in May, 1968, went into effect on July 1, 1969. It required the lender to state clearly the terms of sale, including the annual rate of interest if interest is charged. The full amount of any credit charge must also be clearly indicated. And a 1970 federal law required a credit investigation firm to open its files to a person turned down for credit (or insurance or employment) on the basis of its evaluation. The same bill required any information over seven years old to be removed from the file.

Control of Negotiable Instruments. Bills of lading and warehouse receipts are the only two negotiable instruments of special interest in marketing. Standards for interstate carriers and for approved warehouses, both of which may give such negotiable receipts, are under federal jurisdiction and are embodied in federal legislation.

In addition to these government activities, the functions of public bodies such as the Reconstruction Finance Corporation (RFC) have had considerable influence on financing. The RFC is a government corporation that underwrites financing for private as well as for governmental enterprises.

Government Regulation of International Marketing

Generally, the international marketing philosophy followed by the United States up to the middle 1930s was to have high tariffs on imports to protect American products. This policy was reversed with the passage of the Reciprocal Trade Agreement Amendment of the Tariff Act of 1934. Since that time, the tariff on most imports has dropped significantly. In 1947, a further effort was made to reduce tariffs through the General Agreement on Tariffs and Trade. GATT also prohibits quotas on exports and imports and attempts to resolve trade disputes on a bilateral basis. In 1955, Congress approved the Organization for Trade Cooperation, which placed GATT on a permanent basis.

Congress passed the Trade Expansion Act of 1962, which gave the president the power to cut tariffs at his discretion, or even to eliminate them entirely, on categories of commodities in which the United States and the European Common Market jointly account for 80 percent of world trade. This provision was based on the assumption that the United Kingdom would enter the Common Market, which it did in 1973. The president also received authority to cut all tariffs by as much as 50 percent over the next five years and the prerogative to eliminate tariffs entirely on tropical commodities so long as the United States did not produce the commodities in substantial quantities.

Summary of Federal Laws Affecting Marketing

To facilitate the review of the evolution of federal legislation, individual laws are listed in chronological sequence.

Interstate Commerce Commission Act (1887). Controlled rates of interstate freight and passenger carriers and eliminated rebates to large-scale users of their services.

Sherman Antitrust Act (1890). Prohibited combinations, contracts, or understandings that would stifle or tend to stifle competition.

Pure Food and Drug Act (1906). Made illegal the shipping in interstate commerce of any food or drug that is adulterated or misbranded or contains decomposed, putrid, or filthy materials.

Clayton Act (1914). Designed to implement the Sherman Act. Prohibited pricing discrimination and tie-in contracts between purchasers that lead to monopoly.

Federal Trade Commission Act (1914). Established commission commonly known as FTC. Designed to check unfair competition, combinations organized for price fixing, price discrimination, false and misleading advertising, and misbranding.

Cotton Futures Act (1914). Set standards on which price differentials for varying cotton grades could be based.

Standard Barrel Act (1915). Designed to standardize barrel sizes and to eliminate the use of false bottoms, odd sizes, and questionable practices.

Small Containers Act (1915). Reduced the number of container sizes for handling produce.

Grain Standards Act (1916). Established and administered standards of weights, measures, and commodity grades.

Cotton Standards Act (1916). Established and administered standards of weights, measures, and commodity grades.

United States Warehouse Act (1916). Provided for federal licensing of approved commodity warehouses and for issuance of negotiable warehouse receipts.

Webb-Pomerene Act (1918). Legalized combinations and monopolies in export trade.

Packers and Stockyards Act (1921). Gave the secretary of agriculture the power to prescribe trade practices in the meat-packing industry.

Grain Futures Act (1922). Promulgated rules to discourage the manipulation of grain prices.

Capper-Volstead Act (1922). Exempted farmers' cooperatives from provisions of the Sherman Act.

Produce Agency Act (1927) and *Perishable Agricultural Commodities Act* (1930). Controlled unfair-trade practices in central markets for fruits and vegetables.

Standard Baskets and Containers Act (1928). Attempted to standardize the containers used in the shipment of produce.

Agricultural Marketing Act (1929). Created the Federal Farm Board. The first attempt to control minimum farm prices. Also encouraged the formation of farm cooperatives through aid in orderly marketing and offers of loans at low interest rates.

Agricultural Adjustment Acts (1933, 1938). Aimed to restrict production and increase farm income. The 1933 act was declared unconstitutional because of the discriminatory methods used in financing. The two subsequent acts accomplished the same purposes by constitutional methods.

National Industrial Recovery Act (1933). Established the National Recovery Administration (NRA). Shortened work hours, standardized credit terms, forbade sales below cost, and set up codes of fair competition. Declared unconstitutional in 1935.

Amendment to the Food and Drug Act (1934). Extended product inspection, on a voluntary basis, to seafoods.

Robinson-Patman Act (1936). An amendment to the Clayton Act. Prohibited unfair discounts and other forms of price discrimination.

Commodity Exchange Act (1936). Combined provisions of the Cotton Futures Act and the Grain Futures Act to correct speculative abuses and prevent market control by large interests. Also encouraged the use of standards in commodity trading.

Miller-Tydings Act (1937). Permitted resale price maintenance in interstate commerce within limitations set by states, thus safe-guarding the manufacturer against antitrust prosecution.

Agricultural Marketing Agreements Act (1937). Allowed the federal government to control marketing agreements of producers to restrict production and fix prices.

Wheeler-Lea Act (1938). Extended coverage of the Federal Trade Commission Act in order to protect consumers from unfair business practices, with special emphasis on the elimination of fraudulent advertising.

Food, Drug and Cosmetic Act (1938). Extended Pure Food and Drug Act to include any food, drug, or cosmetic that is adulterated or misbranded. Required listing weight and ingredients on labels.

Wool Products Labeling Act (1939). Became effective in 1941. Required labels on wool garments indicating percentages of wool, reprocessed wool, and reused wool.

Emergency Price Control Act (1942). Superseded the OPA Act of 1941. Established the Office of Price Administration, which endeavored to prevent increases in commodity prices through price regulations. Set up a rationing program for civilian commodities and attempted to protect the consumer from unfair practices arising out of the war emergency.

Lanham Act (1946). Stipulated that a properly registered trademark becomes the user's property after five years unless its use is contested within that time.

Office of Price Stabilization (1950). Reinstated price controls.

Fur Products Labeling Act (1951). Prohibited false advertising and misleading labeling of fur products.

McGuire Act (1952). Reinstated the binding effect of the single-contract agreement whereby one individual agrees to subscribe to a fair-trade price. In this way, the individual manufacturer or wholesaler compels all other distributors of the product to adhere to the price fixed under the fair-trade agreement.

Agricultural Act (1964). Provided a shift away from support prices above world market prices.

Labeling Act (1966). Provided for federal regulation of industry's packaging and labeling practices.

Consumer Credit Protection Act (1968). Compelled lenders to disclose, in both dollars and yearly percentages, the actual cost to the consumer of borrowing money. Provided for the establishment of a new National Commission on Consumer Finance.

Truth in Lending Act (1969). Required lender to state terms of sale (including annual rate of interest) clearly.

REVIEW QUESTIONS

1. What marketing function has been most regulated by government? Why?
2. In what ways is the manufacturer affected by government regulation of marketing?
3. In what ways is the consumer affected by government regulation of marketing?
4. In what ways is the retailer affected by government regulation of marketing?

13

PLANNING AND STANDARDIZATION OF PRODUCTS

Before turning out any product, whether it is a television set or a cold cereal, experienced producers consider the buying habits and preferences of consumers and try to anticipate market conditions.

Marketing conditions affect the producer's activities in two ways: (1) In formulating his production plans, the producer attempts to forecast marketing conditions and consumer preferences, knowing it is wise to produce only those items that will be in demand. (2) In actual production, every product must conform to certain standards. These may be set up by the producer for various reasons, for example, in the interest of economy or of consumer preference. Outside agencies, including the federal, state, and local governments, also may impose standards on the producer. In some industries, voluntary associations may adopt standards for their products.

Planning the Product

Decision on the Product Line. A manufacturer's product may be either a single item or a large number of related or diversified items. Du Pont, for example, makes about 1,200 products, from cellophane to industrial alkali. Efficiently operated companies determine their product line in part on the basis of market information. If a producer has had sales experience with his goods, he can analyze his sales records to determine whether he should drop or retain certain lines. However, if he is not able to undertake an adequate sales analysis of his own, he may use helpful sales figures that have been made available to his industry.

Market research or sales analysis may call for two alternative steps: (1) reduction of product line or (2) diversification of product line.

REDUCTION OF PRODUCT LINE. Reduction of a product line is merely a type of simplification, one of the procedures involved in standardization. A reduction in the variety of goods manufactured or carried in stock helps to eliminate unprofitable operations. It also decreases the capital required for inventory. At the same time, it minimizes the danger that a product will be out of stock and thus improves service to consumers. Finally, by making possible the fuller use of large-scale manufacturing, it tends to lower the price of commodities. The federal government, through the National Bureau of Standards, encourages industries to reduce their product lines. Thus, the varieties of cans for fruits and vegetables have been cut from 200 to 39; paint brushes, from 480 to 138; and sheet steel, from 1,809 to 209.

DIVERSIFICATION OF PRODUCT LINE. Diversification is the opposite of reduction. When demand changes, a producer frequently must adapt his operation to the new requirements of consumers. For example, when automobiles first became popular, buggy companies had to practice diversification in order to survive, and therefore they manufactured both automobiles and buggies. Another common example of diversification occurred in the television industry when the popularity of portable models impelled it to produce both console and portable models.

Standardization

Standardization is "the establishment of criteria of limits to which grades of goods are expected to conform."[1] Grading uses

[1] Shapiro, *Marketing Terms*, p. 160.

these criteria. Grading is "the activity of comparing goods with a previously established criterion . . ."[2] and sorting into classes or grades.

In the manufacture of goods, the process itself produces the desired grades. The grades of agricultural and extractive products are obtained by sorting because the producer has little control over the grades he obtains.

The producer standardizes his product to meet market requirements, which he determines by market research. Production research and laboratory research are important for standardization, but from a sales viewpoint, market research is a more fundamental necessity because it discloses what the market wants and, therefore, how the product is to be standardized.

Prevalence of Standardization.   Standardization is a widespread practice in agriculture, the extractive industries, and manufacturing.

AGRICULTURE.   Standardization is essential in agriculture because grain, wool, cotton, and other commodities must be sold by sample and description, particularly on commodity exchanges.

EXTRACTIVE INDUSTRIES.   Standardization is widely used in such industries as iron ore and lumber because purchasing is largely by description, less often by sample. By means of standardization, buyers are able to identify precisely the merchandise they are purchasing.

MANUFACTURING.   Through standardization of their products, manufacturers can utilize more fully the techniques of mass production and can thus produce in quantity for distribution to a wider market.

Advantages of Standardization.   Standardization facilitates all the principal functions of marketing.

IMPROVEMENTS IN PHYSICAL HANDLING.   Functions of storage and transportation are aided by standardization. Elimination of grades and qualities of merchandise for which there is little or no market means a saving in storage and in transportation. Products of the same grade may be stored together. This procedure facilitates the mass handling of merchandise by reducing unit han-

2 Ibid., p. 73.

dling cost whether for storage or for transportation. Standardization also contributes to the prompt settlement of claims for loss and damage because both owner and handler can agree readily on the value of a lost or damaged commodity.

IMPROVEMENTS IN BUYING AND SELLING. Producers who have standardized their products have, in a very real sense, established a code of ethics for themselves. They are thus morally obligated, particularly if they use a brand name, to guarantee that their products are always the same. This helps consumers to find and purchase the merchandise they want. Use of standards assists the consumer in comparing the prices of different products of the same grade or quality. It is especially helpful in connection with unbranded commodities, such as farm goods, which may differ greatly in quality. Selling and buying are also aided by standardization because it eliminates the need to keep the entire stock of the product on hand for inspection. For example, before standards for wheat were established, the purchaser had to examine almost the entire lot of wheat before he could bid on it. The use of standards permits sale by description. This method of selling is characteristic of transactions on a commodity exchange.

IMPROVEMENT IN FINANCING. Standardization makes financing much simpler by enabling the financing agent to identify easily the quality of the merchandise offered as security for a loan. The amount and terms of the loan can be adjusted readily to the quality of the borrower's inventory.

IMPROVEMENT IN RISKING. Standardization tends to decrease the amount of risk involved, particularly for producers. If the standards have been determined by the preferences of the customer, risk is reduced inasmuch as the producer has some assurance of a market for his goods. In addition, he may be able to reduce the inventory of raw materials once his products have been standardized on the basis of size, color, composition, and other criteria.

Commodity exchanges could not operate were it not for the fact that risking in distribution of agricultural products has been minimized by standardization.

IMPROVEMENT IN MARKET INFORMATION. A newspaper report that Chicago Corn sold for $2.70 has significance because everyone agrees on what Chicago Corn means. Before agricultural standards were set up, market reports of this kind had little value because no one knew the variety or grade of a commodity reported by an outside market. One of the major advantages of standardization is that it gives consistency to many types of market information.

IMPROVEMENTS IN OTHER PHASES OF MARKETING. Producers of standardized goods can concentrate upon the efficient mass production and mass distribution of items that have the widest market. They may find it possible and profitable to reduce prices. Often they will be encouraged to improve product quality as soon as they discover an adequate demand for superior merchandise.

Standardization augments the appearance of merchandise. This effect is particularly noticeable with packaged agricultural products, such as fruits and vegetables, which are often grouped by size and color in transparent containers.

Determination of Product Standards. Standardization affects the physical makeup of a product. Because most products must be packaged and labeled, these two functions are also affected. Note the difference between determination of a product line and determination of product standards. The producer must first decide upon his product line; he may then establish standards for the various products included in his line.

SELECTION OF STANDARDS. Two considerations usually govern product standards: (1) What does the public want in a commodity? A producer collects and evaluates market information of all kinds to ascertain the preferences and expectations of the public. (2) How can a product of the highest quality be manufactured at a price acceptable to the buying public? To obtain this information, the producer utilizes the skills of production engineers, designers, and industrial management specialists. These two points are equally important. Specifications that would make an item a best seller should never be adopted at the sacrifice of efficiency in production.

BASES FOR STANDARDIZATION. Standards may be either quantitative or qualitative. *Quantitative standards* refer to such things as size, weight, quantity, and packaging. *Qualitative stan-*

dards refer to such things as color, flavor, appearance, and degree of ripeness.

Many qualities of products cannot be described adequately in quantitative terms. For this reason, qualitative standards are most often used in marketing. Considerable progress has been achieved, however, in describing some qualities of merchandise in quantitative terms. For example, the color of a product can now be measured with a high degree of accuracy. New scientific instruments measure the wavelengths of the various colors, which can then be designated precisely and identified by numbers that represent wavelength standards.

Control of Product Standards.   After standards for a product have been specified, steps must be taken to make sure that the merchandise to be marketed meets those standards. The producer is not the only one keenly interested in this problem; for example, buyers of a product want to know whether it measures up to the standards claimed by the producer. Various private agencies, such as commodity exchanges and trade organizations, have a similar interest in adherence to designated standards. In addition, governments are concerned with the observance of standards that protect the public welfare.

Control of Standards by Producers.   The *manufacturer* probably has the simplest job of maintaining standards. He sees to it that the proper raw materials are used and that his manufacturing equipment is in good working order. However, despite his precautions, errors may occur along the production line, and an entire lot of merchandise may have to be discarded as worthless or sold as seconds. To make certain that the products he sells are up to his minimum standards, the manufacturer utilizes a procedure known as *quality control,* by means of which he orders the inspection or testing of a representative sampling of his manufactured units.

The *farmer* has some production control over his commodities. Through variety in planting, the use of fertilizers, and crop rotation methods, he endeavors to control the grades of his products. But he is not always successful in this attempt because the weather and insects exert variable influences. Consequently, he must depend primarily upon sorting as his method of determining the degree to which his commodities meet accepted standards of industry. He rarely does the grading himself; usually it is done by the purchaser.

The *producer of natural goods* has virtually no control over the grades of commodities he obtains. He must accept what nature has made available. Thus, the producer of iron ore can only inspect what has already been extracted and state the specifications that identify each lot. Technical products whose qualities cannot be measured by inspection may require various laboratory tests. For example, the purchaser of coal will probably want its British Thermal Unit rating, that is, its heat potential, which must be determined by laboratory test.

CONTROL OF STANDARDS BY OTHER PRIVATE AGENCIES. A number of private organizations (other than the producer) control standards: (1) The *purchasing organization* makes certain that industrial products meet all the specifications agreed upon before it accepts each item. (2) The *ultimate consumer* does this also in a more limited and haphazard way. If either the purchasing organization or the ultimate consumer feels strongly enough that a product is below standard, it will be returned. (3) The *commodity exchange* also administers standards to make certain that every commodity traded meets the standard claimed for it. Inspectors are employed to ensure conformity. (4) Many *retail stores* put some of the merchandise they buy through a series of tests. This procedure helps their buyers to obtain the best values; it also enables the sales staff to provide their customers with accurate information concerning the tested goods. (5) Certain *professional* or *trade organizations* set minimal standards for their industry. Among them are the Underwriters' Laboratories, the American Society for Testing and Materials, and the American Standards Association. *Consumer testing organizations* fall into two broad groups: those that evaluate products and provide information on a subscription basis and those that offer advice to consumers as a service subordinate to other major services. Consumers Research and Consumers Union, the two best-known examples of the former type, test or otherwise investigate and report the relative acceptability of various branded commodities. *Parents' Magazine,* an example of the second type, identifies products that meet its minimal requirements with its seal of approval.

CONTROL OF STANDARDS BY GOVERNMENT.   Agencies of the federal, state, and local governments all participate in controlling standards. Several federal agencies have important responsibilities in this field. One of the duties of the FTC is eliminating containers with false bottoms or other containers that mislead the consumer about the amount of the commodity they contain. It controls the labeling of foods and drugs, ensuring a required minimum of information on every label. The National Bureau of Standards maintains standards for the exact measurement of quantities, such as the inch and the pound. As has been mentioned, the U.S. Department of Commerce encourages and aids various industries to set their own standards. The U.S. Department of Agriculture also engages in this work and administers standards for both food products and agricultural raw materials.

State and local governments are especially active in the maintenance of standards for weights and measures and for the purity of food products. Most states have legalized the federal standards and have enacted additional statutes of their own. State and local officials inspect and test equipment, verify the weights and measures of merchandise, and issue licenses to approved distributors.

REVIEW QUESTIONS

1. What are the major activities involved in product planning and standardization?
2. Show by means of a specific example how diversification and reduction of line may go hand in hand.
3. What marketing functions are primarily affected by standardization? In what ways?
4. What groups of people are active in product planning and standardization?
5. What are the principal federal government legislative acts dealing with product standardization? State the influences of each act.

14

FACTORS IN BUYING

Buying, which includes title transfer, is the marketing function of controlling or concentrating goods to facilitate sale, purchase, production, or use. This function is divided into three classifications: buying for business use, buying for resale (by middlemen, such as retailers), and buying for ultimate consumption.

Buying for Business Use

Types of Business Purchaser. *Producers* buy products (e.g., raw materials) for use in production or processing. They buy other products (e.g., operating supplies and plant-maintenance equipment) for use in business operation. *Business firms, institutions,* and *government agencies* buy products for consumption in their everyday operation. When a retailer purchases display cabinets, he is considered a part of the business market; but when he buys products for resale, he is considered a middleman.

Characteristics of Business Buying. The operations of *business buying* vary; nevertheless, their general characteristics may be stated.

Small Number of Business Buyers.   The business market is numerically smaller than the ultimate consumer market because the latter has a much larger number of potential buyers.

Size of Average Purchase.   In contrast with the ultimate consumer, the business purchaser tends to buy large quantities.

Specifications for Business Buying.   Technical considerations are decisive factors in the purchase of many products. The results of laboratory tests or of other investigations may provide a means of choosing the best products. But the ultimate consumer rarely requires these indications of performance as the basis for his purchases.

Responsibility for Buying Decisions.   Buying decisions are rarely made by a single individual. In many large business organizations, it may be difficult to determine who is chiefly responsible for buying. Even the board of directors, in certain situations, may have to make decisions concerning purchases. If a firm has a purchasing agent, his function may consist merely of placing orders for products specified by production specialists, engineers, maintenance men, or a purchasing committee.

Reciprocal Buying.   Many businesses make it a practice to buy from firms that buy from them. As an extreme example of this policy, one company goes as far as computing the percentage of business other companies give it and then restricts its purchases from each to an equal amount.

Prompt Delivery.   In some instances, prompt delivery may be more significant than price. Although price and performance are usually important, a business cannot operate without merchandise. To ensure uninterrupted operation, the purchaser may be willing to pay a higher price for products that can be delivered immediately.

Dependence of Demand on Business Cycle.   Business demand is a derived demand, depending upon consumer demand. When the economy and consumer demand decline, the business market contracts. Conversely, the business market expands with economic recovery. However, these are only broad trends; consumer demand for many products does not always rise and fall in a precise relationship to the business cycle.

Channels of Distribution to the Business Market.   Goods sold to the business market move along well-defined distribution channels.

MANUFACTURED GOODS. Low-cost items in general use by business are most often distributed through wholesalers. For instance, nuts and bolts, needed by every manufacturer, are typically purchased through the mill supply house. But high-cost items less frequently used and specialized merchandise tend to be sold directly. Woven wire, for example, which must meet technical standards, is usually sold directly by the manufacturer to the industrial consumer. (See Chapter 24.)

RAW MATERIALS. Raw materials, including agricultural products and basic metals, are generally marketed through middlemen for several reasons: (1) The average producer of raw material is not equipped to standardize his commodity; whereas the middleman has become a specialist in this function. (2) The user may be located at a considerable distance from the source of production. (3) Producers tend to be small-scale operators, and a manufacturer cannot depend entirely on such limited sources of supply.

Buying for Resale

Types of Resale Buyer. All merchant middlemen buy commodities to make a profit through resale. They often resell goods to other middlemen. *Wholesalers* bring together a large variety of similar items, such as packaged food products, or many unrelated items, such as needles, paint, or novelties. This merchandise is resold to retail stores. *Retailers* also assemble goods for resale to the ultimate consumer. The actual variety of goods assembled depends upon the type of retailer. A wide range of unrelated goods may be found in a department store; a complete line of a single commodity can be found in a women's shoe store.

Characteristics of Resale Buying. The middleman buys a product in order to make a profit from resale; the ultimate consumer buys a product to gain physical and psychological satisfactions. Still, there is a definite relationship between resale buying and consumer buying. Resale buying is affected constantly by the business cycle and the consumer's reaction to a product.

DEMAND DEPENDENT UPON BUSINESS CYCLES.   Business cycles affect the consumer market, whose size depends upon the general condition of the economy. Total sales reflect the state of the consumers' economic health.

CARE IN PURCHASING.   The middleman is a careful buyer because he must be certain that the quality of his product is high enough to satisfy his customers. His estimate of the probable demand for each product is the basis for his purchasing decisions. He is interested in quality primarily as it affects demand.

Buying for Individual Consumption

Ultimate consumers also perform the function of buying when they purchase any commodity. Because the consumer does not buy anything in order to resell for a profit, he need think only about satisfying his personal desires. It is often difficult for him to estimate the extent of satisfaction he derives from a product, and he is not expert enough to evaluate the quality of many products. Consequently, buying for personal consumption is one of the weakest links in marketing. When the consumer does not know how to buy skillfully, businessmen can easily mislead him concerning the utility and value of their merchandise.

Steps in Buying

Selection of Kind of Goods.   Manufacturers who buy raw materials are usually thoroughly informed about the products needed in the manufacturing process. For business operations other than production, the head of the operating department concerned knows what type of product is required. Middlemen, who buy products for resale, make their selection in terms of the demand and the required markup. Ultimate consumers buy whatever merchandise they need and can afford; they do not commonly purchase on the basis of deliberate conclusions concerning quality, quantity, source, and price.

Determination of Stock on Hand.   The size of the inventory on hand influences decisions relating to the purchase of additional goods. Comparison of the quantity in active demand with the amount of stock on hand yields a figure called the *stock-sales ratio*, which is a basic consideration in determining how much merchandise should be bought.

Determination of the Quality Needed.   For this step in buying, no specific, uniformly applicable procedure can be outlined. Quality requirements vary with the standards set by the buyer.

Determination of the Quantity Needed.   As indicated in the preceding paragraphs, the size of the inventory and the magnitude of demand are prime considerations in decisions concerning quantity. But these are only two of many factors that must be taken into account; in large organizations, decisions concerning quantity sometimes involve excursions into higher mathematics.

HAND-TO-MOUTH BUYING.   This term refers to buying that occurs when the need arises; it is the opposite of quantity buying. Only enough of a commodity is purchased to meet immediate requirements. This kind of buying is increasing because improved facilities for transportation and storage make it possible for a purchaser to obtain what he needs immediately or on short notice. Furthermore, middlemen have become cautious about buying certain commodities that have been subject to rapid changes in demand. Hand-to-mouth buying usually involves a limited inventory; it is thus subject to the disadvantages of an inventory that is too limited to meet the demands of the market.

QUANTITY BUYING.   Purchasers who buy in quantity may obtain special prices and discounts. Quantity buying is desirable when there is a good prospect of an early price increase or of a substantial shortage of supply. In addition, quantity buying offers unit savings in transportation.

On the other hand, quantity buying is problematic. If carried too far, it can result in a decreased rate of stock turnover, with accompanying disadvantages. Also, a decline in prices after large purchases have been made may result in considerable loss to the buyer. Moreover, a purchaser of large quantities of a commodity cannot easily adapt his purchases to changing conditions of supply and demand.

In general, there are four types of quantity buying: (1) *Antici-*

pation (forward buying). The purchaser buys or makes a commitment to buy in advance of actual needs. (2) *Advance buying for the season's needs.* The total amount of goods required for the period is purchased and stored. (3) *Contract for future delivery.* The buyer agrees to accept delivery of a stated quantity of the item at some specified future period. (4) *Control of source of supply.* To be certain that he will have enough of any commodity, the user owns, leases, or otherwise controls the source of supply. Steel companies, for example, control the output of various coal mines. Such control is a form of vertical integration.

Selection of the Source of Supply. The purchaser may choose his commodities from several sources of supply.

BUYING BY MARKET VISIT. The buyer or his representative may go to the different sources to examine the product that interests him.

BUYING ON PURCHASER'S PREMISES. Salesmen visit the buyer to show him samples of their merchandise, and the buyer selects the samples he prefers.

BUYING THROUGH BUYING OFFICES. In a buying office, which is always located in a central market, purchasing representatives of retailers or wholesalers buy merchandise on a commission basis. A purchasing representative is not an employee of the buyer; he is merely an advisor acting on the buyer's instructions. Buying offices are more common in the retailing than in the wholesaling field.

BUYING THROUGH AGENT MIDDLEMEN. Agent middlemen, such as brokers, search for sources of the goods desired by the buyers whom they represent. Business purchasers, especially those who buy raw materials, utilize the services of these agent middlemen.

Agreement on Price and Terms. The buyer and the seller of merchandise negotiate until they reach agreement on price and terms. Although price and terms may be affected considerably by such negotiation, general market conditions often are the decisive factors in solving these buying problems. Nevertheless, the process of negotiation commands the earnest attention of buyer and seller because it may affect the buyer's choice of what merchandise to buy and in what amounts.

Specification of Delivery Date. Since delivery time may be a significant matter to buyers, they frequently require specification of exact delivery date. If material is delivered too soon, it may occupy valuable storage space needed for other purposes; if delivery is late, important production processes may be delayed.

Actual Placement of Order. After quality, quantity, price, source of purchase, and date of delivery have been decided and the terms negotiated, the buyer or his purchasing agent places the order. It may take the form of a contract, a job order, or a requisition.

Receipt and Inspection of Goods. When a shipment has been received, the buyer or his purchasing agent must inspect the material to verify the quantity and the quality. If the shipped order is found to be satisfactory, merchandise is stored for future sale.

Principles of Buying

All buying entails risks, but these can be minimized by application of the following fundamental business principles.

In a rising market (inflationary period), the buyer must avoid the temptation to overbuy in the expectation of price changes that may be to his advantage. It is always possible that a price trend will reverse itself and will result in a loss from depreciated inventory.

In a deflationary or falling market, it is advisable to buy in small quantities (hand-to-mouth buying). This will reduce losses that result from further decreases in price and from price reductions required to sell the stock.

In a normal market, buying should be based upon the computed turnover ratio so that a fresh stock will be maintained and no loss of orders will result from an out-of-stock condition.

The market in which the trading is done should be known thoroughly. Only goods that will meet potential demands of the consumers and give the businessman an adequate net profit should be purchased.

Brilliant promotional advertising rarely sells a commodity for which there is no demand.

Adequate inventory and sales records should be maintained, as well as records of quantities, brands, price lines, colors, styles, and all other elements characteristic of a particular business.

In conclusion, it should be kept in mind that profit is the return received for risks undertaken. Profits usually depend upon skill in purchasing, which in turn depends upon the efficient application of the foregoing principles.

REVIEW QUESTIONS

1. Briefly describe the characteristics of business buying.
2. List the steps in buying.
3. What types of middlemen buy for resale?
4. What kinds of buying policies may be considered in determining the quantity of merchandise to be ordered?
5. Describe the methods by which a buyer may reach his source of supply.

15

SELECTION OF CHANNELS
OF DISTRIBUTION

Changing conditions in retail and industrial marketing force
manufacturers to reconsider their choice of distribution channels.
The trend toward large-scale marketing organizations makes the
producer increasingly responsible for policy decisions in distribution. For instance, he must give more thought to the feasibility
of marketing directly to large-scale retailers if these retailers should
decide to buy from producers instead of wholesalers. Marketing
institutions are always in a state of flux, and the problem of
selecting marketing channels demands continuous attention.

The traditional procedure for moving goods from producer to
wholesaler to retailer to consumer has been changing rapidly. Now
the great bulk of industrial goods is being distributed directly to
the industrial consumer market. Nevertheless, in this market, a
few wholesalers are still distributing certain commodities, such as
operating supplies.

The manufacturer must consider which distribution channel is
most effective at the lowest cost. Contrary to popular belief, the
elimination of middlemen *does not* automatically reduce distribution costs. The manufacturer who obtains the most effective and
least costly distribution is likely to earn the greatest profit; he may

be able to deliver his product to the consumer at the lowest price.

There is no single channel of distribution that will always result in optimum profit. With the trend toward scrambled merchandising and integrated marketing, many manufacturers will employ several channels concurrently.

Factors Affecting Choice

Nature of the Product. Style, perishability, unit value, mechanical aspects, and newness of the product influence the choice of distribution channels.

STYLE. To reduce risks involved in the marketing of goods subject to frequent shifts in style, it is essential to move them as quickly as possible into the consumer's hands. Producers often accomplish this by selling style goods directly to the retailer. Goods of this kind tend to be shopping or specialty goods, which are handled by relatively few stores in concentrated shopping areas. Thus, there is less need for middlemen inasmuch as a manufacturer's sales force can readily cover the market.

PERISHABILITY. Whether perishable products will be distributed through all the traditional marketing channels or be marketed directly depends largely upon distance between the producer and the retailer. Many perishable agricultural commodities require middlemen because they must be transported long distances to reach the retailer. Processed perishable goods, on the other hand, are usually produced and marketed locally to lessen the possibility of deterioration before final sale; in such instances, direct marketing is advantageous.

UNIT VALUE. Generally, the greater the unit value of the product, the greater the possibility of successful direct marketing; the manufacturer is better able to meet the costs of direct marketing if the individual unit is sold at a price high enough to cover such costs in addition to the costs of production. To realize a profit on items of low unit value, the manufacturer must sell to a mass market; consequently, he must utilize traditional channels of distribution.

MECHANICAL ASPECTS. Products with mechanical parts require installation and periodic servicing. A manufacturer may feel that customary marketing channels will not provide these or similar facilities needed to keep his consumers satisfied with his product. He may then try direct marketing, in which case he may contract with middlemen to service the merchandise.

NEWNESS OF THE PRODUCTS.   New products may call for the development of new marketing channels. Cellophane is an example; because it was very widely used for many different purposes, no one existent marketing channel could take care of distribution to all its potential users. The manufacturer had to establish a type of distribution system that would most effectively perform this task. The automobile is another example; when this invention became a traditional part of American life, the major automobile companies were forced to set up their own distribution channels, including exclusive franchises, to ensure the kind of market service required by such an intricate product. However, not all new products require new distribution channels; for instance, manufacturers of television sets made use of channels that had been successfully utilized for the distribution of radios.

Nature of the Market.   In selecting distribution channels, the producer must analyze various factors, such as consumers' buying habits, the size of the average sale, the total sales volume, the scope of distribution, the concentration of purchases, repeat sales, the seasonal character of sales, and competition.

CONSUMERS' BUYING HABITS.   Convenience goods generally require the use of the complete marketing channel. Shopping and specialty goods can be marketed more directly (from producer to retailer to ultimate consumer) because these products are handled by a relatively small number of retailers located in central shopping areas. Much the same is true for industrial goods. Operating supplies are the only products that are likely to be purchased through middlemen, largely because they have a low unit value and are more or less standardized. Other industrial goods are purchased directly from the producer; over 80 percent of all industrial goods are marketed without the use of wholesalers.

SIZE OF THE AVERAGE SALE.   The smaller the sale to the ultimate consumer, the less chance there is for direct selling. A cigarette manufacturer, for instance, could scarcely expect to attain mass distribution by means of direct selling. The marketing cost per sale would be much too high. On the other hand, an industrial product such as a machine selling for $20,000 allows the producer a markup large enough to enable him to sell directly.

TOTAL SALES VOLUME.   Only if a manufacturer's total sales volume is substantial can he seriously consider eliminating middlemen. If his sales volume is very small, he may decide to utilize agent middlemen rather than typical wholesale channels. The selling agent is one type of agent middleman distributing for small-scale manufacturers; another is the manufacturer's agent who provides the manufacturer with a ready-made sales force, making it unnecessary for the producer to invest cash for this purpose.

SCOPE OF DISTRIBUTION.   A commodity may have a narrow or a wide distribution. In narrow distribution, the manufacturer has the choice of marketing directly or using middlemen; in wide distribution, the costs and complex marketing problems involved make it difficult for him to market directly.

CONCENTRATION OF PURCHASES.   The market for a product may be concentrated, or it may be scattered. If it is concentrated, direct marketing is a distinct possibility; if it is scattered, it becomes essential to use existing channels of distribution. A manufacturer who operates within a scattered market probably will not consider opening private offices or private warehouses because the expense would be excessive in view of the relatively small volume of business obtainable within a given area.

REPEAT SALES.   Some articles are staple goods in that they are bought repeatedly by the same consumer. Frequency of purchase affects the producer's choice of marketing channels. Thus, the manufacturer's salesman cannot afford to spend time developing new accounts if each customer buys a low-priced article only once. For such merchandise, traditional wholesale channels will be utilized.

SEASONAL CHARACTER OF SALES.   It is imperative to utilize continuing marketing channels for merchandise characterized by seasonal production or consumption. Distribution facilities that function only part of the year are ineffective. Because the producer of seasonal goods has fewer contacts with the market, he must depend upon wholesaling middlemen to distribute his commodity. A substantial part of the sales to consumers on a time-payment basis are made in December, but producers of seasonal goods (e.g., toy manufacturers) can rarely afford to set up new channels each year.

COMPETITION. When he selects his channel of distribution, the producer must consider the activities of his competitors. He must examine the methods of distribution used by leading manufacturers in his field. Ordinarily, he will utilize the channels used by his competitors because they are familiar to the majority of purchasers.

Availability and Attitude of Middlemen. Although the producer must consider the kinds of middlemen available and the adequacy of their facilities, he must remember that the mere presence of middlemen equipped to distribute his product is not the decisive factor. Much depends upon the attitude of the middlemen. They may be perfectly satisfied with the products they are already handling and may be unwilling to devote sufficient time and effort to assure the successful distribution of a new commodity. To obtain the necessary aggressive representation, the manufacturer may be impelled either to search intensively for suitable middlemen or to undertake a program of direct marketing.

Financial Considerations. Producers generally select marketing channels that will yield the largest profits. They must consider the costs involved in using each channel and the investment required, and the potential net profit from sales.

COSTS OF CHANNEL DISTRIBUTION. Distribution through established wholesalers who have specialized in the traditional marketing functions of wholesaling is frequently most economical. If a manufacturer distributes through certain types of agent middlemen, he may have to absorb some marketing functions that will add to his out-of-pocket expenses. If he markets directly, he must perform virtually all the marketing functions normally carried on by wholesalers and possibly some of those performed by retailers as well. Consequently, direct marketing generally involves more out-of-pocket expenses for the manufacturer than any other channel, and he must have adequate funds if he selects this channel.

PROFITS OF CHANNEL DISTRIBUTION. When he compares the relative advantages of the various channels, the producer is influenced mainly by the factor of potential profits. He studies the probable costs of distribution for each channel and the net profit per item (to be multiplied by the total expected sales). This procedure yields a reasonably accurate estimate of the distribution channel that offers the manufacturer the maximum potential profit.

The Effects of Retail Marketing Organizations

Each type of retail marketing organization has its own buying habits that affect the choice of distribution channels.

Channel Requirements of Small-Scale Retailers. The independent small-scale retailer purchases in small quantities. For this reason, he normally is unable to buy from the producer but must order from the local wholesaler. The small-scale retailer needs a variety of services that, for the most part, only the local wholesaler can provide. These services include immediate delivery on short notice, transportation to the store door, concentration of a diversified stock of merchandise, and the granting of credit. Furthermore, as we have indicated, convenience goods generally handled by small-scale retailers must be marketed through wholesalers because it is not economical for producers to market them directly.

Channel Requirements of Retailer Groups. Small-scale retailers have found it increasingly difficult to cope with large-scale competitors. For this reason, many such retailers have united into groups that perform cooperative wholesaling functions in order to obtain the advantages of large-scale purchasing. Such retailer groups commonly purchase either directly from producers or from agent middlemen who handle large quantities of merchandise.

Channel Requirements of Chain Stores. Ordinarily, chain stores operate warehouses to service their retail outlets in a given area. Even a chain with only one outlet in each community frequently maintains branch warehouses for this purpose. Thus, the chain store performs many wholesaling functions within its own organizational structure and, in effect, purchases goods from ample stock in its warehouses. The use of large quantities of merchandise enables the chain to purchase directly from the producer. Occasionally, merchandise is obtained through brokers or, in some cases, even through integration with the manufacturer.

Channel Requirements of Department Stores. Most department stores (chains and independents) operate their own warehouses, which perform functions similar to those of wholesaling establishments. A department store with one outlet in a given community usually maintains a warehouse for the area. If it has branch stores in the community, these obtain most of their stock from the same warehouse. In contrast with the chain store warehouse, the department store warehouse carries relatively small stocks of a large variety of goods. (The chain store warehouses carry large stocks of a relatively small variety of goods.) Department stores frequently utilize the services of a specialized type of middleman: the resident buyer or purchasing agent.

Channel Requirements of Mail-Order Houses. Like its other large-scale retailing counterparts, the mail-order house operates its own warehouse. Such warehouses are often strategically located in a few major cities in order to reduce shipping time to a minimum. Because the mail-order house performs virtually all the wholesaling functions, it commonly purchases directly from the producer. In many cases, it integrates its activities with those of the producer by purchasing a majority of the stock in the producing firm, by leasing the producing firm, or by making a long-term contract to absorb part of or all the output.

Channel Requirements of the Supermarket. The supermarket traditionally avoids use of wholesalers by operating its own warehouse. Like the chain store, it purchases either directly from the producer or from agent middlemen.

Channel Requirements of Discount Houses. These large-scale retailers, either as individuals or members of a chain, buy in such large quantities that the need for wholesaling middlemen has largely been eliminated.

The Effects of Industrial Consumer Firms

About 83 percent of industrial goods are sold directly by the producer to the industrial consumer. Direct marketing is feasible because individual purchases of the consumer of industrial goods are much greater than those of the ultimate consumer. Furthermore, unlike the ultimate consumer, the business firm generally orders the same goods repeatedly because they are required in its everyday operations. Industrial purchasing is mainly a technical responsibility; frequently, the requirements of an industrial firm can be better determined by its own specialized personnel than by any intermediary. This factor constitutes another reason for the direct purchase of industrial goods. To serve their local customers more efficiently, many producers operate branch offices and warehouses wherever there is sufficient demand for their products.

The Effects of Distribution Techniques

The producer must choose not only a type of distribution channel for his products but also the middlemen within that channel who will most efficiently perform the marketing functions. The producer may adopt any of the following three methods of distribution: general, restricted, or integrated.

General Distribution. Commodities whose sales depend upon maximum customer exposure are usually distributed on a general (or *buckshot*) basis. This is not necessarily an inefficient method. It is advantageous for a manufacturer who produces convenience goods and industrial supplies to be able to offer his merchandise to every middleman interested in carrying it. The producer knows that middlemen who do not handle his product will distribute competing merchandise because the purchaser of such goods readily accepts substitutes for standardized items, such as candy bars, at the consumer level, or nuts and bolts, at the industrial level.

Restricted Distribution. In this situation, the producer limits the number of middlemen who handle his commodity. He reasons that not all middlemen will distribute his product efficiently and that it may even be unprofitable to deal with some of them. The producer may adopt any one or a combination of the following three forms of restricted distribution.

FRANCHISE DISTRIBUTION. The manufacturer offers the retailing middleman a protected territory and, in return, expects that this middleman will handle only items under franchise. Comparable competitive goods cannot be included in inventory.

Franchisers build national chains by licensing others to invest in and operate stores or offices selling products or services. The franchiser makes money from the license royalty and also by selling to the franchisee supplies, techniques or recipes, and nationally advertised slogans, signs, and decor. Such franchising operations now do a combined annual business of $131.6 billion and are growing at a rate of 10 percent each year.

EXCLUSIVE DISTRIBUTION. The retailer is offered a protected territory, but it is understood that he will carry comparable and competitive lines. In return for exclusive distribution, he is expected to put additional effort into promotion and sales of that product.

SELECTIVE DISTRIBUTION. After studying the market, the manufacturer recognizes that there will be a need for a number of outlets to maximize sales in a particular territory. A carefully chosen set of criteria is employed in the selection of the best type and quality of stores to handle the line. As in all forms of restricted distribution, retailers are expected to emphasize the sale and promotion of those manufactured items given to them on a restricted basis.

ADVANTAGES OF RESTRICTED DISTRIBUTION. Several advantages are likely to accrue to the *producer* who limits the number of middlemen handling his goods: (1) Distribution costs are reduced because he does not need to maintain contact with so many accounts. (2) The amount of effort the middleman expends to sell the producer's line is generally increased. (3) New products can be introduced on the market with less difficulty. (4) The consumer prestige of the product is likely to be increased; the consumer is believed to associate quality with exclusive sponsorship by distributors. (5) Prices can be better maintained by the producer; he knows that the resale prices he has set will be maintained because he can refuse to sell to middlemen who cut the price.

The *middleman*, too, may derive several advantages from restricted distribution. It generally reduces his marketing costs. Several factors account for this saving: (1) Less promotion is required because the product already has prestige, and the limited number of retailers who are the middleman's customers appreciate the beneficial results of the producer's promotional efforts in the market area. (2) The middleman can easily increase the sales volume of a restricted or exclusive line of merchandise, assuming that the line is well promoted. (3) He can readily obtain new customers for the merchandise; his sales activities tend to become more and more effective because they are correlated with those of the producers. (4) The middleman acquires more prestige by marketing restricted or exclusive goods. (5) He is likely to achieve an increase in total sales and profits.

DISADVANTAGES OF RESTRICTED DISTRIBUTION. The disadvantages for the *producer* are: (1) His sales volume may be reduced if middlemen who do not handle his product distribute brands of a competing producer. (2) Restricted distribution may make for difficult relationships between producer and middlemen; a producer may find himself too dependent upon the efforts of his group of middlemen. (3) Many complex problems occur. For example, it may be difficult to select middlemen, particularly for handling distribution on an exclusive basis. Problems may arise when the producer's promotional efforts must be integrated with the distributors' marketing program. The latter difficulty is especially vexatious if some of the middlemen fail to fulfill all terms of their agreement with the manufacturer.

The disadvantages for the *middleman* are: (1) He may lose independence by having to accept marketing policies required by the producer. (2) He has little assurance that the producer will continue the relationship, and loss of the line may be financially disastrous for him. (3) He may find that his business policies are virtually dictated by a producer who is so demanding that he feels impelled to relinquish the distribution of the product. (4) He may suffer a loss in prestige if the producer terminates the relationship or is forced out of business. (5) He may find it difficult to meet competition. Because the producer is likely to specify the resale prices for his merchandise, the middleman may be unable to cut prices in order to meet competition. Furthermore, his competitors may handle lines that are subject to restricted distribution, a serious problem if the competing brand is more acceptable than the one handled by the middleman in question.

Integrated Distribution. On occasion, a producer will decide that none of the available middlemen meets his requirements. He then performs certain functions of one or several types of middlemen. He may, for instance, take on the functions of a wholesaling middleman, in which case he will have an organization of branch offices or branch warehouses; or he may perform the functions of retailing, either through the operation of one or more retail outlets or through direct marketing by means of house-to-house selling. This is direct marketing as described in Chapter 11.

The Effects of Pricing Techniques

The producer may follow any one of three basic policies in regard to the resale prices of his merchandise: (1) He may exercise no control. (2) He may suggest resale prices. (3) He may dictate resale prices. The amount of control he can exercise over pricing may influence his selection of distribution channel.

No Resale Price Control. The producer who expects a sizable sales volume from large-scale retailing institutions must realize that he can exercise little or no control over the resale prices charged by the chain store, the supermarket, or the mail-order house. These institutions have developed a reputation for offering goods at prices generally lower than the prices charged by their small-scale competitors. Large-scale retailing institutions are reluctant to handle merchandise subject to resale price dictation. They may refuse to sell a product whose resale price is set, or they may stock it but concentrate on selling competing brands or their own private brand.

Control by Means of Suggested Retail Prices. Many producers suggest the prices which they want middlemen to use in selling their goods. The middlemen, however, are not obligated to accept these suggestions. Suggested prices are merely guides designed to aid the middleman's pricing procedure. Frequently, this policy results in price cutting; some middlemen who dislike price competition may refuse to handle the product or, if they do, may distribute as little as possible.

Control through Dictated Resale Price. There are two ways for the producer to dictate the resale prices of his commodity. One is the use of the device of fair trading. This method is found particularly in the marketing of convenience goods through grocery and drug outlets but is declining in use. The other method is the use of price dictation in restricted distribution. In this case, a middleman who refuses to follow the producer's price policies will be excluded from the distribution channel. This type of resale price control is used principally in connection with shopping and specialty goods.

REVIEW QUESTIONS

1. How may the nature of a product affect the choice of its distribution channels?
2. How may the nature of the market affect the choice of distribution channels?
3. Describe the various techniques of distribution, indicating how each may affect the choice of a channel of distribution.
4. What kinds of price control may be used by a producer? How can they affect the choice of a channel of distribution?

16

PRICE DETERMINATION AND FACTORS IN SETTING PRICES

An adequate understanding of the vital role pricing plays in the marketing procedure is essential to the study of marketing. But it is a complicated subject, and the student must be familiar with the precise nature and behavior of prices before he can understand prevailing methods.

Price is the value of a commodity or of a service expressed in terms of money. The general price level is reflected by wages, the standard of living, and profits, all of which are also commonly expressed in terms of dollars and cents.

In economic theory, price is considered from two viewpoints: (1) the *actual* or *market price*, that is, the money a seller receives at a given time under a given set of circumstances, and (2) the *normal price*, which is generally interpreted as the market price averaged over a long period of time. The *short-run normal price* is prevalent when supply and demand are equalized and production costs are not so low as they should be. This typically occurs in the sale of a new product when insufficient demand bars the seller from taking full advantage of mass production. The *long-run normal price* results when the highest profitable volume of distribution has been achieved and when costs of production and distribution have been reduced to an absolute minimum through optimum use of production facilities.

Price Behavior under Various Degrees of Competition

Theoretically, four degrees of competition are possible in an economy: pure competition, monopoly, imperfect competition (a situation intermediate between the two extremes), and semi-monopoly. The behavior of prices differs according to the extent of competition prevailing.

Pure (Perfect or Free) Competition.   This is a static, artificial economic concept of price behavior. It is a description of price changes in a pure competitive state that must be qualified by certain assumptions concerning supply, demand, and selling and buying.

The idea of pure competition assumes an elastic *supply*, made possible by the free entry of new sellers into the market; many small-scale sellers, none of whom controls sufficient supply to affect price materially; and many small-scale purchasers, none of whom demands enough supply to affect price markedly. The notion of pure competition makes three assumptions relating to the conditions under which products are sold, offered for sale, or purchased: (1) All products offered for sale are identical from the purchaser's point of view. (2) All sellers offer products under identical conditions concerning terms of sale, offer of delivery, and offers of installation or service. (3) Market information, especially in relation to price, will be readily available to all buyers and sellers. Only if these assumptions are made can it be concluded that price is the sole decisive factor in buying.

EFFECTS OF PURE COMPETITION.   Under pure competition, the individual business concern would have no control over its prices. Prices would be dependent upon the relationship between supply and demand. This relationship would always be in equilibrium, inasmuch as the price would always be at the point where demand was sufficient to move the entire available supply. Evidently, in a purely competitive society, the seller could exert no influence upon price. To increase his income, he would have to sell more units of the goods. If prices were less than his costs, he would be compelled to sell the merchandise at a loss. If prices were more than his costs, the difference would constitute his profit.

One other potential effect of pure competition should be noted. Advertising or other means of sales promotion would be unnecessary because buyers would purchase solely on the basis of price. They would know that sales promotion could only add to the cost of the goods which would all be identical in price in a purely competitive market.

PURE COMPETITION AND THE U.S. ECONOMY. There is no such thing as pure competition in the American economy. Identical products are seldom sold by different producers. At any rate, advertising and sales promotion have convinced consumers that apparently similar products vary in quality.

Of course, prices can be affected by artificial factors. Large-scale purchasers exert an important influence on the market. For instance, the price of steel is usually the same no matter which company manufactures this product because the smaller steel manufacturers follow the pattern of price set by the United States Steel Corporation. The retail prices of gasoline and of cigarettes are subject to similar influences exerted by concentrated buying or selling. Another illustration is provided by the leading retailing chains, whose purchasing power enables them to buy products directly from manufacturers at reduced wholesale prices.

In a dynamic market such as that which exists in the United States, the supply of, and the demand for, a commodity are seldom in equilibrium. A great surplus of certain products in some agricultural markets and a scarcity in others might arise at any time. Unpredictable influences such as the weather, new production processes, and strikes may affect the supply of, or the market for, a particular group of commodities. The fact that market information is never universally complete or invariably accurate also contributes to disequilibrium between supply and demand.

Other characteristics of the U.S. economy deter it from operating on a purely competitive basis: (1) High overhead costs often prevent a producer from entering or leaving the market quickly. In a period of depression, a producer's investment in capital goods may compel him to stay in the market even though he may be producing at a loss because of reduced demand. (2) Tradition affects price. Many commodities have become associated with customary prices that can be changed only under the most unusual circumstances. For example, people expect to pay ten cents for a certain bar of candy; the traditional price tends to remain the same despite the cost of material and of labor. (3) The activities of government, for example, the farm subsidy program and parity pricing, affect the prices of many basic materials. (4) Commodities of seasonal demand or production or of perishable nature all limit the possibility of pure competition.

Because the theory of pricing under pure competition is artificial, it is necessary to examine price behavior under other circumstances (monopoly, semimonopoly, and imperfect competition) in order to explain price phenomena.

Price Behavior under Monopoly.   Monopoly is the opposite extreme to pure competition. It is the exercise of complete control by a single organization over the supply of a commodity. Monopoly in this sense is a rare occurrence in the U.S. economy.

EFFECTS OF MONOPOLY.   In theory, a monopolistic business organization has complete freedom in setting prices. In practice, however, the price-fixing power of a monopolist depends upon the following factors: (1) *Public need for the commodity.* If the product is indispensable to the consumer, the monopolist may easily manipulate the price. There are few, if any, such products. (2) *Availibility of another product that might be substituted for the item produced by the monopoly.* If there is a substitute product or if one can readily be developed, the monopolist will find his price-fixing power severely limited, especially if the substitute product is promoted on the basis of superior service to customers. (3) *Government action to restrain monopoly.* Even in the case of a necessary product for which there is no substitute, a monopolist will hesitate to fix the price too high for fear of government intervention. Furthermore, since his primary objective is to gain the largest possible net profit, he will set a price low enough to induce consumers to use more than a bare minimum of his product and also to discourage competition.

STATUS OF MONOPOLY.   Nearly all forms of monopoly have

been outlawed. Two notable exceptions are government monopolies (such as the U.S. Postal Service) and public utilities (such as electric, gas, and water companies) that are closely supervised by government agencies.[1]

Price Behavior under Imperfect Competition. Imperfect competition falls between the two extremes of pure competition and monopoly. Under imperfect competition, the *supply* of a commodity tends to be relatively stable because the heavy costs of plant, overhead, and distribution make it difficult for a new seller to enter the market. Either the supply or the demand may be controlled in substantial measure by a single business firm or by several firms. Furthermore, the *selling* and the *buying* of a competitive product takes place in a *trading atmosphere* entirely different from that under pure competition. Each seller attempts to convince his potential buyer that his product is different, a process of persuasion by means of publicity and advertising. His representations may or may not be factually correct. Appeals are made on the basis of special prompt delivery, liberal extension of credit, or some other advantage unrelated to price.

EFFECTS OF IMPERFECT COMPETITION. Supply and demand are seldom in equilibrium. As a result, prices tend to fluctuate considerably, varying with the geographic area and the source of supply.

STATUS OF IMPERFECT COMPETITION. Imperfect competition is typical in the American economy. The great majority of business organizations operate under the conditions described above as characteristic of imperfect competition.

Price Behavior under Semimonopoly. Semimonopoly is not really a distinct form of competition; it is a specialized form of imperfect competition. Under semimonopoly, a few buyers and sellers effectively control a substantial part of the supply of a commodity.[2] The business organization with semimonopoly control

---

[1] The justification for monopolies in public utilities is the fact that in a given area the capital investment required for equipment is usually too large to warrant costly duplication.

[2] A state of *oligopoly* prevails when the firms operating in any one field are so few that a price change by one firm affects the price policies of the others. A state of *monopsony* prevails when a single buyer's purchases affect the price of a commodity.

may exercise this control in either or both of two ways: (1) It may monopolize the marketing channels through an exclusive method of distribution. (2) It may, through an intensive promotion and advertising campaign, succeed so well in product differentiation that it will eventually supply a significant portion of the consumer demand.

Price Variations in the U.S. Economy

There are few fixed prices in the U.S. economy. Even when *actual* prices are fixed by the government (e.g., the price of gold), the *real* prices vary. Considerable variation in both real and actual prices is a distinguishing trait of the American economy.[3]

Types of Price Fluctuation. There are three principal types of price variation, depending upon whether they are attributable to the geographic area, the time of occurrence, or the marketing channel utilized.

PRICE VARIATION BASED ON GEOGRAPHIC CONDITIONS. Prices of a product may vary in different locations. The broader the market area, the smaller the geographic price variation. Thus, the price of wheat in London tends to be similar to the price in Chicago because most of the difference is attributable merely to differences in the cost of transportation. The price of bricks in New York City will bear little or no relationship to the price in Los Angeles because bricks, as a local product, are rarely transshipped.

PRICE VARIATION BASED ON TIME OF OCCURRENCE. Price fluctuations may be seasonal, cyclical, secular, or irregular. *Seasonal* fluctuations occur where there is a more or less regular pattern of change in supply and demand. For example, in December or January when the supply of oranges is greatest, the price approaches a low point. Conversely, the price of toys reaches its annual peak during the maximal demand in the weeks before Christmas. *Cyclical* fluctuations occur in response to business cycles, with prices rising on the upward swing and falling on the downward curve of the cycle. *Secular* fluctuations, involving long-

---

[3] Real price is the price in terms of the purchasing power of the dollar. Actual price is the market price expressed in terms of dollars and cents.

term price trends occur when prices rise or decline over any long period of time. The gradually rising or declining price resulting from secular fluctuation is known as the *normal price*.[4] The *short-run normal price* prevails where supply and demand are temporarily equalized; production costs have not yet been decreased as much as possible. The *long-run normal price* prevails where production costs have been reduced to a minimum through the use of mass production facilities and the attainment of optimum distribution. *Irregular* price fluctuations are unexpected and unpredictable price shifts. For example, should a hailstorm damage the wheat crop, the price of wheat would immediately rise.

PRICE VARIATION BASED ON MARKETING CHANNEL. There are three customary levels of prices: producers' prices are lower than those of wholesalers, which in turn are lower than retailers' prices. In a period of substantial price fluctuation, producers' prices vary more rapidly and widely than wholesalers' prices, and these vary more rapidly and widely than retailers' prices.

Producers' prices are the most sensitive because producers are closest to and have more knowledge of basic economic factors. They know immediately when their costs increase or when the demand for their product is increasing. Except in the field of price-maintained products, producers' prices vary with changing conditions. These fluctuations are especially severe in the case of agricultural goods because the marketing situation may be radically altered in a short time. The housewife may see strawberries drop ten cents a box in price in a matter of days where a large shipment hits the retail market. However, manufactured products also are frequently subject to abrupt price variations.

On the *wholesale* level, prices tend to vary directly with changes in producers' prices. However, wholesalers' prices are not likely to change at a moment's notice (except in the organized exchanges), even though they still follow rather closely the path of producers' prices. A degree of stability is attained through the wide and rapid dissemination of market information.

On the *retail* level, prices show the least variation.[5] One reason

[4] *Market* price is the actual day-to-day price.
[5] Resale price maintenance allows practically no retail price variation.

is that the retailer makes no effort to adjust his prices to fractional changes in the wholesale price. The margin on which the average retailer operates is sufficiently large to permit him to absorb the wholesalers' slight increases in price; his customers have generally become accustomed to prices to such an extent that any shift in the retail price might affect sales adversely. Another reason for the relative stability of retail prices is the fact that the ultimate consumer often is not a skilled buyer; if he does not know how to compare the quality of merchandise, he cannot buy upon a strict price basis.

Causes of Price Variation.   To answer the question of why prices fluctuate, several factors must be analyzed.

SUPPLY OF THE PRODUCT.   One type of seasonal price fluctuation is exhibited by oranges. When their supply increases, their price drops. Conversely, when weather hurts crops, the decreased supply causes prices to rise. Agricultural goods as a whole demonstrate this phenomenon. In general, the lower the supply, the higher the price.

DEMAND FOR THE ITEM.   Demand is either *inelastic* or *elastic*. With inelastic demand, changes in price do not result in sizable changes in sales. With elastic demand, changes in price may affect sales. Of course, the demand for a particular commodity or service may be inelastic at one time and elastic at another.

ECONOMIC CONDITIONS.   Prices related to cyclical change may increase as the business cycle tends toward prosperity. Normally, the converse is also true when there are no artificial price supports; in a declining business period such as a recession or a depression, prices used to decrease. In today's economy, however, prices seem to rise regardless of economic conditions.

NATURE OF THE MERCHANDISE.   Unstandardized goods, bought by inspection, show the greatest price fluctuation. Perishable goods also show great price fluctuation; the grocer who on Saturday afternoon sees that he still has many boxes of strawberries left may offer them at half price rather than risk their complete loss through spoilage over the weekend. A similar procedure may be followed with seasonal wear. Swimsuits may be closed out at a reduction just before the end of the summer season to ensure that a style change before the next year will not leave unsalable goods on the dealer's shelves.

SIZE OF THE MARKETING AREA.   The smaller the marketing area, the greater the price variations between areas. This is another way of saying that supply and demand tend to become equal on a local rather than on a broad basis.

GOVERNMENT ACTION.   Price variations and/or fluctuations may result from actions of the Department of Agriculture to establish limits for commodity prices or to subsidize the farmer. Acts designed to prohibit price cutting tend to keep prices high. On the other hand, government action may work in the opposite direction. High consumer taxes may decrease purchasing power and cause a decrease in prices, and government competition, common in the field of utility operation, may also lower prices.

COMPETITION.   Under the U.S. system of imperfect competition, small-scale producers tend to follow the price leadership of the dominant company in the field. Therefore, smaller businesses may not really set prices according to their costs and accepted net profit; instead, they may sell at prices that will give them a competitive advantage over, or at least competitive equality with, the leaders. Sudden decisions by the leaders in the field to change prices may force competitors to do the same, although the latter may have no true economic reasons for making the change.

SUPPLIERS' SUGGESTIONS.   It is not unusual to find that suppliers will suggest resale prices to their wholesalers or retailers for those commodity prices that are not fixed under the fair-trade acts. Although this action has no legal standing, suppliers may boycott outlets that do not abide by the suggestions. Thus, prices may vary as the supplier wills, with little or no consideration for the effect of the price changes on the wholesaler's or retailer's markup.

Governmental Influence on Pricing

Before we discuss the methods used by business to set prices, it will be valuable to consider how the government may affect prices without using *direct* legislative methods.

Indirect Regulation of Natural Monopolies. On all inter-state transportation, the government has attempted to regulate prices through review of rates. For example, the ICC passes on changes in utility, motor, and railroad transportation rates. The Civil Aeronautics Board reviews air carrier rates. At the state level, various public utility commissions regulate utility rates on an intrastate basis.

Legislation of a Nonprice Character. The tariff on imports from other countries affects the prices paid by American consumers for foreign products. In many cases, the United States imposes such high tariffs on imported goods that native marginal manufacturers can sell products of equal quality at lower prices or products of lower quality at prices equaling those of imported goods. Federal, state, and local taxation also affects price indirectly. For example, there is a federal tax on air transportation.

Antitrust Activities and Government Competition. The government, by means of the Sherman Antitrust Act (see page 125) and its subsequent amendments, may sue large and powerful monopolies that restrict production to maintain artifically high prices. *Trust busting* seeks to restore active competition by encouraging the entry of companies into a field containing only one or two competitors. It also seeks to prevent any firm from gaining control over all competitors.

In some cases, the government has become a competitor of business, particularly in the manufacturing of hydroelectric power, with the result that certain private utility companies which have furnished electric power to nearby communities have been forced to reduce their rates. In the early 1970s, President Nixon took a series of steps to control prices directly.

The government finances basic research to discover new or cheaper products; for example, the federal government subsidized the synthetic rubber development program. The research programs that utilize the remarkable scientific discoveries of great contemporary physicists and that have been developing the practical aspects and applications of atomic energy are also supported by the government in the United States and in various foreign countries.

Factors That Affect the Setting of Base Prices

Business organizations exercise their prerogative of price setting through price-determination procedures derived from a consideration of the cost of the merchandise, the customers, the competition, the supplier, the sales areas, and the list prices. The final price is usually the result of a combination of these factors.

Pricing Based on Cost of the Merchandise. A percentage, called the *markup*, is added to the cost of the goods. This percentage is carefully calculated in order to reimburse the seller for the overhead and operating expenses involved in handling the merchandise and also to allow him a profit on the transaction.

SPECIAL FORMS OF PRICING PROCEDURE. A business organization with many departments and products may use different markups for different departments, each markup theoretically reflecting that department's cost of doing business. A sales technique sometimes adopted is the *markdown*, or reduction in price, which stimulates immediate sales or clears out a particular class of merchandise, usually outdated in style, shopworn, or damaged. Sometimes a business may ignore its own standard markup procedure and make use of the *price leader* (or *loss leader*), a product sold at a loss. The price leader is usually adopted in the hope of attracting customers who will make other purchases.

LEGISLATION PERTAINING TO PRICING METHODS. Two kinds of legislation *directly* affect pricing by regulating the use of markdowns and of price leaders. These are *resale price maintenance laws (fair-trade acts)* and *unfair-trade acts.*

By 1971, laws permitting resale price maintenance had been enacted in all but five states. The Miller-Tydings Act (1937) legalized such agreements for goods in interstate commerce. Under resale price maintenance, the producer may fix wholesale and retail prices below which the middleman is not allowed to sell. The small independent dealer and his major source of supply, the wholesaler, favor resale price maintenance because it provides a means of meeting the price competition of the large-scale retailer. The large-scale retailer is the principal opponent of price maintenance.

In 1951, the Supreme Court ruled that fair-trade agreements are not binding upon merchants who do not sign them. This ruling threatened to destroy their practical efficacy until the passage of the McGuire Act in 1952, which restored the binding effect of fair-trade agreements upon all distributors of a product.

Unfair-trade acts are designed to prohibit a resale price below the middleman's own standard markup. Such acts are now law in twenty states, but the problems of enforcement are difficult. The arguments for and against these acts are similar to those concerned with the fair-trade acts.

Arguments Favoring Price Maintenance (Fair-Trade Acts). Price maintenance emphasizes nonprice competition, which is sometimes claimed to be more ethical.

It prevents the consumer from underestimating the value of the product (as he may if its price varies).

It prevents what is sometimes called *cutthroat* price competition by large-scale retailers.

Arguments Opposing Price Maintenance. Some manufacturers and many retailers (particularly the large ones) use price cutting as a means of stimulating sales. Price maintenance prohibits this practice and thus tends to reduce sales volume.

A price maintenance policy subjects a manufacturer to pressure from retailers wanting higher margins of profit or those who want volume-priced merchandise.

Manufacturers may unknowingly encourage sales of a competitor's nonmaintained product.

Retailers may refuse to handle the product or to push it if they do handle it.

Large-scale retailers oppose the policy on the ground that the manufacturer has no right to tell them how to run any part of their business.

Certain large-scale retailers believe that price maintenance merely subsidizes the inefficient retailer. (Studies indicate that many price-cutting retail practices actually are correlated with a lower cost of doing business.)

The large-scale retailer maintains that the inflexibility of the system permits no adjustment in times of changing price levels.

Profit margins may be reduced under price maintenance. (Retail profits are high on many products that have not been sold on a resale price maintenance basis.)

Price is no longer necessarily related to the cost of merchandise.

From the retailer's point of view, price competition is not necessarily eliminated because the consumer still has freedom in purchasing competitive products on a price basis.

From the consumer's point of view, the system does not encourage careful buying.

Price maintenance encourages the use of private brands by merchants who can sell large quantities of a product at prices lower than those of national brands that may be price fixed.

The manufacturer is responsible for the enforcement.

Pricing Based on Quality of the Merchandise.   Many business firms attempt to relate their prices to the quality of their merchandise through the technique of price lining. *Price lining* is the offering of merchandise at several different and distinct prices that may or may not be related to quality of the merchandise being sold. For example, in a store that sells home tools, there will usually be offerings at a low, medium, and high price.

ADVANTAGES OF PRICE LINING.   Price lining simplifies the problem of the firm's buyer because it helps him to evaluate the cost price of the merchandise. It offers the added advantage of broadening the market of the business enterprise. The firm can cater to more than a single customer class; if the lining is broad enough, the business organization may be able to cater to all price classes. The selection problems of the customer are simplified because he need consider only those items falling within the price classification that interests him.

DISADVANTAGES OF PRICE LINING.   It is difficult to maintain price lines for commodities subject to frequent price fluctuations. It is difficult to make adjustments in lines during times of rising or falling prices, regardless of commodity class. Not all items in the various price lines will increase or decrease in cost simultaneously, so that some items in the high-quality group may fall in price to such a point that they will rank with the middle-quality line. Then, if price stability is restored, the prices of each line must be sufficiently different to meet the consumer's expectation of higher prices for better quality.

Pricing Based on Customer Habits or Preferences. To a certain degree, sellers are influenced by consumer habits and preferences in determining the prices of their products. In this sense, there are five kinds of prices: prices based on demand, prices based on custom or convenience, odd prices, negotiated or uniform prices, and prices based on use.

PRICES BASED ON DEMAND. The current viewpoint is that pricing must be based upon an analysis of demand. Such an analysis indicates the price that the customer must pay and the quantity that he must buy in order for the sellers to realize the greatest *total profits.* Unit profit is of relatively minor importance. For instance, a selling price of $.12, yielding a profit of $.02 per unit, may be considerably better for the seller than a price of $.15, yielding a profit of $.05. If total sales at $.12 are 20,000 units and total sales at $.15 are 5,000 units, obviously the greater total profit will result from the lower price.

PRICES BASED ON CUSTOM OR CONVENIENCE. Despite variations in wholesalers' and manufacturers' selling prices, many prices are traditional and tend to be maintained. This is particularly true in the case of retailers. (Examples are the prices of thread, beer or soft drinks, and chocolate bars.) However, when prices decline drastically, the businessman may still earn the same profit, inasmuch as the lower his price, the more units he will be able to sell.

ODD PRICES. Odd prices, especially at the retail level, are those in odd amounts, such as $1.99. It is contended that the customer is psychologically more ready to spend $1.99 than he is to spend $2.00; he reacts favorably to the slight cut in price. Whether odd pricing is really successful is a moot question.

NEGOTIATED OR UNIFORM PRICES. In general, retailers offer uniform prices to all customers. This policy is relatively recent in the United States. In the latter part of the nineteenth century, John Wanamaker urged retailers to follow a uniform system of prices. At the wholesale level, except in the case of certain manufactured goods, buyer and seller still tend to negotiate prices. A one-price policy has distinct advantages: (1) It builds confidence and good will for the seller; the buyer never need worry that he is being discriminated against because he is not a good negotiator. (2) It saves time for both buyer and seller. (3) It diminishes the power of the buyer to dictate prices. (4) It tends to result in higher selling prices and, in this respect, is especially advantageous to the seller. Of course, if a one-price policy is not common within a particular industry, the seller who attempts to use it may find his sales adversely affected thereby because many buyers, knowing that he has only one price, may buy elsewhere in the expectation of obtaining lower prices through negotiation.

PRICES BASED ON USE. This is a relatively uncommon criterion for pricing; it is applied frequently by the utilities. The industrial purchaser is offered lower unit rates than the ultimate consumer for water, gas, and electricity, regardless of the quantities used. Nevertheless, the consumer who purchases large quantities of gas, water, or electricity may be offered special industrial rates. Farmers sell milk at various prices, depending on whether it is to be used for fluid milk or for ice cream, cheese, and butter.

Pricing Based on Competition. The owner of a well-run business continually compares his prices with those of his competitors. Manufacturers generally check competitive list prices. Large-scale retailers may employ comparison shoppers to keep a continuous check on the prices of other similar concerns. Once they have this information, they may take one of three steps: underselling, meeting competition, selling above competition.

UNDERSELLING. Some business firms have a standard policy of selling below competitive prices. Macy's department store guarantees its customers prices 6 percent lower than those of competitors on merchandise not subject to fair-trade agreements.

MEETING COMPETITION. Retailers and wholesalers attempt to meet the prices of their competitors. In the tire industry, for example, under price leadership, prices are largely determined by the action of a single producer. Price leadership is found under certain conditions: where highly standardized or widely advertised goods are marketed; where there are relatively few producers, with different degrees of control over their output; and where there are high, fixed operating expenses among members of the industry. No company can afford to drop out of a market controlled by price leadership, and it is difficult for new ones to enter. The leader's prices may rise above those of a monopoly and may influence marginal producers to employ high prices. However, the leader may not be able to maintain his price position because his competitors may refuse to follow suit. In the long run, the position of a leader who has increased prices may become untenable.

SELLING ABOVE COMPETITION.   A business organization may decide to sell at prices higher than those of its competitors. It must then utilize other appeals, such as prompt and efficient service, a complete assortment of goods, and product differentiation. This type of pricing at the retail level is utilized by local merchants, for example, the corner delicatessen, which sells at higher prices than many of its competitors but boasts of a wider assortment and a superior quality of merchandise and provides service twenty-four hours a day. A producer may sell many branded items at prices higher than those used by other competing manufacturers because he has convinced consumers that his product is different.

Pricing Influenced by the Supplier.   Suppliers influence pricing (particularly in the case of sales to the middlemen) either by dictating prices under price maintenance agreements or by simply suggesting appropriate resale prices. The supplier's influence is especially effective in the sale of a new product to small-scale middlemen.

Geographic Pricing Techniques.   A common method of pricing is the negotiation of shipping costs between buyer and seller in the transfer of merchandise. This unsystematic procedure is based upon the bargaining position of the two principals. The ICC has ruled that for shippers working on a basis of "constant charges" for shipments of 300 pounds or less, the rates would be determined by weight and distance alone. These rates may become negotiable.

Prices Constant over All Areas.   This is a systematic form of pricing (known as *postage stamp pricing*) whereby the seller maintains a single price regardless of the buyer's location. It would appear that the seller absorbs all transportation costs, but in reality, these costs are averaged out, so that buyers who are close to the shipping point absorb more of the transportation charges than those who are farther away. A modification of this is *zone pricing* whereby all buyers within a zone pay the same price.

Basing Point Prices.   In this system, the producer offers a similar price to all buyers located within a single sales area. The cost of transporting commodities is computed with the understanding that they all will be regarded as coming from the same point of origin, regardless of the fact that they may actually be shipped from different locations. The *single basing point system* has only one such point of shipment for the entire nation. The *multiple basing point system* uses one of the group of basing points nearest to the purchaser as a basis for the calculation of transportation costs. In 1948, most basing point pricing systems were held illegal, on the ground that they were evidence of price collusion among sellers. Today, the basing point price system is relatively rare.

Pricing Based on List Prices.   There are two kinds of prices based on list prices: flat list prices and prices at a discount.

FLAT LIST PRICES.   A flat list price is a uniform price, most commonly found at the retail level.

SUGGESTED LIST PRICES.   Many manufacturers furnish their dealers with suggested list prices. In many cases, these are artificially high prices that permit retailers ostensibly to discount so that the consumer believes he is getting a bargain.

DISCOUNTS FROM LIST OR TRADE PRICES.   A discount is any reduction allowed from a list price. Discounts are a common feature among producers and wholesalers who sell to the trade. If the trade price is quoted, it is assumed that the trade discount has automatically been included. By using a system of discounts, sellers can modify their prices without having to set new list prices. A disadvantage is that, in addition to possible annoyance to customers, the use of discounts may lead to price cutting and price wars.

The Effect of Discounts on Pricing

Types of Discounts.   Discounts may be trade or functional, quantity, cash, anticipation, promotional, brokerage allowance, seasonal, or special.

TRADE OR FUNCTIONAL DISCOUNT.   The trade or functional discount is offered to the buyer in accordance with his position in the channel of distribution. Ordinarily, the amount of his discount depends upon whether he is a wholesaler, an industrial purchaser, or a retailer. Discounts are lowest for the retailer and highest for the wholesaler.

The purpose of a trade discount is to compensate the purchaser for his performance of marketing functions. It also protects the wholesaler from cut-price competition should the same type of product that he is handling be sold directly to the retailer by the producer. For example, a product with a list price of $1.00 may be sold to the wholesaler at a 40 percent discount, that is, at a net price of $.60. The same product, when sold directly by the producer to the retailer, may carry only a 20 percent trade discount and cost the retailer $.80, presumably the identical price that the retailer would pay the wholesaler for the same product.

A *chain* or *string* of discounts is a variation of the trade discount. For example, the wording of this discount may be "list 30–10." This means that the purchaser is entitled to two trade discounts, of which the first is 30 percent of the list price and the second is 10 percent of the remainder. From the purchaser's viewpoint, trade discounts of the chain variety are not signally advantageous. They make it difficult to compare prices of competing vendors because computations must be performed in order to determine the net prices.

QUANTITY DISCOUNT. The quantity discount is offered on the basis of the amount of the commodity purchased. For example, the list price of a commodity might be $1.00 per dozen, with a 1 percent discount for every dozen over twenty purchased, up to fifty dozen. An additional 1 percent might be allowed for every dozen purchased in excess of fifty dozen. Quantity discounts may be *cumulative* or *noncumulative*. Cumulative quantity discounts are based upon purchases made from a single source during a designated period of time, such as six months. Noncumulative discounts, which are more common, apply only to a single purchase.

Quantity discounts, whatever their form, offer definite advantages. From the *manufacturer's* viewpoint, they encourage purchasers to buy more frequently from a single vendor; they stimulate larger orders; and they result in production economies, since greater production is made possible by the increased demand.

From the *wholesaler's* viewpoint, quantity discounts are advantageous because he is able to buy at lower net prices. The ultimate consumer and the industrial consumer also benefit from the decreased price level that results. All vendors must either sell at quantity discounts, like those offered by any one vendor, or grant some other form of equivalent price concession.

Quantity discounts also have disadvantages. A producer, overestimating the savings that may result from obtaining a large order, may allow too much discount. Moreover, small-scale buyers may resent the fact that lower net prices are offered to large-scale purchasers.

CASH DISCOUNT.   A cash discount is offered for payment of bills in advance of the due date. The cash discounts offered are often in excess of the modal interest rate of 6 percent per annum.

Some bills are dated at the time of sale; others, at the time the merchandise is received by the purchaser (ROG, for "receipt of goods"). Still others are dated at the end of the month in which they are received (EOM, for "end of month"). The most common discount period is ten days. Thus, the invoice may state terms of "2/10 net 30," indicating that 2 percent may be deducted if the bill is paid within the first ten days but that the net amount is due thirty days after the date of the bill or twenty days following the end of the cash discount period. The amount of the cash discount will usually be either 1 percent or 2 percent.

ANTICIPATION DISCOUNT.   Anticipation is another form of cash discount sometimes permitted by the seller. When no cash discount is indicated, or when the dating of the bill is such that there is an interval between the arrival of the bill and the offering of the cash discount, the buyer may be allowed to deduct an amount that is prorated on the basis of a 6 percent annual interest charge for prepayment of the bill, prior to due date.

PROMOTIONAL ALLOWANCE DISCOUNT.   A promotional allowance discount is a special price reduction offered to the purchaser for specific activities of sales promotion in behalf of the product. It is used especially in retail advertising to compensate the retailer for emphasizing a particular make or brand in his sales.

BROKERAGE ALLOWANCE DISCOUNT.   A brokerage allowance

discount compensates the purchaser for performing a brokerage function and is a special form of the trade or functional discount.

SEASONAL DISCOUNT.   A seasonal discount stimulates the purchase of seasonal goods during off periods. The objectives are to move the seasonal produce of the seller out of the warehouse and to maintain a more balanced production throughout the year in order to reduce overhead costs.

SPECIAL DISCOUNTS.   These may include free installation, trade-in allowances, adjustments, free goods, and PMs.[6] A retailer's discount is sometimes given to employees, the clergy, and teachers.

Governmental Restrictions on Discounts.   In the 1920s and early 1930s, small-scale retailers were in difficulty. Chain stores grew at a rapid pace in the twenties; in the next decade, with the advent of the supermarket, price competition that hurt the small-scale retailer increased steadily. Much of this competition was unfair because large-scale buyers frequently dictated their own terms to suppliers. To discourage unfair competition of this kind, the Robinson-Patman Act of 1936 outlawed discounts unrelated to the cost of doing business. Since passage of this law, all buyers have had to offer the same discounts, provided that the factors involved in these transactions have been substantially identical. The law has affected the various types of discounts.

TRADE OR FUNCTIONAL DISCOUNTS.   This discount must be uniform for buyers in similar positions.

QUANTITY DISCOUNTS.   Every retailer must be offered the same opportunity to receive quantity discounts. The scale of discounts must be related to the reduction in costs of production and distribution resulting from quantity purchases. Special rebates and discounts formerly given to large-scale purchasers because they commanded tremendous purchasing power have been outlawed.

CASH AND ANTICIPATION DISCOUNTS.   Both of these must be offered to buyers in similar positions. The buyer must be given the

[6] PMs are special inducements offered the retail clerk for every unit of a particular brand sold. They are special commissions offered usually by the manufacturer, not by the store. PM is said variously to stand for "pin money," "prize money," or "push money."

opportunity to obtain cash or anticipation discounts by making his payments within the required period of time.[7]

BROKERAGE ALLOWANCES.   Before passage of the Robinson-Patman Act, it was common for the large-scale purchaser to claim brokerage allowances regardless of whether he performed a broker's functions. It is now illegal to allow such discounts unless they are actually earned.

OTHER DISCOUNTS.   Seasonal discounts and promotional allowances are offered to all purchasers falling within similar categories. A seasonal discount is one offered at a season of the year when the manufacturer's sales are typically slow. A promotional allowance may be allotted to retailers for the use of demonstrators in the store, or for advertising featuring a specific brand.

Net Effect of Government Restrictions on Discounts.   One of the principal effects of government restrictions on discounts has been to raise prices on purchases by large-scale retailers. Chain stores, mail-order houses, and similar organizations now must pay higher prices for branded products because they are no longer granted extra discounts. Consequently, many large-scale retailers have increased their purchases of private brands to counteract governmental restrictions on their business practices.[8]

Special Pricing Techniques.   Some of these promotional techniques are considered unethical.

Bait pricing is advertising a product at a phenomenally low price. The product usually cannot be bought; rather, it is used merely as a stratagem to trade up interested customers.

Comparative pricing is also unethical because it presumes to show on a price ticket a series of reductions. Usually, the prices crossed out were never meant to be used with the product.

Price packing, used with durable goods, permits the dealer to

---

[7] Large-scale buyers sometimes take such discounts even when not entitled to them. The vendor hesitates to make them adhere to the rules for fear of losing an important customer.

[8] Private brands are those products controlled by the retailer or wholesaler for which he makes arrangements with the producer about price and that are to be branded with his own trade name. In such cases, of course, restrictions on discounts do not apply because these private brands are not offered for sale to all middlemen.

offer an unusually high trade-in discount for the purchase of a new product. The original price was fictitious.

A more legitimate pricing technique is *loss-leader selling*, in which the price is set below invoice cost in order to reduce inventory size or to attract customers. *Leader pricing*, on the other hand, is merely a reduction from the going price, but it is also intended to reduce inventory.

1. What are the characteristics of pure competition, and how do they differ from the characteristics of an economy typified by imperfect competition?
2. Compare price behavior in economies of pure competition and of imperfect competition.
3. List the factors that may cause price fluctuations in the contemporary U.S. economy.
4. Compare the advantages and disadvantages of resale price maintenance.
5. Describe briefly the kinds of discounts in common use today.

17

PROMOTION

Promotion is communication about the product or the company to the consumer. It consists primarily of personal and nonpersonal selling. *Selling* is the personal or impersonal process of assisting and/or persuading a prospective customer to buy a commodity or a service or to act favorably upon an idea that has commercial significance to the seller. Promotion refers to activities immediately preceding transfer of title to a commodity. It attempts to accomplish that transfer, to make the purchaser sufficiently receptive so that the transfer can be consummated. Promotion is a most important step in the distribution process because without it, all preceding marketing steps go for nothing.

Promotion of the product is not always the final step in the selling process. If the commodity needs service, this must be furnished. Sometimes other forms of follow-up are required to keep the customer satisfied.

The United States has reached that stage in economic and technical development where overproduction is a major characteristic of the economy. Manufacturers may produce more than can be currently purchased by consumers. Therefore, promotional activity is of utmost importance. The bottleneck of all production may be the width of the retail counter separating buyer from seller.

At one time, promotion was considered the last step in a series extending from producer to the consumer. Today, with rising complexity of markets and growing competition for the consumer's dollar, it has become an integrated marketing activity, along with product planning, merchandising, and marketing research. Most businesses have accepted this marketing concept.

Promotion by Marketing Functions

In Chapters 2 and 3, we pointed out that the promotional staff faces numerous problems. For example, there is little homogeneity within the national or even a regional market. In one area, 90 percent of sales may go to one customer type; the figure for that same type may drop to 45 percent in a second region. There is no one method by which a market can be described. For the sake of simplicity, we have adopted the functional classification to highlight the hierarchy of a market. However, any number of classifications could be used.

Promotion to Manufacturers. Manufacturers usually purchase raw materials and equipment from salesmen, some of whom sell only to them. Normally, if his company is large, the manufacturer makes all purchases through a purchasing agent.[1] However, the shop superintendent, chief engineer, treasurer, or in some cases, a purchasing committee may make the final purchase decision.

Promotion to industry, often termed *industrial selling*, is generally a highly skilled job. The salesmen, sometimes called *sales engineers* because of their technical knowledge, are specially trained, familiar with the industry's problems, and prepared to sell by specification when necessary. Advertising and other sales promotional materials directed to industry are of a superior and informative nature.

Promotion to Wholesalers. Wholesalers are merchant middlemen who sell to other middlemen or to industrial and commer-

[1] In this case, a company employee, not an agent middleman.

cial users but not to ultimate consumers. Their role depends on a demand for their products that can be resold profitably by other middlemen in the distribution channel.

When he purchases for resale, the wholesaler's chief objective is to maintain an acceptable profit level. Therefore, his emphasis is on quality of inventory maintained to accelerate resale, unlike industrial buyers, who demand the best quality available for production. Wholesalers must be convinced that the product offered to them is a commodity normally carried in stock by their customers. A highly specialized inventory will restrict their potential market.

Promotion to Retailers. Retailers usually sell merchandise in small quantities to ultimate consumers, although they may purchase large amounts directly from manufacturers. Usually, they spread orders among several salesmen who represent varying kinds of wholesaling middlemen.

Promotion to Ultimate Consumers. Ultimate consumers purchase goods or service for personal use only. At one time, most were unskilled buyers. However, as a result of better education and communication and with rising standards of living, some consumers have become highly informed and disciplined purchasers. This trend has been aided by a variety of consumer movements; by inspection or regulatory activities of the federal, state, and municipal governments; and by explicit labeling now required on many products. Retailing changes such as the prevalence of supermarkets, the advent of discount houses, and growth of shopping centers have helped develop the skill and knowledge of consumers.

Personal Promotion

Personal promotion, or selling, is a face-to-face situation involving the seller and one or more prospective buyers, in which the seller attempts to complete the sale.

The sales function is an essential element of marketing management. In a large company, the sales function may comprise a hierarchy of responsibilities and corresponding supervisory positions. At the apex is the sales manager. If the company is large enough, there may be regional sales managers, district sales managers, and/or supervisors responsible for the activities of their salesmen in a particular territory. In some cases, there is only a sales manager or supervisor and salesmen. In a small firm, one salesman covers a whole territory. In a large organization, a salesman may be responsible only for a particular product or group of products within a territory. Sometimes, salesmen may be organized on the basis of the type of customer being served.

In a more complex sales organization, an individual or a group of individuals is responsible for the recruitment, selection, training, and retraining of salesmen. Other members of the sales team will devise compensation plans to motivate salesmen toward optimum effort.

Steps Preceding Personal Promotion.   The marketing research department generally provides the sales department with a market analysis showing market size and composition (kind and location). The analysis may cover either regional or local markets. However, once potential demand is established, further study indicates the problems of established competition, determines the value of advertising, and recommends use of certain kinds of sales promotional techniques. The marketing research department can also give the sales manager a forecast of sales for each territory to help establish a quota for each salesman.

During the year, continuing sales analysis is made by territory. This is a continuous collection and analysis of sales data by product, customer, various territories, and price lines.

Prospecting and the Preapproach.   Two basic steps precede the actual selling operation: prospecting and preapproach. Prospecting concerns collection of names of potential customers. These names are put on "call sheets" arranged by territory or area and help the salesman to route his calls most efficiently.

The preapproach integrates the data from marketing research with knowledge of prospects and customers to be called on during the selling process. Complete knowledge of the product is the key to making an effective sales presentation. The salesman must know the advantages and disadvantages of his own product and of competitive products. He must be aware of product care, use, and service problems.

Personal Promotion Procedures. The salesman must master selling techniques. He must understand the integral basic steps of a sales presentation, which follow a definite sequence. A sales interview requires the salesman to obtain a series of reactions from his prospect, in the following order: attention, interest, desire, action (AIDA).

GETTING ATTENTION. Regardless of the form of selling used, the prospect's attention must be attracted and held.

AROUSING INTEREST. Once the buyer's interest has been aroused to the point where he cares to hear details about the merchandise, the salesman may be confident of a favorable attitude toward his ideas and merchandise.

STIMULATING DESIRE. As the sales presentation unfolds, the prospect should be made to see the advantage of the product or service. The salesman must be able to overcome any objections raised by the prospect, but this refutation must be done with considerable tact to avoid offending the prospect. If the salesman is successful in this effort, he has awakened in the prospect an active desire for the service or product.

OBTAINING ACTION. The salesman's objective is to obtain a favorable reaction culminating in an order. In good personal selling, the customer must feel that he has made a purchase rather than that he has been sold a product. Moreover, a purchase does not end the salesman's responsibility. He must follow up to determine whether the customer needs additional products or services or any other help.

Nonpersonal Promotion: Advertising

Advertising, sales promotion, public relations, and mechanical selling devices are forms of nonpersonal promotion. Advertising is "a nonpersonal, paid message of commercial significance about a product, service, or company made to a market by an identified sponsor."[2] The goal of most advertising is to communicate information about a product, service, or idea. Its objective is to facili-

---

[2] Shapiro, *Marketing Terms*, p. 3.

tate the work of a salesman by stimulating demand. Usually, advertising is an indirect method of selling, although it is direct selling in cases such as a mail-order catalog or a coupon attached to an advertisement.

Importance of Advertising. Large-scale production, mass distribution, and accelerated forms of communication make advertising a necessary part of the marketing economy. Because of constant competition for the consumer's discretionary dollar, information about products, services, or ideas must be constantly directed toward potential buyers. In 1972, approximately $23 billion, an important part of the gross national product (GNP), was spent for advertising.

Advertising is important to the manufacturer whether he sells locally, regionally, or nationally. He must inform the public about the advantages of his product. It is difficult for manufacturers to sell to middlemen unless their products are backed by advertising. The middlemen (wholesalers or retailers) are also required to advertise. For wholesalers, this may be by direct mail, catalog publication, or trade press advertising.

Retailers are the greatest users of local advertising, usually in the newspapers. They must advertise frequently in order to move the products they carry.

Advertising makes the consumer aware of the large choice of available products and services. It improves his knowledge and may also minimize strenuous, time-consuming shopping.

Timing. Typically, a product or brand has four stages in its life: an *introductory* or *pioneering stage*, in which it is a new thing or a new type of thing; a *market growth stage*, in which innovators enter the market and help expand its total size; a *market maturity period*, in which followers enter and try for a share of the existing peak market; and a *market decline period*, in which total market size is falling, perhaps because of the development of new products or changes in consumer needs.

The type of advertising used depends partly on the period of the product's life cycle. The introductory stage requires selling the concept of a new product. The market growth stage requires less advertising emphasis on the idea of the product and more on the particular brand and its advantages. The market maturity period requires still greater emphasis on the competitive aspects in order to try to hold the line against the latecomers to the market. The market decline period requires the advertiser to cut his advertising to the bone, perhaps using reminder methods only, in order to milk the brand for the last possible dollar of sales and profit before it dies.

Copy Appeals. A review of Chapter 3 will help the reader understand the social-psychological implications of the various basic copy appeals. The following list is not meant to be all-inclusive or to reflect all work undertaken in the social sciences. However, a superficial study of almost any kind of advertising indicates that most advertising copy utilizes one or more of these appeals.

APPEAL TO HUNGER. "Hunger" comprises the individual's needs for food, shelter, and clothing. The appeal is based upon the awareness of physical discomfort when these requisites are unavailable.

APPEAL TO LOVE. This emotional reaction, based upon the relationship between the sexes, includes paternal and maternal affection and mutual understanding resulting from companionship and friendship.

APPEAL TO COMFORT. All of us like creature comforts; within limits, the more of these we can have, the happier we are. The desire for a warm place to live during the winter is elementary. A comfortable bed has a strong appeal.

APPEAL TO VANITY. This appeal emphasizes the desire to possess something that distinguishes an individual from others in his group. At a professional level, the appeal may carry a high-sounding name such as "the responsibility of leadership." At the more common consumer level, it is known as the "pride of ownership" or, more simply, "keeping up with the Joneses."

APPEAL TO FEAR. This appeal is based on fear of the unpredictable, such as the possibility of physical injury, economic or material loss, or social humiliation.

DESIRE FOR LONGEVITY. Most people want to live as long as they can. Advertisers, knowing this, often base advertising appeals on it. Many health products are stressed for this reason, as are vitamin additions to foods.

DESIRE FOR SOCIAL APPROVAL. Man is a social creature; he wants social acceptance. Thus, such social attributes as offering the right brand of beer to guests or being able to play the piano well are emphasized by advertisers as highly desirable.

Sometimes these appeals are used in combination form. Insurance advertising appeals to fear (based on unpredictability of events) and to love (based on desire to protect the family in the case of accident or death). Perfume exemplifies another combination appeal to vanity, love, and social approval.

Illustrations. In addition to copy, an advertisement may include illustrations (drawings, photographs, or diagrams) in black and white or in color. The advertisement may utilize symbols, slogans, and other identifying marks.

Basic Advertising Approach. There are three different basic approaches to advertising: product advertising, institutional advertising, and reminder advertising. Each is employed according to how much of the sales job it is intended to achieve.

PRODUCT ADVERTISING. Such advertising tries to influence the consumer to buy a particular product or brand. There are two degrees: hard-sell advertising and image-building advertising.

Hard-sell advertising is evident in much advertising of consumer medicinal products. Typical examples are a diagrammatic sketch of a man with a pounding headache and a direct attempt to relate use of the particular brand of medication to alleviation of his symptoms. In image-building advertising, there is a subtler attempt to emphasize the advantages the customer will derive from the particular brand. The advertising says little about direct advantages of the product but implies many nice things about it or its use. The slogan "Come to Marlboro country" is an example.

INSTITUTIONAL ADVERTISING. Institutional advertising says nothing about a specific product or brand; rather, it concerns only the institution (company). Although its aim is not product-oriented, it may be designed to build prestige of the advertiser's brands.

REMINDER ADVERTISING. Reminder advertising is product-oriented but says or implies nothing about the product. Its only goal is to develop or maintain product familiarity. When the product has reached its peak, this advertising aims only to remind the public of the brand name. Sometimes there is a product shortage, and such advertising is used to keep the name alive.

Media. Many considerations affect the decision about the medium or the combination of media to employ. The choice depends on kind of product, location and level of markets (as determined by marketing research), and the money available.

PRINT MEDIA. These include magazines, newspapers, and supplements (the magazine sections or comic sections in Sunday editions of newspapers). Some of the types of magazines commonly used by advertisers are those reaching the general executive market (e.g., *Newsweek* and *Business Week*), those reaching homemakers (e.g., *Ladies' Home Journal* and *McCall's*), and farm magazines. Specific business publications, called *trade press publications*, reach specialized segments of the business market.

Newspapers can be categorized as daily and weekly publications. They can be classified as metropolitan or suburban. They can be classed according to type of consumer reached (general versus special ethnic groups) and according to whether they are paid for by the consumer or are free (*controlled circulation*, such as the shopping newspaper).

BROADCAST MEDIA. These include radio and television, which account for a large share of the advertising dollar. Commercials are presented at intervals during a broadcast or between shows. In the *straight announcement* (usual in radio, occasional in television), the advertiser makes a direct statement about the product. In the *demonstration* (usual in television), the product is shown at work in a viewer-interest situation.

OUTDOOR MEDIA. These include billboards, posters, painted billboards, and spectaculars (electric signs, with or without moving parts, which are found in most major North American cities). Transportation advertising (*car cards*) is found in or on subways, streetcars, buses, taxicabs, and in or around waiting rooms and transportation platforms. Because the physical size of the advertising area usually limits the amount of copy, these media are most often used for straight reminder advertising or a simple and short claim for the product.

DIRECT MAIL. Direct mail is any advertising sent to potential buyers through the mail. It ranges from simple postcards to expensively produced, colored, multipaged catalogs. Direct mail is useful in cases when the advertiser wants to reach, not all members of the population, but only those he considers prime prospects.

OTHER MEDIA.   Other forms of advertising are novelties or specialties such as calendars, balloons, memobooks, pens. Some 95 percent of motion picture theaters show advertisements for brands or services. Media such as skywriting and special menus and programs are less often used.

Management of Advertising.   Thus far, we have discussed advertising in terms of its planning (and, to some degree, its techniques). Management and execution of advertising campaigns are just as important. To assure reasonable success, campaigns usually require the following basic steps: budget preparation, planning of copy strategy, copy preparation, developing media strategy, media selection, and testing effectiveness of the advertising.

BUDGET PREPARATION.   First, the amount of money to be allocated to advertising must be determined. Second, this sum must be allocated to the several company divisions or products participating in the campaign. A certain percentage may be spent on advertising the products of the company; a smaller percentage, on institutional advertising. After the total advertising budget has been approved, decisions are made on how to execute specific advertising programs.

COPY STRATEGY.   The copy strategy or platform is the basic campaign idea or theme around which all advertising is to be built. The problem is to find a copy strategy based on a sound framework of consumer psychology, yet meeting all general and specific campaign goals. To achieve this, it is important not only to understand consumer drives but also to have full knowledge of the product and consumer reaction to it.

COPY PREPARATION.   The preparation of copy requires a wordsmith to translate copy strategy into a finished written or spoken advertisement. The copywriter must achieve an appealing blend and arrangement of words, appealing in the sense that the consumer's buying interest is aroused. The content of the copy will generally tie in with the entire strategy of the marketing plan.

Media Strategy. Sometimes known as the *media mix*, this strategy requires that the basic objectives of the campaign be kept clearly in mind. Media objectives relative to these overall goals must be specified, particularly in terms of desired numbers and kinds of people to be reached and the frequency of reaching them within the advertising budget.

Media Selection. Individual media choice is integrated with total campaign objectives. Each specific medium is classified by coverage and nature of the audience. For his advertising campaign to be effective, the advertiser must reach the kinds of people he regards as prospects.

Testing Advertising Effectiveness. It is impossible to measure the effect of advertising through sales; too many other factors also affect sales. However, through marketing research, the number of people reached by advertising can be measured. It is possible to estimate the information these people receive from the advertising and the influence of the advertising on their attitude toward the product. There are audience-size measures, "playback" measures, and attitude measures of advertising impact. There is even a service (available in two eastern cities) that enables the advertiser to offer two different television commercials to balanced groups of people within the area (without their knowledge) and measure the sales effect through keeping records of their purchases. This is accomplished by having two sets of cable wirings. One-half the homes are on one set, the second half on another, without their knowledge. It is mechanically possible to see that one set of homes receives one commercial while the other set receives an alternate commercial. When samples of these homes are selected for study, family members keep records of what they buy—unaware that their records have anything to do with television.

Building the Image

The concept of the image has become important in marketing strategy. The *image* is the final impression of a product or company that a consumer receives through both his physical senses and his psychological experiences. There are six basic kinds of images: corporate, product, brand, wholesaler, retailer, and consumer's self-image. All are interdependent.

Corporate image transcends all other types of images because a company with a poor image will have difficulty in gaining optimal market penetration for its product. Corporate image depends upon the selection of the advertising media and the quality of the public relations program. The customer must feel that the company's major objective is to satisfy customer demand.

Product image depends upon the image-building operation of the several companies making the same product line. A product may be considered as being for the young or for the elderly, as connoting high or low social status, as being feminine or masculine. Associations helping to build product image for an industry should try to communicate that the product is of good quality and is dependable.

Complementing the corporate and product images is the brand image. Once a product line has been accepted by the public, each company making that product tries to have its own brand accepted. Brand acceptance depends upon packaging, labeling, brand name, identification, advertising, and the promotional efforts of a company. The corporate image of the company can help or hurt brand acceptance, and hearsay evidence from neighbors or friends may modify a brand's acceptance by consumers.

Even if the other images in the several steps of the channel of distribution are acceptable, a sales barrier may arise if the wholesaler's image is poor. If a product is carried by a retailer with a poor image, the sales of the product to customers will not reach optimal level.

The consumer's self-image is a very important factor in marketing. The self-image is the role the consumer believes he is playing or the way he believes others regard him. It is composed of basic physiological, sociological, and psychological elements. No matter how good the corporate, product, and outlet images may be, if they do not conform to the self-image of individuals in a market segment, acceptance of a brand will be negatively affected.

Marketing managers must consistently weigh all these image components. If any one image component is weak, appropriate steps must be taken to correct the situation.

The Advertising Organization

Three types of advertising organization are basically important in producing advertising: the advertising agency, the manufacturing advertiser, and the retail advertiser.

Advertising Agency. The advertising agency is responsible for preparation of most national advertising. This independent organization prepares the advertisement and inserts it in the medium according to a predetermined schedule. The agency bills the client at the standard media rates, obtaining its income through a discount or commission. Until 1956, 15 percent was the standard discount with most agencies and media. In that year, the American Association of Advertising Agencies signed a consent decree with the Justice Department affirming that its members would not force clients to accept this figure. Actually, the 15 percent fee is still the most common procedure. However, there is a trend toward a 100 percent fee compensation agreement. Annual billings for fee clients are computed from the disbursements and costs involved in handling a client's project. Most national advertisers do not attempt to place their advertising directly with the medium because they would not be granted the discount offered to the agencies.

The advertising agency may be organized in several different ways. Some agencies follow the product group method, in which a team of specialists by function report directly to the account executive responsible to the advertiser. A large agency will probably be departmentalized functionally. Generally, the larger agencies have the following structure.

CLIENT RELATIONS DEPARTMENT. This department has a dual responsibility: It convinces advertisers of the desirability of the agency's ideas and reconciles the agency with what the advertisers think should be done. The account executives, who maintain relationships between agency and advertisers, are found in this department.

COPY DEPARTMENT. Ideas for the copy platform often originate here. This department creates written and spoken words for the campaign. Copywriters translate copy strategy into actual copy for individual advertisements.

Art Department. The art department develops art strategy to accompany the copy platform; it also determines the type of artwork required. It chooses artists or photographers to prepare the material and accepts general responsibility for seeing that artwork meeting the campaign requirements is provided on schedule.

Media Department. The media department recommends the media mix for the campaign, selects individual media, and prepares the placement schedule. Its work is sometimes restricted to print media.

Radio and Television, and Outdoor Advertising Departments. Because radio and television and outdoor advertising are highly specialized media, some large agencies have a separate department for each. The radio and television department recommends the network or station to be used.

Merchandising Department. Since advertising can work only within the framework of sound merchandising, some agencies also perform a merchandising operation for their clients. The department may advise the advertiser about the most suitable or effective distribution channels, pricing policies, point-of-sale material, and personal selling activities. Occasionally, it may perform live merchandising activities for the client, such as dealer contacts and placement of point-of-sale material in outlets.

Research Department. The larger agencies also have a research department, which specializes in copy testing and measurement of advertising effectiveness.

Production Department. Many aspects of advertising require attention to mechanical detail, such as the preparation of cuts and other types of engravings for printing use. Also, it is the agency's responsibility to see that all advertising paid for has actually been distributed to the public. Therefore, the agency must scan newspapers and magazines on dates when advertising has been scheduled. The more mechanical duties of the advertising agency's business are usually handled in a department of this sort.

Plans Board. Many agencies have a plans board, generally composed of the principal executive specialists of the agency. Responsible for overall strategy in advertising, the board discusses pros and cons of a proposed program and determines, either through its own approaches or by a review of plans developed by others, what broad recommendations will be made to the advertiser.

OTHER DEPARTMENTS.   An agency usually has personnel responsible for development of new business prospects. It also has a unit responsible for financial operations and, if it is sufficiently large, a personnel department.

Many advertising agencies are small. Although not all are organized into the formal departments listed, each must perform the functions described.

In recent years, as increasing economic pressures made it more and more difficult for agencies to make a profit, a great many cut back on or completely eliminated some of the departments not directly connected with the preparation of advertising or the buying of advertising time or space. The research department, for instance, is far smaller in the typical agency than it used to be. Some groups of advertising specialists have even set up so-called *boutiques*, where all that is offered is the creative service of preparing the advertising; other groups have set themselves up to do only media buying.

Manufacturer Advertiser.   The large manufacturer advertiser performs the functions of marketing planning. Included with this may be specialized functions of advertising planning, media selection, and sales promotion. If the company is large enough, these specialized functions will be handled by specific individuals; otherwise, the product brand manager will perform them in addition to his general brand marketing planning. The company may have specialists in each of these areas so well established that they become (for the entire marketing program, regardless of brand) the dominant force in decisions about their functions.

Retail Advertiser.   The retail advertiser normally uses no advertising agency because advertising media offer lower rates for retail advertising than for national coverage and therefore allow no retail discounts. Hence, for financial reasons, no advertising agency could accept such retail assignments. In addition, the advertising agency could not meet the daily advertising demands of the usual retail operation or become sufficiently familiar with the thousands of products handled by a retail establishment.

The small retailer cannot afford the luxury of his own facilities for advertising production. He must depend upon help offered by suppliers and media. Manufacturers selling nationwide often provide cooperative advertising for small retailers who carry their products.

The large retailer has a department to prepare advertising. Headed by a department manager, its staff may include copywriters, artists, scriptwriters, and other specialists.

Nonpersonal Promotion: Sales Promotion

Sales promotion consists of "those sales activities that supplement both personal selling and advertising and coordinate them and help to make them effective, such as displays, shows and expositions, demonstrations, and the non-recurrent selling efforts not in the ordinary routine."[3] It is usually used to publicize a product or service. Examples of sales promotion activities include printed materials displays, sampling, price promotions, premiums, contests, and publicity.

Printed Materials.   These include circulars, booklets, inserts for direct mail provided for the trade.

Displays.   Displays may be supplied by the advertiser to his retailers. They may be simple counter boxes to hold the product or complex, intricate mechanisms, lighted and with moving parts, designed for show windows. The advertiser's salesmen sometimes help arrange the retailer's displays.

Sampling.   The seller provides prospects with a free product sample or a special coupon offering a free product or a reduced price on first purchase of the product. In-store demonstrations with samples are another type of sampling.

Price Promotions.   The manufacturer may offer special prices for his brand to stimulate sales. The offer may take varying forms: two for the price of one, the $.01 sale (where a second may be had for $.01 over the "regular" price for one), a banded offer (where the price of the product includes some other product, such as a

[3] Ibid.

free toothbrush with a tube of the toothpaste), or a refund (where all or part of the purchase price is refunded if the consumer sends in or uses a coupon).

Premiums.   Premiums are growing in importance as a marketing tool, and like other types of sales promotion, their purpose is to increase sales. Premiums include trading stamps, in-package premiums, and premiums offered, with or without cash, for sending in a coupon.

Contests.   Contests are promotional devices used with salesmen, middlemen, and consumers. In contests directed to consumers, proof that the sponsor's product has been purchased is often required.

Publicity

Publicity is "any form of commercially significant news about a product, an institution, a service, or a person published in space or . . . time that is not paid for by the sponsor."[4] It has been claimed that publicity is more uncritically accepted by the consumer than advertising because he is likely to believe that the information is being impartially reported for its news value. Sellers try to obtain this type of publicity as part of their selling effort. Some large advertising agencies have even organized special departments to perform this function for advertisers.

Mechanical Promotion

Advertising and promotion seek to *prepare* the prospect for the sale; mechanical selling is designed to *complete* the sale. To make automatic selling feasible, a product should have a mass market, must be amenable to automatic merchandising, and should usually be a standardized item.

Forms of Mechanical Promotion.   There are three major forms of mechanical selling: the turnstile machine, the coin-stimulated electric machine, and the vending machine.

[4] Ibid.

TURNSTILE-TYPE MACHINE. With this mechanical device, the depositor is permitted access to the product or service on deposit of a coin. This is often found in transportation.

COIN-STIMULATED ELECTRIC MACHINE. With some mechanical devices, developed for other than vending purposes, there is a coin device that activates the electric current necessary for their operation. Among these devices are telephones, laundromat washers and driers, and television sets (in hotel and motel rooms).

VENDING MACHINE. This has been discussed in the section Large-Scale Retailing in Chapter 10. Upon deposit of appropriate coins, the machine vends or dispenses the particular product or service.

REVIEW QUESTIONS

1. Define personal promotion, and describe the steps that should precede it.
2. What basic principles are used in all personal promotion?
3. Define advertising, and describe the steps followed in the organization and execution of an advertising campaign.
4. Define sales promotion, and describe the various types used.
5. Define image, and explain why it is important in marketing.

18

THE PHYSICAL HANDLING OF GOODS: STORAGE AND TRANSPORTATION

The transfer of goods from the producer to the consumer necessitates a great deal of physical handling. Goods must be stored, either on the premises of the producer or on those of a middleman; and eventually they must, of course, be transported to the consumer. The two principal procedures involved in physical handling are, therefore, storage and transportation.

Functions of Storage

Storage is "a marketing function characterized by the creation of time utility by holding and preserving goods for varying periods of time."[1] Practically all commodities require storage at some time during their distribution.

Creation of Time Utility. If consumption lags behind the production of goods, the excess product is stored until needed. This procedure narrows the gap between consumption and production. For example, many farm products (such as wheat, vegetables, and fruits) have a more or less stable consumption rate

[1] Shapiro, *Marketing Terms*, p. 162.

throughout the year, but only certain seasons favor their growth. Consequently, excess wheat is stored as is, and surplus vegetables and fruits are canned or frozen and then stored so that they will be available to the consumer whenever he desires them.

Creation of Form Utility.   Storage may modify or improve the quality of commodities, thus enhancing their value or desirability. Many commodities benefit from aging, as in the curing of tobacco, the aging of meat, and the aging of liquor.

Creation of Place Utility.   Storage encourages standardization and grading by providing space and facilities. A principal function of storage is to make goods available to a buyer at his place of business when he needs them. For example, a retailer who runs out of a particular item, precooked cereal, can simply telephone the wholesaler's warehouse and have the merchandise delivered within twenty-four to forty-eight hours.

Results of Storage

Expedition of Financing.   The warehouseman with whom goods are stored may offer a financing service to the owners of the merchandise. If he does not offer such a service, he will give the owners a negotiable warehouse receipt that will make it possible for them to obtain outside financing.

Reduction of Risking.   Certain risks are inherent in ownership. It is possible, however, for the owner of goods to reduce his risks by storing merchandise with a reputable warehousing firm. The warehouseman absorbs part of the risk. In addition, the operations of the commodity exchange, which are based largely upon the provision of safe storage, reduce the producer's risk. The commodity exchange permits hedging, a transaction that often eliminates the risk caused by price fluctuations, an inevitable risk involved in commodity ownership.

Cutting of Transportation Costs.   Transportation costs are often reduced through storage that allows greater quantities of a commodity to be accumulated. Because shipments of merchandise in quantities of less than carload lots are subject to higher transportation rates than carload shipments, the opportunity storage provides for increasing the size of a shipment helps to decrease transportation costs.

Encouragement of Quantity Buying.   Storage enables the purchaser to increase the size of his purchases. For instance, the mill supply house system, through its warehousing, makes it possible for the industrial firm to buy in large lots. Thus, larger assortments of goods are available, so that potential buyers can make their selections more efficiently.

Facilitation of Selling.   Storage makes selling more efficient through its effects upon the quantity and variety of available merchandise. It enables the seller to improve his services, and it makes hand-to-mouth buying possible because little or no advance notice of intent to buy need be given to the seller.

Stabilization of Pricing.   Through adjustment of supply and demand, prices tend to be stabilized. One of the principal advantages of storage is the part it plays in helping to stabilize prices. For example, before frozen orange juice concentrate was popular, the price of fresh oranges fluctuated seasonally; but with popular acceptance of the concentrate, price fluctuations for fresh oranges have been considerably reduced because the oranges can be processed and stored so that juice will be available when they are scarce. In this way, the orange surplus is diminished during a large-crop season, and the dearth is eliminated during the off-season.

In the long run, storage also helps to reduce prices of commodities. If storage facilities are available, producers are encouraged to store their excess produce because immediate disposal of their output is not an urgent matter. The opportunity to store merchandise makes increased production possible and thus reduces unit costs and prices. Storage also helps to reduce prices by eliminating spoilage.

Standards for Good Storage

Proper Conditions and Handling.   Goods must be cared for properly during storage. They must be inspected at regular intervals. Special storage equipment may be necessary, especially for perishable products and products that must undergo processes such as curing.

Convenience of Storage Facilities. Goods must be kept where the facilities for transportation and financing will be convenient for the producer, the middleman, and the consumer.

Control of Storage. The storage organization must be dependable. It must be prepared to supply requested services, such as grading and curing; and to facilitate the financing process, it must be in a position to furnish proof of title of goods in storage.

Kinds of Storage: Classified by Ownership and Use

The kinds of storage may be listed either in terms of ownership and use of the facilities or in terms of the services performed and specialties handled. In terms of the former, types of storage include four kinds of warehouse facilities: public, private, field, and government owned.

Public Warehouses. Public warehouses are operated for the benefit of the general public and charge fees. They are privately owned, but their operations and fees may be regulated by government agencies.

Private Warehouses. Private warehouses are owned and operated by an organization principally for its own use. The storage facility of a retail store is an example of a private warehouse.

Field or Custodial Warehouses. In a field warehouse, space for storage is set aside on the premises of the owner of the merchandise. The space is leased to a public warehouseman, or custodian, who has physical and legal control of the goods, even though the goods remain on the owner's premises. The principal purpose of field warehousing is to assist financing. Field warehousing provides a warehouse receipt that can be used as collateral for loans.

Government Warehouses. Federal and municipal governments own many warehouses, including customs storage warehouses, internal revenue repositories, and those that correspond to the private warehouses of industry.

Customs Warehouses. Sometimes the owner of the goods

and the federal government disagree concerning the amount of customs tax due on a product. When this happens, the goods are impounded in a customs warehouse until the question is settled.

INTERNAL REVENUE WAREHOUSES. The government owns warehouses that are utilized for the financing of goods not yet ready to be marketed and upon which a tax is due. Liquor and tobacco, for example, must be aged before they can be marketed. The federal government will provide storage space for such commodities for a fee and will postpone collection of the internal revenue tax until the products are withdrawn for marketing. These commodities are called *bonded* products.

WAREHOUSES MAINTAINED EXCLUSIVELY FOR STORAGE OF GOVERNMENT PROPERTY. Many agencies of the federal, state, and local government have their own warehousing facilities. One of the best examples is the national military establishment, which has many arsenals. Of course, such warehouses are not used for marketing activities.

PUBLIC WAREHOUSES OPERATED BY GOVERNMENTS. Municipal governments may have storage facilities that offer all the services of a public warehouse. They are especially likely to maintain such warehouse facilities in a commodity market or port city.

Kinds of Storage: Classified by Services Offered and by Nature of Product Stored

Nature of Service Offered. An examination of the services provided by warehouses indicates that each type performs one or more of all the marketing functions. They break up large lots into small for shipment to buyers, and they operate billing services to relieve their customers of this task. In performing the incidental activities necessary to improve or maintain the quality of products, the warehouse provides fumigation services for such products as cereals and flour to prevent losses from the ravages of pests, and it assumes the job of reporting any damage to stored articles. It sometimes installs products after they have been purchased. For convenience, a manufacturer or a wholesaler may also maintain one of his offices in the warehouse, where space is generally available.

Nature of Product Stored.   There are special storage facilities for manufactured goods, agricultural products, and raw materials. Some warehouses provide special services in connection with products they store. They may gin cotton, clean and grade wheat, and provide cooperage. There is also the public cold-storage locker, where space is available to individual consumers for the freezing and/or storage of their foods.

Effects and Standards of Transportation

Transportation is the physical transfer of products from producer to consumer. Often it involves transmittal through, or handling at, intermediate points.

Transportation creates *place utility*; it makes goods available where the demand is greatest. The time when goods arrive at their destination is also important. Transportation must supply *time utility*; goods must reach their destination according to schedule. If they arrive before or after the period of peak demand, time utility has not been properly created.

Effects of Transportation.   Marketing is affected by transportation in several ways.

LOCATION OF MARKETS.   Marketers are strongly influenced in their selection of market locations by the availability, convenience, and cost of transportation. Wholesalers, for instance, need to be as close as possible to their retail customers.

COST OF MARKETING.   Transportation affects marketing costs. A bulky item that has a high transportation cost in relation to its value will tend to have a high marketing cost. Sand and gravel have high marketing costs because a high percentage of their selling price pay for transportation. Less of the retail price of wheat flour and fresh meat goes to transportation costs.

AREA OF MARKETING.   The ratio between the amount paid for a product and its transportation costs determines, in part, the size of the potential market. The addition of transportation costs to the selling price usually indicates that compared with the total value of a commodity, the cost of transporting it is high and the market area is small. This factor helps to explain why bricks are produced and marketed on a strictly local basis and why diamonds can be distributed from any one center to market areas in many different parts of the world.

CHANNELS OF DISTRIBUTION.   Goods shipped in less than carload lots have a higher unit transportation cost than those shipped on a carload basis. Therefore, a middleman may be selected as a channel of distribution because he will be able to consolidate his shipments and transport them in carload lots. This procedure is preferable to having a manufacturer ship directly to customers who often require less than a carload.

Standards of Transportation.   Efficiency requires that transportation meet certain standards.

ADEQUACY FOR BOTH NORMAL AND PEAK LOAD REQUIREMENTS. To handle products with a seasonal production or demand, transportation facilities must be capable of carrying more than the normal or average load. They must be equipped, for example, to move the peak citrus production of Florida at the right time.

CONVENIENCE OF TRANSPORTATION TERMINALS TO BOTH SELLER AND BUYER.   It would not be economically sound for a wheat terminal transportation point to be located in Portland, Maine, if the grower were in Iowa and the buyer were in Buffalo. Desirable terminal points would be Omaha, St. Louis, or Chicago. Easily accessible terminals are required for convenient transportation.

CAREFUL HANDLING OF GOODS EN ROUTE.   Careless handling may cause goods to lose the demand value that they should have when they arrive; form utility will suffer. It is imperative that goods be transported to the buyer in undamaged condition.

MINIMUM TIME FOR TRANSPORTATION.   To allow the full advantage of time utility, the merchandise being shipped must be handled with the least possible delay en route; otherwise, demand for the commodity may have slackened by the time it is delivered.

PROPER RELATION OF TRANSPORTATION COSTS TO THE VALUE OF THE COMMODITY.   If the cost of transporting an item rises too much in relation to its value, the excessive cost will hamper or prevent distribution. Conversely, if the value of a commodity increases, the cost of transporting it is likely to rise.

Kinds of Transportation

Transportation may be classified by nature of the arrangements made with the user. This grouping includes the *common carrier*, which transports goods for all companies at uniform rates; the *contract carrier*, which transports good for one company or a limited number of companies, with rates varying with specific situations; and the *private carrier*, which is operated by the company whose goods it transports. However, transportation may also be classified in terms of the physical facilities that are used for land transportation by railroads, trucks, and pipelines; for water transportation; and for air transportation.

The following table indicates the relative importance of the various merchandise carriers.'

Percent Distribution of Freight, by Ton-Miles, by Carriers in the United States in 1964

Type of Transportation	Percent (Ton-Miles)
Railroads	41.09
Inland waterways	15.80
Pipelines	21.65
Motor vehicles	21.28
Airplanes	.17

SOURCE: U.S. Bureau of the Census, *Statistical Abstract of the United States: 1971* (Washington, D.C.: U.S. Government Printing Office, 1971).

Railroads. In the United States, the railroads are still by far the leading carriers.

TYPES OF EQUIPMENT. A railroad typically has nine kinds of freight cars: (1) the *standard freight car*, which may be either a boxcar or a flatcar; (2) the *gondola car* (low sides and no top); (3) the *ore car*; (4) the *tank car*; (5) the *refrigerator car*; (6) the *cattle car*; (7) the *piggyback flatcar*; (8) the *automobile car* (to carry new automobiles); and (9) the *container car*, which is not typical because it is a sectional boxcar with removable sections designed for truck pickups and deliveries.

GENERAL TYPES OF SERVICE. (1) *Fast freight* service offers rapid, scheduled service, with speed approximating that of the better passenger trains. This kind of freight service is utilized especially for highly perishable commodities. (2) *Slow freight* service (*drag* or *tonnage freight*) has a slow, irregular schedule and is used for nonperishable or less valuable commodities. (3) *Way freight* service is used principally for short local hauls of shipments in less than carload (LCL) size. (4) *Railway* (*REA*) *Express* service is provided by a separately organized company. Special Railway Express cars are run on fast freights. They are useful for the shipment of small packages with a high unit value or of goods whose shipper or buyer can afford the relatively high costs of transportation. This service includes speedy door-to-door delivery and special care in handling.

Parcel post service, inaugurated by the U.S. Post Office in 1913 and now handled by the U.S. Postal Service, has provided inexpensive transportation by rail.

SPECIAL TYPES OF SERVICE.   The following special services are offered by the railroads.

Diversion in transport.   Because market prices are subject to almost continual change, shippers sometimes find it advantageous to change the destination of a product en route.

Reconsignment.   After the freight arrives at a specified market, it may be reconsigned, that is, sent to still another destination.

Rolling or tramping.   When markets are in a state of flux, it often happens that after a shipment has been dispatched in the general direction of a certain market, the shipper may receive information concerning which market will offer the highest prices for his commodities. He will then wire the railroad, designating the market to which the tramp shipment is to be sent.

Transit privileges.   Certain raw materials must be processed before they are distributed. A transit privilege enables the manufacturer to ship his product from the point of origin to a processing plant and to a final market at a rate lower than the combined rate for two separate hauls. The transit privilege is also used in the case of seasonal produce stored at central storage warehouses.

Piggybacking. Piggybacking combines the long-haul advantages of railroads with the short-haul advantages of trucks. Truckers contract to have railroads haul their trailers long distances on rail flatcars, and the railroads also carry their own trailers. A shipper is permitted to use his own or a leased trailer and to have it hauled by the railroad for a flat fee based on mileage.

Special rates for LCL service. LCL service is much more costly than CL (carload). However, railroads have evolved special rates for certain shipments less than CL. These special rates, which are neither so low as the CL rates nor so high as LCL rates, apply to the following methods of shipment:

PACKAGE CAR. One car is dispatched to a single destination, but it carries the freight of more than one shipper. This car is usually attached to a scheduled freight train known to shippers.

POOL CAR. A single shipper assigns a carload to many local consignees. A freight forwarder in the receiving area is usually responsible for reshipping.

CONSOLIDATED CAR. Two or more shippers make up a carload together. At the receiving end the shipment is broken up into smaller lots by a freight forwarder.

MIXED CAR. The shipper of several different products may ship them together, in a single car, at the CL rate for the product which costs most to ship. This rate will still normally be lower than combined LCL rates for each.

Demurrage. The railroad usually allows shippers and receivers twenty-four to forty-eight hours to load or unload their freight cars before the railroad charges for the detention of the car. Consignees often prefer to pay a *demurrage charge* and hold their goods in the freight cars until they are sold, rather than unload them at a siding and then later reload them into the buyer's truck.

PROBLEMS OF RAILROADS. Railroads face five major problems:

Competition. In recent years the railroads have lost much of their business to trucks and pipelines. This loss is attributed primarily to the relative inflexibility and high rates of most railroads.

High break-even point. The cost structure of the railroad is so high that scarcely a railroad in the country today shows a reasonable profit. A high break-even point is probably the most serious problem of the railroads.

Rate-making. In the case of interstate carriers, the complex task of rate-making is subject to review by the Interstate Commerce Commission. Various public utility commissions review local and intrastate carrier rates. It is difficult to allocate costs of operation equitably, for railroads are subject to joint costs. There are so many factors involved in computing rail transportation joint costs (length of haul, value of the commodity, and size of shipment, among others) that it is extremely difficult to evolve a rate that will cover all operating and fixed costs and give the railroad an acceptable net profit. Moreover, railroad rate computers are burdened with the additional problem of establishing rates that will not be prohibitive for bulky goods with low unit value and that will be equitable for relatively small-sized articles of high unit value. In practice, the following three types of freight rates have been used:

A *class rate* is set for groups of commodities with similar value, method of shipment, or quantity. Such commodities are designated as a class, and a general rate is set for all commodities of this category. This type of rate making applies principally to *general merchandise* (i.e., general manufactured goods).

A *commodity rate* is a special rate for bulky items, usually raw materials. Shippers of wheat, iron ore, coal, lumber, and petroleum are usually granted this rate.

An *exception rate*, applying to some 10 percent of all CL freight, is allowed for especially bulky items in order to reduce their freightage.

Freight car supply. A shortage of freight cars has sometimes resulted in crop losses. The remedy is to be sought in a planned increase in freight equipment.

Freight car control. The problem of freight car control may be even more serious than that of supply, as indicated by the figures on the next page obtained from a recent study of time distribution for a typical freight car.

Clearly, there is something wrong when only one-tenth of a car's life is spent in movement and when it makes only twenty-five pay trips annually. Such inefficiency may be attributed to a poor layout of terminals that encourages excessive or wasteful handling,

Distribution of Time for a Typical Freight Car

Activities of Freight Car	Percent of Time
Loading and unloading	27
Switching	39
Movement	11
Holding for loading and unloading	6
Reconsignment	3
Repair	9
No demand	5

to congestion in central markets, and to delays in loading or unloading. However, through the use of data processing systems, a revolution is taking place in freight car control. The average car spends only one hour and fifteen minutes a day doing its job, but under a computerized system, it appears possible to increase a freight car's working day to two and one-half hours. This would in effect double the nation's fleet of 1.5 million cars. Shippers could be supplied with empty cars more quickly, and they would be able to pinpoint the location of their shipments at any time.

Trucks. At the turn of the century, there were fewer than 500 trucks in the United States. In 1970, there were more than 17 million in use. Flexibility sufficient to cope with the various requirements of customers is the basic reason for the growth of the trucking industry. At first, trucks were used merely to haul freight to and from transportation terminals; but in the past twenty years, they have become complete carriers, from pickup through final delivery. Another reason for the growth of the trucking industry is the vast increase in highway facilities, particularly the interstate system.

ADVANTAGES OF TRUCK TRANSPORTATION. Truck transportation offers the following advantages: (1) *Flexibility*. Trucks can go almost anywhere. Not only can they serve producers in isolated areas, but changes in routing caused by market fluctuations are easily made. (2) *Speed*. The speed of the truck in short hauls usually cannot be equalled by other kinds of transport. (3) *Low cost.* Trucking is inexpensive not only in terms of out-of-pocket payment for transportation but also in terms of packaging. (4) *Reduced damage.* Fewer losses from damage occur in trucking than in most other forms of transportation. Efficient manipulation of the small shipments used in trucking is possible, and fewer individuals are likely to handle each shipment than in the case of any other means of transportation.

Pipelines. World War II stimulated the use of pipelines. Today, the pipeline is an important medium of transportation for crude oil, gasoline, and natural gas. There are 1.030 million miles of pipelines in the United States, of which more than 83 percent are used for the transportation of natural gas. Two types of pipeline convey natural gas; a large line carries gas from the wells to smaller, local lines, which redistribute the gas.

Crude oil obtained from wells is collected by small pipelines, or *gathering lines,* that move it to concentration centers. From these centers, it is transported by a *trunk line* or a tanker either to a port city for shipment by tanker or to a refining center. After being converted into gasoline, it may be transported from the refining center via another trunk line leading to a reshipping center.

CHARACTERISTICS OF PIPELINES. Unlike railroads, trucks, and airplanes, pipelines do not, of course, move with the commodity. They are a highly specialized means of distribution that does not provide facilities for storing the commodity at a receiving point. Because of the nature of pipelines, some of the material they transport is unavoidably lost in transit. This loss must always be absorbed by the shipper. In many cases, pipeline transportation requires that the products of various shippers be intermingled, a factor that affects quality.

Water Transportation. Early trade was almost entirely dependent upon water transportation. In the eighteenth century, Americans depended upon Europe for their products, and their own trade within America was largely waterborne. The first cities in the United States were located on waterways; today, each of the seven largest cities is a port city.

ADVANTAGES AND DISADVANTAGES OF WATER TRANSPORTATION.

Usually, water transport can be utilized economically only by those shippers or receivers whose businesses are located near water routes or by those whose products are neither perishable nor apt to become obsolete during the comparatively long period required for transportation. The greatest advantage of water transportation is that it costs less than any other form of transport; however, it is the slowest mode of transportation in the United States. Another disadvantage is the fact that icy northern waters hinder or entirely stop navigation at certain times.

To overcome these disadvantages of water transportation, shippers are developing *container ships* that can carry more profitable cargo by providing faster door-to-door service. Products are enclosed in containers that can be loaded and unloaded by cranes on ships and that give protection against pilferage. Container ships can be loaded and unloaded in twelve hours, compared with seventy-two working hours for the conventional freighter. These ships also carry truck trailers between the East and West coasts of the United States, with resulting decrease in delivery time in a combined sea-land operation.

Air Transportation. Since World War II, the tonnage of air freight has increased greatly in volume. Despite this increase, however, airplanes carry only a small part of the total freight tonnage of the United States.

Advantages and Disadvantages of Air Transportation. *Speed* is a principal advantage of air transportation. Airplanes easily outstrip all competition in this respect. Speed is important in transportation of perishable goods or goods critically needed. Products of great value also may benefit from the *special care* provided for short periods of time by air transport. *Flexibility* is another advantage of air transportation. The airplane is able to penetrate areas that no other transportation medium can reach.

However, the high cost of air transportation has worked to its detriment in the past. To combat the cost factor, more than 30 percent of airline freight is handled by airfreight forwarders who pick up goods to be shipped by air; consolidate them into larger, easier-to-handle loads; and then purchase the actual transportation from the airlines.

Management of the Physical Supply Function

The systems approach emphasizes the need to have the right goods in the right place at the right time. This is accomplished by proper management and integration of the two aspects of physical supply: storage and transportation. It may be less expensive, in the long run, to ship by air and to eliminate warehousing. By making use of air shipments, the Raytheon Company was able to cut average delivery time from about eleven days to some sixty-four hours and consequently decided to sell its field warehouses.

Some of the most dramatic increases in efficiency of marketing have come about through proper management of the warehousing function and through general progress in materials handling. In 1940, most products were handled by manpower. Today, there is widespread use of efficient mechanical devices to streamline and economize the warehousing function. Modern warehouses are largely one-story affairs because it is simpler and more efficient to mechanize materials handling on a one-floor than on a multifloor basis. There are highly efficient conveyor systems and forklifts for the handling of palletized merchandise. Containerization is common, so that handling of individual packaging cartons is often unnecessary until the goods reach the retailer.

Transportation, like storage, has become more efficient over the years. This is occurring even with the railroads, which we often think of as being generally poorly run because of their curtailment of passenger service. But freight trains have become longer and are moving faster than before. They offer containerization. They have developed three-tiered automobile cars that compete more effectively with truck automobile carriers.

Trucking has become more effective with the development of the interstate highway system. It is now possible to get coast-to-coast delivery in as little as seventy hours.

REVIEW QUESTIONS

1. Define storage, and describe its functions.
2. State the results derived from the proper use of storage facilities.
3. What are the standards for good storage facilities?

4. List the kinds of storage facilities available in terms of the owner-ship and use of the facilities.
5. In what ways has the storage function become more efficient in recent years?
6. What are the standards for a good system of transportation?
7. Describe the kinds of transportation facilities available, indicating the strong and weak points of each.
8. What special types of services in the transportation of freight are offered by the railroads?
9. Define container car, way freight, LCL, and class rate.
10. In what ways is transportation becoming more efficient?

19

MARKETING RESEARCH

Marketing research is "the use of the scientific method in the solution of marketing problems. . . . It involves the gathering, organization, and analysis of market data . . . for the guidance of management in the making of marketing decisions. . . ."[1]

Marketing research is an essential business activity, and its importance has grown greatly in the last fifty years. Marketing research managers are always a part of the marketing management team and in many cases are responsible for the basic information that is used in the construction of a company's marketing plan. Marketing research techniques are often utilized in problem solving when it is necessary to have the right information to make an immediate decision or to take a specific step.

Marketing research may be applied to each marketing function. It may be used to analyze a potential market for a product or service, to measure brand preference, to evaluate consumer attitudes and opinions, to measure the impact of advertising, and to test-market product innovations.

Marketing research managers may also be responsible for fore-

[1] Shapiro, *Marketing Terms*, p. 99.

casting a company's sales, laying out sales territory that should result in optimum returns, and performing sales analysis so that a company may take immediate action if a problem becomes apparent.

Techniques of Marketing Research

Research Plan.   The researcher must first define the marketing problem that his study is to help resolve. It may be a regional sales drop, a decision about whether to go national on a new product, or some other problem area.

Once the major problem area has been defined, the researcher may break it down into a series of single problems. This is followed by further reducing the problems into their elements, sometimes called *subproblems*. In order to avoid excessive expenditures of time and money, the researcher then goes to available sources such as company records, government reports, business and trade publications, and university research findings. From these, he may find several tentative answers to the problems, or he may discover where answers may be obtained.

In many cases, information is not available; but by perusing current yet germane sources, the researcher may be able to construct a series of hypotheses for each problem area that will help him to decide what kind of research techniques will be necessary to obtain an answer.

When all this is put into an organized form, the researcher has a working guide or research plan that permits him to estimate time and cost for the solution of each problem. In some cases, the budget may not permit the solution of all the individual problems uncovered around a problem area; and the researcher, in conference with other members of the marketing team, may then set up a priority. That is, the problems that appear to be most important will be researched immediately; others may be postponed.

Sources of Background Information.   As indicated above, it is always good procedure to uncover what has already been said about a problem before undertaking actual research. For example, company records are one of the finest sources of information. Data may be obtained not only from public statements such as the balance sheets and profit and loss statements but from detailed records of sales, advertising, promotion, and other marketing activities. Sometimes manufacturers receive reports from their wholesalers or retailers that may also be important sources of information.

Secondary information may be obtained from government bureaus such as the Bureau of the Census, Bureau of Domestic Commerce, Bureau of Labor Statistics, and the Federal Reserve Board. Government publications such as the *Survey of Current Business*, the *Statistical Abstract of the United States*, and censuses of housing, population, business, manufacturers, and agriculture may also be useful.

In almost every case, a business organization belongs to at least one trade association, and the association's publications become important in the evaluation and solution of a problem. There are also important business publications, such as *Business Week, Barrons, Dun's Review, Sales Management*, and *Advertising Age*.

In unusual situations, the researcher may be able to obtain data from private research sources that will sell their findings.

Internal Analysis.   One research technique often overlooked by marketing researchers is *ratio analysis*, which is analysis of pertinent company records. These records may be salesmen's call reports, factory shipments, orders, or financial statements. For example, one important financial ratio is net profit divided by net sales or net sales divided by average inventory. If the researcher chooses the appropriate ratios and places them on a graph and then obtains standards by which the ratios may be judged, he is in a position to uncover significant elements in a problem area and may even unearth additional problems. He may want to relate the ratio analysis to other kinds of historical evaluations that may help him to arrive at a solution. For example, he may wish to plot the GNP and the net or discretionary income figures for the same period as he would for the ratios. He may also wish to graph industry sales, profits, and other figures that can be obtained from trade associations.

All this information, whether or not it is directly related to the problem, will give the researcher greater understanding of the problem area so that he will be in position to further refine the research plan.

External Analysis. Often in marketing research, it is difficult to obtain an answer to a problem through any form of internal analysis; and in such cases, the researcher turns to external analysis, more commonly known as the *survey method*.

It should be understood that a survey can be used to obtain only four kinds of information: measurements of consumer behavior, measurements of consumer knowledge or attitude, measurements of consumer opinions, and facts concerning socioeconomic and psychographic (psychological attributes or emotional reactions to a product) characteristics, known as *profile data*. These profile data permit the researcher to sort and classify the answers to the survey questions according to the characteristics of the people who have been interviewed.

APPLICATION TO MARKETING PROBLEMS. The survey procedure is a very useful marketing research tool. It can help solve problems relating to measurement of intent to purchase, to product acceptance, to package design, to advertising measurement and impact, to selection of wholesale or retail distributors for a product, and to evaluation of possible sites for retail stores or shopping centers.

BASIC TECHNIQUES OF GATHERING DATA. The marketing researcher has several kinds of techniques available, including observational methods, that is, observing or taking pictures of consumers shopping or making purchases. Sometimes it is appropriate to send a sample group of people a questionnaire by mail. To measure the popularity of a radio or television program, viewers may be questioned by telephone; this is the telephone survey technique (also known as the *coincidental method*). However, much of the marketing research in this country is done through the face-to-face interview, in which selected respondents are individually questioned.

Another method that combines both personal interviewing and mail surveys is the panel, composed of a constant sample of people who are questioned periodically on their behavior, attitudes, or opinions. This method has the advantage of being a continuing source of information. Sometimes *mechanical devices* are used with a panel. These include electronic devices attached to receiving sets to record what program a sample of families is watching on television or listening to on radio; eye cameras that record eye movements in viewing print ads and packages; and the tachistoscope, which exposes material for a time so short that the viewer cannot see it all. This tachistoscope determines what advertisement or package elements are first perceived. A truck or trailer may be used as a portable laboratory to take equipment to consumers.

SAMPLING.   No matter what technique is used to collect the information, some form of sample is employed so that the findings will be representative of the population. There are two major kinds of samples. *Nonprobability sampling* permits the interviewer to select the people who are to be questioned. The interviewers are sent to selected locations to collect information from individuals. This kind of sampling may result in bias and does not allow the research director to measure closeness of fit of a sample to its population. In contrast, *probability sampling* embraces a number of sophisticated techniques. The basic assumption is that those who are to be questioned are selected mathematically in such a way that every member of a population has a known chance of being chosen. The interviewer never has a choice of whom to question because the individuals to be interviewed have been preselected mathematically. Moreover, the research director is able to measure the precision of the sample.

QUESTIONING PROCEDURE.   No matter what kind of sampling plan is used or what kind of technique is employed to collect the information, a data form must be designed so that information can be collected methodically and completely. In many cases, the data forms are questionnaires, which may be unstructured or stuctured. In the *unstructured* questionnaire, a series of statements is provided for the interviewer, who reads the statements to those being questioned. All information elicited is recorded, and often the interviewer is instructed to probe the answers so that additional information may be obtained. The *structured* questionnaire is usually tightly designed, and respondents are to answer "yes" or "no" or to select one answer from a series.

Data obtained from questionnaires are not sufficiently complete to furnish information on all the ramifications of a problem.

Sometimes researchers resort to an adaptation of psychological techniques that are included in a conventional questionnaire. *Free association* is a method wherein a list of stimulus words is read to a respondent who answers each one with the first word that comes to mind. At other times, information is obtained through *sentence completion tests*. In other cases, a *cartoon* is designed showing people in an appropriate setting; the situation or conversation calls for the respondent to provide the words of response in an open balloon attached to one of the cartoon characters. Another technique is to provide a picture and ask the respondent to write a story about the picture; this is an adaptation of the *thematic apperception test* used in clinical psychology. In marketing research, these psychological techniques are utilized in what is known as *motivational research*; because of the nature of the information obtained, the responses are considered qualitative rather than quantitative. Although many marketing researchers use qualitative research by itself, the authors believe that when this kind of research is part of the research plan, it is always necessary to have quantitative verification of the findings through a large sample from which structured interview data are obtained.

Tabulation and Interpretation. After the data have been collected by either internal or external means or both, the tabulation plan is designed. First, the questionnaire is edited to ensure completeness and to eliminate bias and inconsistencies. If the data are quantitative, it is necessary to set up intervals by which the data may be tabulated so that meaning can finally be derived from them. If the data are qualitative, categories are constructed that are logical, psychologically sound, and mutually exclusive.

Once this has been done, the questionnaire data are put into a computer, where they are processed. For full disclosure of meaning, many questions are cross-tabulated; that is, the percentages computed for a series of answers are related to the answers from another question. One of the standard forms of cross-tabulation is to relate answers to socioeconomic characteristics.

If the data are to be tabulated by computer, many of the answers will have to be coded before they are transferred to a card or tape for mechanical tabulation. With computers, many more advanced methods of statistical analysis are now possible;

and as a result, research is becoming that much more helpful to the marketing manager.

Once the data have been summarized through tabulation, percentages have been derived, averages computed, and any other relevant statistical computations made, the material is ready for interpretation. The marketing researcher reviews the findings and writes a report that attempts to answer the problem or question which occasioned the research. The final report may be made orally to the marketing team along with a written summary of the findings.

Once his report has been made, the marketing researcher has the responsibility to do all in his power to see that his recommendations are seriously considered in the formulation of the marketing plan. Otherwise, money and time have been wasted.

The Marketing Research Firm

The marketing research firm gathers and may interpret market and marketing data. It is usually an independent organization, unattached to any other business. It may be a one-man business, or a firm offering full-time employment to hundreds of people. It can take so many different forms that its nature will be considered here by geographic area of operation, type of broad field of specialization, type of narrow field of specialization, the amount of interpretation of data offered, and degree to which the services are custom-tailored.

Specialization by Geographic Area of Operation. Marketing research firms operate in virtually every country in the world with the exception of Communist areas. There are marketing research firms in the United States, Canada, Mexico, various countries of the West Indies and Central and South America, Japan, India, other free-economy countries of the Far East, and some African nations. Marketing research firms are found in every European nation. There are several associations of firms operating in different countries, so that a research buyer, through dealing with a single source, may have international studies conducted.

In the United States, firms offering services on a national basis can be found in such cities as New York, Chicago, Philadelphia, San Francisco, and Los Angeles. There are also firms offering regional coverage, and firms of local scope can be found in almost every large city. The firm giving local coverage tends to be smaller, with less specialization and usually less proficiency in diagnosing a marketing problem and writing an interpretive report.

Broad Field of Specialization.   Most firms engaged in marketing research tend to operate within the broad limits of one discipline, such as economics, accounting, statistics, personnel research, or the sampling survey.

Narrow Field of Specialization.   Within the limits of the discipline utilized, a marketing research firm will tend to be either a general practitioner or a specialist.

GENERAL PRACTITIONER.   The general practitioner will accept almost any kind of marketing problem study falling within the scope of its discipline and will collect and analyze facts pertinent to the assignment. The general practitioner most often works on a project basis.

SPECIALIST.   The specialist works in one of several ways.

By stage in the marketing study.   There are specialist firms that will undertake just one of the following steps in a marketing study: design of the study (usually done by independent consultants rather than by firms), collection of the data (field work), data processing, or interpretation of the data (usually done by consultants).

By type of facility offered.   There are also specialists who make use of only a single type of research facility. In the United States, several firms offer only panel types of study; several others specialize in store inventory kinds of work. One firm conducts only telephone surveys; another, mail.

By concepts.   A third method of classifying specialists concerns the concepts they tend to use in designing a study. One American firm always takes a motivation research approach to a problem; others have a purely quantification orientation.

By type of problem handled.   Certain firms concentrate in the direction of the kinds of problems on which they work. Some marketing research firms seem to do more consumer product testing than anything else. Others concentrate their efforts on the measurement of radio and television audiences. Still others seem to do more in the field of publication research than anything else. There are several firms in the United States and Canada that offer laboratory testing (such as attention measurement) in package testing. One American firm conducts primarily image studies.

Comments about Marketing Research

Limitations of Marketing Research.   The technique of marketing research has several limitations.

DATA ARE NOT PREDICTIVE.   Despite the considerable progress that has been made in the field of marketing research, it is still impossible to predict accurately certain types of consumer behavior (such as purchases) on the basis of research.

DATA ARE SUBJECT TO MANY SOURCES OF ERROR.   The very nature of sampling procedures means that there is a built-in error, regardless of the soundness of the study's experimental design. Results are never entirely current and are subject to sampling error. There are also other sources of error; the observer himself is subject to error in his observations and reports.

RESEARCH COSTS ARE HIGH.   The cost factor is one of the greatest hindrances to the wide application of marketing research. This is no restriction for the large corporation, but it does mean that the small business firm is rarely in a position to make much use of marketing research. Even though small business firms have access to information of trade associations, they often are unable to utilize it.

RESEARCH RESULTS CANNOT DICTATE ACTION.   It is sometimes assumed that once a probem is defined and research results are secured, these results indicate the marketing action that should be taken. This is far from the truth. Research results can seldom dictate action; they can only suggest facts to be taken into account in arriving at the particular marketing decision.

Value of Marketing Research.   If used carefully, with full understanding of its strengths and weaknesses, marketing research can be a valuable aid to marketing efficiency. Like accounting and the other tools used in the administration of a business, it can help increase the accuracy of executive judgment.

No properly trained market researcher would claim that marketing research is a panacea for all the problems of business. Market study is no substitute for the experience and training that a man in business has acquired in his particular field. Even so, a businessman is sometimes so close to his own operation that he cannot see the forest for the trees. Thus, he may make a decision based on limited observations that ignore what is going on beyond the narrow scope of his own business activity. In such cases, marketing research may make its greatest contribution by furnishing the businessman with an objective and dispassionate analysis of all the related data, which will enable him to make a realistic judgment or decision.

REVIEW QUESTIONS

1. Briefly describe the various applications of marketing research.
2. Outline the steps into which a research procedure may be divided.
3. What kinds of data are usually obtained through questioning individuals in a sampling survey?
4. What techniques may be used to obtain information in a sampling survey?

20

FINANCING OF THE MARKETING PROGRAM

Market financing is "a marketing function which includes the provision and management of money and credit necessary to get goods to the consumer or user. . . ."[1] It covers financing necessary to carry stock and the offering of mercantile and consumer credit, including installment credit. It excludes financing of a building to carry on a marketing business and the consumer's borrowing of funds to finance a purchase.

There are certain basic sources of financial aid. *Invested capital*, comprising funds borrowed on a long-term basis for expanding or replacing capital equipment, is probably the most important source. Another is *short-term credit*, obtained either through commercial paper brokers or directly from banks. A less acceptable method of obtaining funds is the *hypothecating of accounts receivable* or the *discounting of accounts receivable*. If none of these financing methods is sufficient, the marketing organization may postpone payment, which shifts the burden onto a seller through such devices as an open-book account, a promissory note, or a draft.

[1] Shapiro, *Marketing Terms*, p. 65.

Financing is an integral part of all marketing. Organizations specializing in distribution constantly need both short-term and long-term capital. Without adequate financing, distribution is crippled, and the cost of marketing rises.

Marketing organizations must deal with problems of seasonal production and distribution. To reduce fluctuation, intelligent management attempts to produce and distribute during off-season periods. If this operation is properly financed, marketing costs are usually decreased.

Sometimes the selection of a channel of distribution may depend upon whether the channel can finance the marketing activities of the firm in question. Therefore, the buyer or seller likes to deal with an organization that will offer financing. The wholesaler may finance the producer, the retailer, and the industrial consumer. The producer may finance the ultimate consumer and sometimes a jobber or a wholesaler.

With adequate financing, a corporation's sales volume may be increased. With credit available, more salesmen may be hired, and more sales promotion, including advertising, may be used. In other words, expansion of credit may bring about an expanded total sales volume.

Capital requirements affect a firm's credit policies in two ways: (1) The requirements themselves will determine how much credit a company needs to finance its own operations. (2) Any limitation on a company's credit will negatively affect its own credit extension to customers. The extension of credit is the lifeblood of business.

Market financing may be divided into two major groups: *credit*, which is the postponement of payment to some period following purchase of a commodity; and *loans*, which are the advancement of money on either a short-term or a long-term basis for the financing of an undertaking.

Credit

Function of Credit.   Credit facilitates the movement of commodities from producer to ultimate consumer. It is estimated that

60 percent of all retail sales are made on a credit basis (47 percent charge accounts and 13 percent time payments). Some 95 percent of mercantile transactions (i.e., sales to business firms) involve the use of credit.

Types of Credit. Credit may be classified in several ways: (1) *Recipients.* On this basis, there are *consumer credit* and *mercantile credit.* Consumer credit is given by the seller to the ultimate consumer. One business organization supplies another with mercantile credit. (2) *Period of time.* There are long- and short-term loans. (3) *Presence or absence of inducements* to pay before the end of the credit period. With *open-book credit,* no special inducement is offered to pay before the total amount is due. This procedure is typical of the charge account. With *cash credit,* a discount is offered to the debtor to induce him to pay prior to the end of the credit period. This cash discount is common in mercantile transactions and is often indicated by a shorthand statement such 'as "2/10; net 30." This means that the creditor will permit the purchaser to deduct 2 percent from his bill if he pays it within ten days and that the bill is due at the end of thirty days. Some bills bear the date of the day of sale; others are dated as of the first of the following month (EOM). In either case, a ten-day discount offer runs for ten days after the date on the bill. The typical cash discount is 1 percent or 2 percent. The purchaser may receive additional discounts. Some possible types (discussed in Chapter 16) are: anticipation discount, quantity discount, and trade discount. (4) *Credit card types.* It is said that today we live in an almost cashless society. Certainly there are many credit cards in use. These mainly fall into two types: those offered by the seller (department store, gasoline company, airline, car rental firm) and general credit cards offered by a firm in the credit business (Carte Blanche, American Express, BankAmericard, local banks).

Factors That Determine the Granting of Credit. Criteria that guide the granting of credit differ from industry to industry. However, they may be discussed in terms of certain generalizations.

Several factors affect the time and amount of *consumer credit.*

THE INCOME PERIOD OF THE CONSUMER. Credit will normally be extended over a longer period to the farmer with seasonal income than to the urban dweller with a weekly income.

THE VALUE OF THE COMMODITY. Because automobiles are more expensive than appliances, those who purchase an automobile on installments will usually receive a longer credit period than those who buy an electrical household appliance on credit.

In *mercantile credit,* the standards are a bit different. (1) The *rate of stock turnover* influences the extension of mercantile credit. Usually, the more quickly a middleman moves his goods, the shorter the credit period. (2) The *buyer's location* and the *availability of transportation* also affect his credit standing. The farther away a buyer is from his source of supply, the greater the chances are that he will receive an extended credit period. (3) *Tradition* plays a very important part in American business, almost to the point where it creates a certain inflexibility in the economic system. It is difficult to persuade a creditor to extend credit beyond a traditional time period without special collateral. (4) The *nature of the commodity,* including its perishability, turnover rate, and depreciation, must be considered when credit is allowed. (5) If *income of the buyer* is seasonal, longer credit may be extended. (6) The *character of the credit risk* also affects mercantile credit. If an organization or an individual has a bad record, this information is transmitted to mercantile establishments by credit exchanges. Moreover, much can be learned about a firm's operations through examination of its balance sheet and profit and loss statement.

Advantages of Credit. (1) Credit may raise the standard of living by allowing buyers to purchase commodities on anticipated income. (2) To buyers, credit usually signifies a charge account, which makes the return of an undesirable article relatively simple. (3) Credit may relieve the buyer temporarily by allowing him to buy necessities during a period when it is impossible for him to pay for them. (4) Credit aids those who are paid too infrequently to pay cash for things as needed (e.g., those who receive monthly pay).

Disadvantages of Credit. Credit may encourage overspending; some retailing data show that the average size of a cash sale is smaller than the average size of a charge sale. Under lax credit conditions, a buyer may easily abuse his credit privilege, with resulting unhappiness. In the scramble for peak sales and turnover, sellers may extend credit to poor risks. This policy leads inevitably to expensive collection procedures and to excessive bad debt losses.

Overextension of credit may lead to price cutting. Assume that two sellers have equivalent services, commodities, and prices. The one who offers a sixty-day credit period against the thirty-day credit period of his competitor may be indulging in what amounts to price cutting.

Loans

There are two types of loans: long term and short term. *Long-term loans*, covering a substantial period of time, are most frequently made for capital outlays. Commercial, equipment trust, collateral trust, and income or debenture bonds may be the means of long-term financing. *Short-term loans*, which have a normal repayment period of thirty days to six months, are usually used to finance a company during a short period of need.

Short-term Loans. Short-term loans have both advantages and disadvantages.

ADVANTAGES. Short-term loans are relatively *inexpensive*. As a result, they are often obtained by borrowers who wish to take advantage of cash discounts. They are *simple to obtain* once a credit line has been established. They allow a purchaser to *avoid dependence on his market sources or channels* and thereby simplify the complex process of making a purchase.

DISADVANTAGES. The bank may *place restrictions on short-term loans*. It may be unfamiliar with the peculiarities of an individual business and thus hesitate to grant short-term financing.

SOURCES OF SHORT-TERM LOANS. For producers and wholesalers who need funds to finance marketing operations, a commercial bank is the most common source of short-term loans. Financing middlemen in certain commodity fields also grant this type of loan. Three kinds of financing middlemen merit special attention.

Factors. These middlemen specialize in the purchase of accounts receivable. Upon purchase of such accounts, they handle the complete marketing of the commodity. They are found principally in the textile field.

Cattle loan companies.   These companies specialize in lending money to cattle producers after thoroughly investigating their resources and proficiency. They provide a higher loan on such collateral than the banks could, and they take a low interest rate.

Warehouse companies.   These companies lend money on goods stored with them, particularly in the case of farm commodities. Their principal advantage is convenience for the borrower.

Either the retailer or the ultimate consumer may require financing to complete the marketing process. The consumer may finance his installment buying directly through one of the *investment and commercial banks* or *finance companies,* with or without the use of goods as collateral. The store that offers installment-buying privileges may finance such arrangements itself, or may discount the installment paper, or lending institutions may provide the store with funds on a note basis.

Retailers who require financing for marketing needs other than installment purchases may often obtain *ordinary short-term bank loans.*

Types of Collateral.   When a borrower's financial stability or dependability is in question, collateral may be demanded to guarantee repayment. The following are some of the most common kinds of acceptable collateral: *accounts receivable,* as in the cast of the factor; *goods purchased,* as in installment buying; and *outside collateral,* which may be required to finance installment buying and certain other types of marketing loans. In agricultural commodity fields where the warehouse is under close government supervision, the warehouse receipt itself may be negotiable, i.e., it can be converted to cash or used as collateral for a loan. Such collateral is termed *negotiable warehouse receipts. Bills of lading* are another type of collateral. Order bills of lading are negotiable. The goods are directed to an agent and can be delivered to a buyer only after the agent has endorsed the order bill of lading. Finally, stocks, bonds, cosignatures, and insurance policies are in many cases acceptable as *miscellaneous collateral.*

REVIEW QUESTIONS

1. Describe the principal types of credit.
2. What standards guide the granting of credit to the consumer? To the businessman?
3. State the advantages and the disadvantages of short-term loans.
4. From what sources may short-term loans be obtained?

21

REDUCTION OF MARKET RISK

In a dynamic, free, competitive economy, risk is inevitable. Risk constantly challenges business acumen, and no one has been able to develop a formula to eliminate it. Even accurate estimation of risk is difficult. Buying goods for resale, as well as for almost every other business activity, involves risk. It exposes business to the danger of financial loss, which may be caused by physical deterioration, obsolescence, theft, damage, waste, changes in supply or demand, or a shift in the price level.

Kinds of Risk

Marketing risks are usually divided into three broad classes: natural, human, and economic. However, many risks belong to more than one of these classes. Losses resulting from human error may also derive simultaneously from nature. For instance, a warehouseman may forget to check a refrigerator thermostat and thus spoil stored butter and eggs. The initial fault is his, but if spoilage were not an inherent characteristic of butter and eggs, the resulting loss would not have occurred. Nevertheless, risks may be classified in terms of the initiating cause if it is understood that the categories are arbitrary and overlap.

Natural Risk.   Risk created by natural phenomena is usually beyond human control. Damages caused by rain, snow, floods, storms, earthquakes, lightning, pests, and extreme heat are types of natural risk. The perishability of farm products and other commodities is usually deemed a natural risk.

Human Risk.   This risk springs primarily from human frailty and unpredictability. It includes the following varieties: (1) *Personnel risks*, such as high employee turnover, dishonesty, incompetence, carelessness, sickness, accidents, deaths, and strikes; (2) *customer risks*, such as nonpayment of accounts and disproportionately high returns or adjustments on items sold; (3) *government risks*, such as increased business taxes, regulations, price controls, and wars.

Economic Risk.   Economic risk, sometimes termed *market* or *price risk*, is caused primarily by price fluctuations. Economists distinguish between two types of economic risk:

Time Risks.   Prices fluctuate with the passage of time. Such fluctuations are related to the supply and demand equilibrium, which, in turn, reflects such conditions as saturation of the market, changes in consumer wants, new inventions and developments, action of competition, general business conditions, and seasonal fluctuations.

Place Risks.   The demand for and the price of a commodity or a service do not remain constant at a given location, and they vary from place to place. This variation generates place risks that are caused by geographic conditions and differing demands at each business location.

Methods of Handling Risk

Business organizations react to risk in three ways: absorption of risk, reduction of risk, and shifting of risk.

Absorption of Risk.   When a business organization speculates on inventory for small profits, the attendant hazard of losses arising from risks peculiar to the business may make a policy of full risk absorption advisable. This practice requires capital over and above that needed for carrying on the business and an extensive knowledge of many fields of trade. For example, one large chain of motion-picture theaters carries no third-party liability insurance. Instead, it has set up a reserve fund to pay claims and maintains its own staff of claim adjustors. This chain requires additional capital as well as special skills not normally used by the motion-picture industry.

Reduction of Risk. Several techniques may be utilized to reduce risk. A business may change its organizational pattern, improve its management methods, increase the efficiency of its physical equipment, and make use of research.

ALTERATION OF ORGANIZATIONAL PATTERN. A business firm may reorganize extensively to reduce risk. Reorganization may involve vertical integration, horizontal integration, or associations and combinations.

Adoption of vertical integration. To guarantee a constant source of raw materials, a manufacturing organization may undertake vertical integration. A vertically integrated organization is one that controls several or all the steps necessary to the production of a commodity. It may also, if the integration is complete enough, control wholesale and retail distribution. Thus, some large oil companies own the producing wells, the refineries, the pipelines or other transportation equipment needed to handle finished products and by-products, and the wholesale distribution facilities. They may also own and operate retail establishments and export agencies. Vertical integration permits control of all processing steps from the original collection of raw materials to sale of the finished product to the ultimate consumer.

Establishment of horizontal integration. A horizontally integrated organization is one that processes or fabricates several closely allied, identical, or competing products. These processes may take place in several different plants. The word *horizontal* means that the processes involved are in the same stage or level in the progressive refinement of the raw material into the finished product. Horizontal integration increases capacity; rising demand can be met without building new plants and going through all the exploratory steps in capital expansion.

Formation of association and combinations. Competitors may cooperate to reduce risk. However, they do this only with expert legal guidance because collusion is illegal under the monopoly laws. Therefore, most such efforts on the domestic front are limited to practices such as the exchange of sales information and the collection of other kinds of information (on trade practices and the like). Under the Webb-Pomerene Act, which permits American businesses to combine for the purposes of export trade, risk is reduced by distributing the export business among several companies selling to foreign markets. Although many kinds of associations and combinations are forbidden by law, they still may persist by avoiding formal agreements.

IMPROVEMENT OF MANAGERIAL METHODS. A business may reduce risk in the following ways: (1) *Producing only to order.* This policy keeps investment in inventory at a minimum. (2) *Diversifying.* For example, a company that formerly produced only industrial products eventually found it necessary to produce consumer goods as well. (3) *Branding the product.* The symbol or brand represents a definite quality or price. Branding reduces competition by marginal producers and in some cases increases a manufacturer's control over his market. Other methods include: (4) *careful grading, sorting, and standardizing of commodities;* (5) *painstaking budgetary planning and control accompanied by strict supervision of inventory;* and (6) *effective sales promotional efforts.*

IMPROVEMENT OF PHYSICAL EQUIPMENT. Much business risk is inherent in the physical plant. Such safeguards as fireproof buildings, adequate vaults, and protection from burglary will reduce not only risk but also the rates paid to insurance companies for assuming these risks.

USE OF RESEARCH. Market research to discover the psychological reasons why people buy or refuse to buy a product may help to reduce risk. Market surveys are used to measure sales efficency, to predict public acceptance or rejection of new products, and to test the results of advertising.

Shifting of Risk. A businessman faced with substantial risks that cannot be reduced may shift the risk to some other person or institution. Five of the most common devices for shifting risk are discussed in the following paragraphs.

AVERAGING OF RISKS. Insurance companies carefully study the risks to which business is subject and determine the probable incidence of losses. Insurance rates are based upon this statistical analysis of probability. The payment of premiums reimburses the insurance company for assuming the risk of the insured. Insurance companies may, for a premium, assume risk of fire, theft, life, or credit loss, to name only a few of the most common risks. The statistical analysis made by the insurance company enables it to predict rather accurately how many fires will occur in a given year and what financial losses will result. Knowing how much money will be required to pay claims, the insurance company can then fix premiums for its fire insurance policies. The income from premiums is used to settle claims and to meet the insurance company's operating expenses.

RISK SHIFTING THROUGH SALES. A merchant with an extensive inventory may suddenly realize that his investment is in jeopardy because of unpredictable price fluctuations, errors in buying, changing tastes or styles, or a downward swing of the business cycle. To meet these unexpected risks, he can sell his goods at a reduced price. The risk is then borne by the purchaser, who accepts it because of the price reduction.

CONTRACTUAL SHIFTING OF RISK. During times of rapid inflation there is always a possibility that prices will increase in the interim between purchase and delivery of merchandise. To protect themselves, many manufacturers demand an *escalator clause* in their contracts which provide that the buyer pay an additional price for the merchandise ordered if manufacturing costs should increase prior to delivery. Sudden price changes are prevalent in deflationary and inflationary market conditions. Through escalator clauses and other contractual arrangements, businessmen attempt to shift the risk of price changes to others who may be in a better position to cope with it.

GOVERNMENTAL ASSUMPTION OF RISK. Governments often attempt to reduce risk for producers, especially agricultural producers. The federal government assures farmers a parity price for

250   MARKETING
certain crops. This means that if prices drop, the government will
lend money on certain crops or purchase them at a minimum
price. In this way, the farmer can expect a definite income, and
the risk of falling prices is absorbed by the government.

HEDGING AS RISK SHIFTING.   The establishment of commodity
exchanges gave farmers and processors an additional weapon with
which to combat risk arising from uncontrolled price fluctuations.
This weapon is hedging. In order to understand the concept of
hedging, it is necessary to understand the functioning of commodity exchanges.

The Commodity Exchanges

A commodity exchange provides a physical trading place and
sets up and administers certain rules governing trading on its
premises.

Exchanges do no trading on their own account; they merely provide facilities in which others transact business. They are incorporated organizations with membership open to those who can pay
the current price of a seat. Applicants must be approved by the
board of directors. Commodity exchanges are nonprofit organizations, collecting membership fees only to meet their operating expenses. Trading is restricted to members in good standing. The
exchanges disseminate market information and establish grading
and inspection systems. Usually, they are located at central or
terminal markets.

Types of Commodity Exchanges. Some commodity exchanges deal in farm products such as wheat, rye, barley, and
oats. Others handle cotton, livestock, hides, and lard; still others
trade in tin, lead, zinc, crude rubber, and copper. Although these
products can be traded on more than a half-dozen exchanges, some
90 percent of all grain exchange transactions in the United States
take place at the Chicago Board of Trade; the New York Cotton
Exchange handles more than 70 percent of the cotton contracts,
and two exchanges (in New York and Chicago) do most of the
trading in dairy products.

Types of Commodities Traded on Exchanges.   To be traded on an exchange, a commodity must be homogeneous and relatively nonperishable. The supply of the commodity must be large enough to warrant trading, and it must be readily available. Moreover, the product must command a high level of demand throughout the year, and a large number of producers and consumers must be actively interested in it. Finally, the magnitude of the supply must be more or less unpredictable. If the supply of any one commodity were constant and completely dependable, there would be no need for the exchange because speculation would be impossible and hedging transactions would be unnecessary. The main purpose of commodity exchanges is to aid businessmen in coping with substantial changes in the prices of commodities.

Types of Transactions on Exchanges. Exchanges allow trading on both present and future values of agricultural products. By buying futures contracts at the current price, processers can make sure they will get a steady flow of raw mtaerials at that price. The transactions consist of *cash* or *spot sales*, wherein ownership of commodities is immediately transferred and the money passes from buyer to seller, and *futures sales*, wherein an agreement is made to deliver or to accept delivery of a specified amount of the commodity at a stated future date and price.

The two principal kinds of trading on a commodity exchange are *speculation* and *hedging*. In *speculation*, the trader buys or sells in accordance with his predictions concerning the direction or extent of price fluctuations. In *hedging*, he endeavors to eliminate potential losses by means of the simultaneous purchase and sale of the same amount of one commodity in the cash and futures market on a specific date. At some future date, these transactions are usually reversed in the two markets to complete the hedge. For example, assume that a hedger enters the market on September 2. He buys in the cash market and sells in the futures market. On September 10, he sells in the cash market and buys in the futures market. The figures on p. 252 illustrate these transactions.

Note that if the hedger had operated only in the cash market he would have lost $.05. To reduce the possibility of loss, he entered the futures market in reverse direction. In this case, the

A Hedging Transaction

	Trading in Cash Market	Trading in Futures Market
September 2	Bought @ $1.00	Sold @ $1.10
September 10	Sold @ .95	Bought @ 1.05
Net Gain or Loss	—.05	+.05

spread between cash and futures prices (amounting to $.10 on September 2) remained constant.

Hedging (1) provides considerable protection against losses from price changes, (2) decreases marketing costs because operators require less margin, (3) increases the effectiveness of competition because less capital is needed in order to enter the field, (4) encourages loans because more stable prices reduce the risk in credit extension, and (5) raises prices paid to producers because hedgers need not absorb all the risk. Nevertheless, the protection afforded by hedging is not complete because the gains and losses *seldom* match perfectly.

Advantages and Disadvantages of the Commodity Exchange. The commodity exchange has both advantages and disadvantages.

The advantages are that it (1) stimulates standardization and grading; (2) makes hedging possible; (3) establishes a free and open market, in which prices are subject to the forces of supply and demand; (4) enables the owner of goods to carry surplus stocks until they are required; (5) equalizes prices between different geographic areas; (6) minimizes price fluctuations; (7) facilitates *arbitrage*, the practice of buying in one market and reselling in another at a higher price; (8) encourages the collection and dissemination of market news and information; and (9) simplifies financing.

The disadvantages are that it (1) often permits destructive transactions to be completed by inexperienced or dishonest speculators and (2) makes possible the unscrupulous manipulation of prices.

REVIEW QUESTIONS

1. Describe the principal kinds of risk.
2. What methods of handling risk are utilized?
3. What are commodity exchanges? What are their functions?
4. Define spot sales, futures sales, speculation, and bedging.

22

THE MARKETING OF SERVICES

A *service* is work done or facilities provided to business or the ultimate consumer for a price. This definition excludes public services provided by the government because usually these are offered to business or the public either without charge or for a nominal fee.

Types of Service

Services may be classified in two ways.

Personal versus Facility Services. Many services are of a personal nature (e.g., beauty shop, house painting, domestic services); others are primarily facilities, where the principal offering is temporary use of physical property (e.g., automobile rental, amusement park, motion-picture theater, hotel, or motel). Some services are really a mixture of the two in that the personal service could not be offered without extensive physical facilities (e.g., hospital, university).

Business versus Consumer Services. Services are offered both to business and to the consumer. Business services include activities such as marketing or management consultation and auditing services. Consumer services include education, motels, amusement parks, laundries, and the like. Like tangible products, some services are for both industry and the ultimate consumer, depending on who the buyer happens to be (e.g., life insurance, transportation, utilities, and motels).

Some Characteristics of Services

General Small Scale. Such services as provided by a beauty shop, barber shop, laundry and dry cleaner, carpenter, lawyer, and physician are typically small scale, often limited to one person in business for himself. However, the large-scale service firm is beginning to appear, and it tends to specialize in one or more facilities (e.g., amusement park, inn).

Lack of Standardization. A room you stay in at one Howard Johnson's may vary significantly from that in another establishment of the same name. One may be larger than the other or have newer furnishings. Even the same room in one outlet may vary from one time to another. It may have been cleaned better on one occasion than another. The television set may be working one time but not another. When you go to the dentist on one occasion, he may be very gentle and sympathetic; whereas on another, he seems cold and merciless. The permanent wave a woman gets from her hairdresser may be very flattering on one occasion but terrible on another.

The key factor in this lack of standardization is the extensive role of *people* in producing the service. As a result, many services cannot be effectively standardized. There is usually no mechanical production line, as there so often is in the case of tangible products.

Moves toward Mass Production and Mass Marketing. Because so many services are basically personal in nature, mass production and mass marketing are not common.

There are, however, signs that mass production and mass marketing are on their way in the service field for at least some services. In some of the larger metropolitan areas, for instance, even the finest restaurants known for their cuisine are buying frozen meals made at a central location and heated electronically when a diner orders them. Automation has come to the new motion-picture house, to the point where a theater can be operated entirely by a cashier and one other person.

Franchising is a major technique that has enabled the service industry to move toward mass production and mass marketing. Franchising emulates the chain store principle of strong central control, but the local outlet, although standardized in many ways so that it appears to be part of a chain, is locally owned. The typical Howard Johnson's outlet, for example, looks like most other outlets carrying the same name. The orange roof and the physical appearance of the inn or restaurant are easily recognizable features. You have the feeling as you enter a Howard Johnson's establishment that you have been there before. There is a standard menu in Howard Johnson's restaurants. Supplies are bought through the parent company, and food is prepared from identical recipes. Furthermore, the Howard Johnson's chain favors mass marketing through use of major advertising media.

General Lack of Marketing Concept. It often appears that the small service specialist regards himself as a skilled craftsman, rather than as a marketer. He seems to feel that the customer should be grateful that he has an opportunity to purchase that particular service. Frequently, the beauty shop or barber shop is dirty or messy. The skilled craftsman (carpenter, plumber, or electrician) often expects the householder to clean up the mess he has made. Service firms, usually small ones, often do not really consider whether their locations happen to be convenient for the customer.

Their codes of ethics prohibit lawyers and physicians from advertising. Both groups clearly have the old-fashioned attitude that they are specialists in their services and that marketing of their services is an undignified kind of operation.

Moves toward Marketing Concept. However, there are signs that the marketing concept is beginning to be applied in the field of services. The more progressive banks and insurance companies are appointing marketing managers. In some of the larger companies in these fields, there is even greater marketing specialization; advertising managers and marketing research managers have been added to the staffs. Some transportation lines (bus and rail) are moving in the same direction; airlines, of course, have had marketing managers for years. It is increasingly common for amusement parks or other entertainment complexes to have marketing managers. Some larger nursing-home chains are now stressing marketing, and institutions such as the telephone company and motel chains have been doing so for years.

Life Cycle.   Services, like products, have life cycles. Already moribund are interurban trolleys, streetcars, tourist homes, and the blacksmith shop. Other services appear to be in the process of dying out, for example, the in-town hotel (except in large cities), the old-style amusement park (featuring rides only), and poolrooms. Candidates for possible oblivion are the dry cleaner (because of the increasing acceptance of wash-and-wear clothing), exterior painting contractors (because of the perfection and low price of plastic building materials), and motion-picture theaters (because of the development of video tape and film rentals for use in the home).

New services are continually appearing. Rental retailing is growing by leaps and bounds, and it is now possible to rent products ranging from lawnmowers to tuxedos. Automated banking has been perfected. Facilities are open twenty-four hours a day, and it is possible for the customer to deposit or withdraw funds, to transfer funds from one account to another, or to make payments on loans.

Generally Direct Major Distribution Channel.   Most services are marketed directly from producer to consumer. Although they are not common in services, there are *some* middlemen. The agent middleman is found in services such as employment, booking, travel, and insurance agencies. None takes title to the service he is offering for sale. The merchant middleman dealing in services is even rarer. When an organization contracts for a charter flight and then sells space to others, it is acting as a merchant middleman because it is now the (temporary) owner of the service. Some laundries operate in the same fashion, offering laundry and dry cleaning at retail prices and then purchasing the service from a vendor. The firm that specializes in offering temporary help is also a merchant middleman because *it* pays the people, makes the necessary deductions from salary or wages, pays employee taxes, and bills the buyer. In effect, it owns the time of the people whose services are being sold.

General Nonportability. Not many services are portable, particularly those that are offered at a facility. The amusement park, the private nursing home, the beauty shop, the bank, the motel cannot easily be brought to the consumer; the consumer must go to them. But there are exceptions. Many personal services (janitorial, yard, household maintenance, and repairs) can be delivered to the consumer. Cable television and utilities fall in this category; so do some transportation services (e.g., moving companies, taxicabs) and some forms of entertainment (e.g., piped-in music, video tape and film rentals). Insurance and correspondence courses are portable.

The Pricing of Services

Although the pricing of services generally follows the practices of the pricing of tangible products, there are some differences.

Decline of Price during Low-Demand Periods. Services are far more perishable than most tangible products. If a service is not sold at a specific time, the sale is lost forever; services cannot be stored. For example, if a room in a motel is not rented during a particular overnight period, that potential income is lost permanently.

For this reason it is common for many services, particularly those that are facilities, to offer low prices during periods of low demand. A Florida hotel may offer bargain prices during the summer just so that it can employ its staff on a year-round basis. The telephone company offers low prices for night and weekend calls. Airlines offer low prices for night flights and for overseas flights during the nonvacation period. Some motels and car-rental companies offer lower weekend prices so that their facilities will be used during a period when they otherwise might not likely be.

Requirement for Advance Payment or Guaranteed Purchase. Because services are so perishable, when a potential customer indicates interest, the seller often wants to make sure that he does not make a commitment unless the buyer also makes a commitment. The motel is not interested in reserving a room past a six o'clock arrival time; if the prospective purchaser does not arrive by then, it may be too late to rent the room. Therefore, a guarantee is asked for late arrivals. You generally pay in advance for an airplane ticket, and if you plan to go to a concert or a play, you are often asked to pay for your ticket and pick it up in advance.

Negotiation for Higher-priced Services. When the price of a service is hundreds or thousands of dollars, price negotiation is common, just as it is in the purchase of higher-priced tangible goods (such as a house or an automobile). This may occur with services such as house painting or foreign travel.

Bids for Higher-priced Services. Bids are common in the case of some specialized high-price services. It is usual to solicit bids, for example, when a business firm is planning to undertake a major marketing research survey that will cost many thousands of dollars. When the individual consumer needs to have his house painted, he is likely to ask for bids.

The Promotion of Services

The promotion of services generally follows the same principles used in promotion of tangible goods. However, there are some differences in emphasis.

More Stress on Consumer Benefits. In the promotion of tangible goods, it is possible to talk about specific product characteristics (even though it may not be desirable to do so). But because services, for the most part, are intangible, it becomes necessary to promote them in terms of benefits to the buyer. The airline that advertises "Getting there is half the fun" demonstrates this principle.

Importance of Personal Selling. Unlike the tangible product, few services can be sold by mail or vending machine (air insurance, other forms of insurance, and automatic banking are exceptions). Detailed explanations are often necessary. Direct and continuing relationships often develop (e.g., the consultant, the physician, the lawyer). Sometimes price negotiation is required.

All these mean that personal selling is important in marketing of services.

Emphasis on Local Advertising.   Local media (newspapers, radio, television, direct mail, the yellow pages of the telephone book) tend to be more important than national media because most services are local in nature. The national franchise chains (McDonald's, Howard Johnson's, Avis) are exceptions. These can and do use national media.

An important medium is word of mouth. The new arrival in town is likely to ask for guidance in selecting a beauty or barber shop, an auto-repair shop, and the like.

Example of a Service: McDonald's

Since franchised services are becoming increasingly important, it is appropriate to consider one of the most successful.

Roy Kroc and His Background.   Roy Kroc, founder of the McDonald's chain of franchised fast-food outlets, came from an unpromising background. A high school dropout at the end of his sophomore year, he played piano with several traveling bands and served as musical director of a Chicago radio station for a period. One winter, he tried his hand selling real estate in Florida but was so unsuccessful that he returned to Chicago in the middle of the winter without money or even an overcoat.

Meeting the McDonald Brothers.   In 1937, Kroc obtained sales rights for a machine that could mix five milkshakes at a time. In 1954, he learned of one shop in California that had eight of these machines. Intrigued, he decided to visit them to learn what their secret was. He saw people lined up to buy $.15 hamburgers. The shop was run by the two McDonald brothers, and Kroc asked why they did not open more shops (presumably so that he could sell them more machines). They were not interested; they were successful as they were and did not care to expand.

Kroc soon saw that there was more than an opportunity to sell milkshake machines here. He obtained the right to own and operate other McDonald's shops for .5 percent of sales. He opened his first McDonald's store in 1955, in Des Plaines, Illinois; six years later, he bought complete rights to the name for $2.7 million.

The Operation Today.   Today, the operation is so successful that it is second only to Kentucky Fried Chicken in number of outlets. Three-quarters of the outlets are franchised; the others are owned by the company. The company likes to say that the total operation uses more beef than any other consumer except the federal government. McDonald's operates in six countries outside the United States; it shows an unusually high return of between 12 and 15 percent of sales to the owner.

How It Works.   The first step in this operation is selection of the franchisee. The company looks for a man between thirty-five and fifty who has a capital accumulation of at least $55,000 (for investment in the franchise). They want someone who has a business background, is level-headed, and has the "proper attitude" toward family life. They also want a man who "can stand prosperity," who does not want to spend his time on the golf course after achieving success with his franchise; they want him to continue to work at it.

When they find the right person, they offer him a twenty-year contract, with the parent firm taking 2.5 percent of the gross and charging another 2.5 percent for the franchisee's contribution to national advertising. The parent firm spells out rigid controls that must be followed, but it sells nothing—no raw materials or operating supplies—to the franchise holder. He buys all these locally.

The company selects the site for the store carefully. It looks for a somewhat-above-average residential area with young families (90 percent of McDonald's customers are local customers rather than transients), preferably near a shopping center. The company buys (and retains ownership of) the site. Standard building design and equipment are provided.

Before the store is opened, the franchisee must attend Hamburger University, in Elk Grove Village, Illinois, where he takes a three-week crash course that includes both classroom instruction and laboratory work (the latter right down the street at the local McDonald's outlet). The new owner learns basic food preparation, equipment maintenance, purchasing, personnel, and quality control.

The thing that really makes the McDonald's operation successful is the running of the individual outlet. McDonald's has put the
hamburger on the assembly line. The operational control starts
with the purchase of the meat. There are rigid specifications about
the cuts of meat permitted and the percentage of fat allowed.
Cooking is on a production-line basis; there is a production control
man near the middle of the counter who calls the order of each
hamburger mix. Eighteen patties are placed on the grill at a time,
and the production control man determines how many of these
are to go into doubles, cheeseburgers, regulars, and custom (special orders, such as no mustard).

To maintain quality control, unsold hamburgers are discarded
ten minutes after cooking; French fries, after seven minutes. All
McDonald's outlets have a standard menu, with only minor variations catering to local tastes in some parts of the country.

There is a national advertising campaign aimed at children. The
local franchisee also does some of his own advertising, generally in
the newspaper. Franchisees are also encouraged to use public relations; it is not unusual to see the franchisee or his manager offering
free hamburgers to some local group (such as children who have
taken their bicycles in for a voluntary police check).

With this sort of program and effective controls (through field
checks), it is scarcely a wonder that the operation has been so
successful.

REVIEW QUESTIONS

1. Why is a service usually unstandardized?
2. Name three national franchise chains that have utilized national
   advertising for promotion of their services.
3. In addition to those listed in this chapter, list three services that no
   longer exist. Name three relatively new services.
4. Why is it that most services depend upon local media for their
   advertising?

23

INTERNATIONAL MARKETING

As the volume of international trade continues to grow (for the year 1970 U.S. exports rose 7.6 percent to an estimated $42 billion, excluding military grant-aid shipments), students of introductory marketing should give some attention to the elements of international marketing. Several factors are responsible for the astounding growth of international trade since the end of World War II.

World trade has been stimulated by the many multinational marketing groups that have been formed for the general purposes of abolishing tariff barriers within their borders and of establishing economic policies that will benefit all members. Probably the most important of these groups is the European Economic Community, usually known as the Common Market, which is composed of France, West Germany, Belgium, Luxembourg, the Netherlands, the United Kingdom, Ireland, and Denmark, with Greece and Turkey as associate members. Those European nations that do not belong to the Common Market have formed an organization known as the European Free Trade Association (EFTA); its members are Austria, Norway, Portugal, Sweden, and Switzerland, with Finland as an associate member. Latin American countries have combined in international organizations such as the Latin

American Free Trade Association (LAFTA), composed of Argentina, Brazil, Chile, Colombia, Ecuador, Mexico, Paraguay, Peru, and Uruguay; and the Central American Common Market (CACM) with Costa Rica, El Salvador, Guatemala, Honduras, and Nicaragua as members.

Another stimulus to international marketing has been the growth in the world population. There were some 2.1 billion people in the entire world in 1930; by 1969, the population had reached 3.6 billion. Between 1963 and 1969, the annual rate of population increase was 2.5 percent for Africa; 1.7 percent for North America; 2.7 percent for Latin America; 2.3 percent for Asia (excluding the USSR); 0.8 percent for Europe; and 2.1 percent for Oceania. The great population increase in Africa and Latin America was accompanied by growth of economic development and per capita income that, when supplemented by improved education, may make these areas potential markets for American goods and services.

The increasing affluence of the countries of Western Europe has stimulated demands for products and services that indicate limited future expansion of United States trade with the highly industrialized areas of Europe. However, Europe's industrialization will finally pose a barrier to some kinds of American exports.

While world markets are growing in affluence, domestic profits of U.S. manufacturers after taxes seem to be dropping off. Between 1947 and 1970, profits had dropped approximately 9.3 percent, as is indicated in the table on p. 265. As the domestic market becomes saturated, U.S. firms must seek greater opportunities in international markets to increase their profit margins.

There no longer are significant barriers in communication and transportation between nations. Newsworthy articles can be sent to all the news media in the world within a day, and television broadcasts can be transmitted internationally by satellite. The most distant parts of the world can be reached by airplane in a matter of hours. Accelerated communications and transportation are important aids in expediting the growth of world trade. The only remaining barriers to world trade may be found among the so-called Iron Curtain or Communist countries. However, with

Rates of Profit after Taxes on Stockholders' Equity in
Manufacturing Corporations, 1947 to 1970

Year	Percent
1947	15.6
1950	15.4
1955	12.6
1960	9.2
1964	11.6
1966	13.4
1968	12.1
1969	11.5
1970	9.3

SOURCE: Federal Trade Commission and Securities and Exchange Commission:
Quarterly Financial Report for Manufacturing Corporations. U.S.
Bureau of the Census, *Statistical Abstract of the United States: 1971*
(Washington, D.C.: U.S. Government Printing Office, 1971).

détente, there are increasing signs of change. Trade between the
United States and China is resuming, and trade between the
United States and Russia is increasing. It is fairly easy now for an
American tourist to visit Russia.

Devaluation of the American dollar in 1971 and 1973 also
stimulated international trade, at least in the sense that more
American goods are being sold overseas (because they became less
expensive).

Feasibility Studies

Before an American business decides to penetrate an overseas
market, it should evaluate many political, social, and economic
elements in the proposed market. A carefully designed marketing
research study should be undertaken to secure detailed information on the size of the market, potential demand, methods of distribution and promotion, kinds of pricing and discounting procedures, and the quantity and quality of competitive products. A
socioeconomic profile of potential consumers should indicate the

size of the average family, the literacy rate, amount of per capita income, buying patterns, occupational and spatial distribution of the population, educational levels by age-group, and local preferences in such matters as color and packaging. In measuring any potential market, mores and institutions of the people and any restrictions related to eating, color, or buying must be taken into consideration. In many countries, religion is an important factor in these matters.

To determine the political and economic stability of the proposed foreign market, a properly administered research program should obtain information on the stability of the foreign government and its policies toward business and foreign trade. The size and growth of the GNP, the amount of disposable and discretionary income, and the extent of private and government investment in business should be investigated. The structure of the political hierarchy and whether the country has hard (or convertible) currency must be studied. The research program should study the banking and financial system, the major industries, the services provided by business, tariffs, taxes, import-export controls, and legislation affecting import trade.

In addition to the company's own research program, supplementary material on any market may be obtained from the U.S. Department of Commerce, the United Nations, foreign embassies, the U.S. commercial attachés in the countries under consideration. The Department of Commerce will perform a trade contract survey to locate firms within a foreign country that meet specific requirements of American business. The charge for this service is minimal, but the survey does not produce all the necessary information. Therefore, the findings of the marketing research study should be coupled with the trade contract survey.

Analysis of these data will provide business with an estimate of sales potential in a foreign market and will suggest methods for efficiently penetrating that market. A marketing plan may be constructed and implemented by appropriate strategy for each foreign market in which the research indicates an acceptable return on investment. The marketing plan must include the objectives or goals of the company in this operation, the availability of human and productive resources that will be required, the problems of financing and insurance, and the costs of the proposed undertaking. Included in these costs would be the channels of distribution and methods of transportation that would be employed. After reviewing the plan and costs, management is in a better position to know whether the international operation should be integrated as part of the domestic company's activity or should be decentralized. When several markets appear to have significant potential, a marketing plan should be prepared for each.

Structure of International Operations

Once the decision has been made to enter a.foreign market, the American company generally has a choice of the method to be employed. If the American firm proposes to do business in a country that is a member of a multinational organization such as the Common Market, it may be necessary to join forces with an established company in that country in a joint venture. In a similar situation, it may be wise to license a foreign manufacturer to make and sell the American product on a royalty or fee basis.

If there are no obvious barriers to penetration of the foreign market, it is usual for smaller American companies to employ an agent middleman to market their products abroad. A larger company that envisions a good-sized potential market may set up a subsidiary in the chosen country for the purpose of manufacturing and distributing its products.

If a company does not want to become involved in such details of overseas sales as locating market representatives, deciding how the products should be transported, and methods of distribution, it usually retains an agent. Generally, this agent sells through foreign distributors and handles many noncompetitive lines.

Conversely, the export commission house is a buying agent for foreign firms. It seeks out U.S. products for foreign customers and is paid a commission by each foreign firm that it represents.

Other methods of entering foreign markets include exporting directly through an export specialist such as a manufacturers' export agent, an export broker, or the combination export management firm. The combination export manager (CEM) is usually a part of an independent firm located in the United States that may take over the total export output of a manufacturer. The CEM usually penetrates foreign markets through his own resident distributors overseas. He may also undertake the advertising and promotion for products or services. The CEM may perform other duties such as evaluating the credit standing of foreign customers. Like all agents, he never takes title to goods or has any financial responsibility to the domestic company. The CEM is usually paid on a commission or fee basis.

Among companies in the United States that are active in international business, one-third own at least a 10 percent interest in a foreign subsidiary or affiliate. The pattern of moving from exporting to direct investment in a foreign operation has become common today. The major reason for investing in foreign operations is to circumvent the local tariff and thus obtain lower costs in reaching world markets. Although airfreight and other modern shipping methods have reduced transportation expenses, import duties and similar obstacles still represent an important problem to the American exporter. Originally, an important reason for owning or partially owning an overseas operation was the lower labor costs that were available, but this advantage is gradually disappearing. Many companies, particularly larger ones, go into overseas ownership to check competitors' moves. For U.S. companies manufacturing in a foreign country, having facilities in that country is an important advantage to the domestic company as well as to the overseas customers. Another reason, which is much more difficult to measure, is the prestige commonly attached to companies having subsidiaries in foreign countries; those businesses feel that being a part of the international business community is important.

Many businessmen believe that it would be foolish for a U.S. company to license a foreign company unless it was assured that the licensee was both a good manufacturer and good marketer, and this combination is often difficult to find. However, licensing provides a means for earning additional income from technical developments without placing a strain on the American company's domestic staff. The major advantage to this procedure is when the American company holds a patent abroad. However, the foreign licensee has little reason to renew once the patent or contractual agreement has run out; therefore, he is in a position to make and sell his own product. To overcome this danger, the domestic company's trademark(s) are registered in its own name in all countries where the product is sold. The licensing agreement usually provides that the licensee must use the company's brand in marketing the product that is made under license. Once the patent or agreement has run out and the licensee wishes to be on his own, he is forced to sell against the domestic company's brand. In some situations, the domestic company may acquire a minority stock ownership in the licensee. This sometimes eliminates the potential competitive problem and makes the licensee feel that he is a partner with the American company.

Smaller companies may build their export business by turning the operation over to a foreign sales specialist who will take care of credit problems, brokerage, and processing of purchase orders. Generally, this representative will require that management make occasional trips overseas to prepare advertising for use in foreign markets and, when necessary, to demonstrate equipment. Before signing any contract, however, the domestic company must assure itself that this sales representative has properly trained and qualified people who can sell its product to foreign customers. Moreover, the domestic company must make sure that the sales representative has the proper financial resources and is sufficiently well organized to handle its product. In a sense, this representative will be the export sales department for the company. The major advantage of this kind of operation is that it eliminates the need for setting up an export organization within the company and permits the company to carry on its domestic market while its overseas orders are carried through by another organization to which a commission is paid.

Another method of selling abroad is to use an export merchant who buys the domestic goods for his own account and sells them overseas.

If the exporter is a novice, he may wish to investigate the piggyback program. The International Traders Index is a registry of companies that are well entrenched in overseas sales and that are interested in expanding their product lines by including noncompetitive products of novice exporters. These firms are known as *carriers*, and the financial details as well as the sales commissions are negotiated by the export company and the novice exporters.

Financing

Export financing is a very complicated problem. It can be accomplished in various ways. American manufacturers may use company resources, sell additional stock, or request a credit line from banks that deal in export operations. Established exporters that are involved either with joint ventures or with subsidiaries may finance their operations through foreign banks or other foreign credit sources so that dollars do not leave the United States. U.S. companies may receive help in underwriting through domestic and United Kingdom bankers and from banks in Hong Kong. In addition, short- and medium-term credit is available in Europe, as are Eurodollars.

Eurodollars are dollars owned by foreign governments or by companies or individuals located outside of the United States and deposited in European banks or in the European branches of American banks. Eurodollars have been used for financing since the late 1950s and have been fed by U.S. balance-of-payments deficits. Many Eurodollars are available for loans, and the short-term demand for this type of money is huge. European companies and even foreign governments borrow in the Eurodollars market. The U.S. government's voluntary restrictions on direct dollar loans to foreigners by American banks have led many foreign companies to negotiate Eurodollar loans for expansion purposes.

Another source of financing is *Eurobonds*. These bonds have been used in Europe since early 1964 and are sold through banks and underwriters located outside of the United States. The bonds are in dollar denominations and pay interest in dollars. Transactions in Eurobonds are growing at a spectacular rate. American corporations have found this method an ideal way to raise money for their foreign operations without withdrawing dollars from the

United States, and in 1967, an estimated $527 million worth of Eurobonds were sold overseas by U.S. companies.

Some economists have said that the Eurodollar activity is a foreign vote of confidence in the U.S. dollar and will permit American companies to handle much of their expansion easily. The money in the Eurodollar pool exceeds the entire U.S. gold stock.

Insurance.   When planning to distribute their products to overseas markets, domestic companies should review the insurance that is available to them. The Foreign Credit Insurance Association (FCIA), in cooperation with the Export-Import Bank of the United States, insures trade credits carried by U.S. exporters to buyers in all friendly foreign countries. This insurance covers the exporter to an agreed percentage against loss resulting from credit risk, political risk, cancellation of export license, or change in governmental decree. The FCIA assumes 100 percent of the liability for commercial credit losses, and the Export-Import Bank assumes 100 percent of the liability for political risks. The FCIA issues four types of policies: short-term comprehensive, short-term political risk, medium-term comprehensive, and medium-term political risk.

The insurance industry, because of its widespread facilities, was invited to join the Export-Import Bank in providing insurance to exporters. Today more than sixty insurance companies are part of the FCIA. This program, in effect since 1962, was designed to aid American industry in increasing its share of the world market at a cost consistent with the risks involved. Since the advent of FCIA, premiums have been reduced by as much as 50 percent. This association and the Export-Import Bank act as coinsurors in underwriting the credit insurance for exporters. All the servicing of the business is done by the FCIA, which acts as an agent for the Export-Import Bank and the insurance companies. When U.S. products are exhibited at foreign trade fairs, the Export-Import Bank covers these products against loss due to political risk.

Foreign Trade Financing.   Exporters prefer to keep their working capital liquid. Many do not care to sell abroad on credit because of the time interval involved in collecting from these customers. Financing of exports by the small businessman becomes difficult because he may not be in position to carry accounts receivable for a very long time.

Funds for exporting are usually obtained from banks and other organizations engaged in financing foreign trade. Generally, the major banks in the larger cities in this country handle most of the foreign trade financing. Two kinds of financing are available to the exporter.

DOCUMENTARY SIGHT OR TIME DRAFTS. The customer has agreed to pay his bills against presentation of drafts drawn against him and on sight. Generally, the exporter will forward a draft with the appropriate documents to his own bank in the United States for collection.

LETTERS OF CREDIT. The buyer agrees to pay the exporter's bill by a letter of credit. The exporter will be notified by his own bank or some other U.S. bank that a letter of credit for a specific amount has been opened in his favor. Basically, there are three kinds of letters of credit: irrevocable unconfirmed, confirmed irrevocable, and revocable. American banks generally will provide financing for the exporter between the time he accepts an order and the date on which he is to receive payment under a letter of credit.

Most heavy equipment and capital goods are now sold on what are known as *medium-term credits*. Generally, the foreign buyer agrees to make a down payment when the order is given and will pay the remaining balance on a monthly, quarterly, or semiannual basis. This balance is normally covered by a promissory note.

With the availability of credit insurance, there are several factoring firms that will factor export accounts receivable. This means that accounts receivable will be purchased at a discount from the exporter so that he has the cash available as soon as the sale has been made. Organizations known as *confirming houses* operate similarly to factors. They are in reality factoring organizations and represent the overseas buyer. Once a confirming house receives word that a sale has been made to a client, it will pay for that export order on previously agreed terms that usually involve a discount for the confirming house. It is through this discount taken on the value of an order that a factoring firm or confirming house makes its money.

Government Aid in Financing. In addition to the private sources that are available to the exporters, there are several public agencies that may directly or indirectly help to finance exports.

The Export-Import Bank of the United States (Eximbank) makes hard loans to foreign borrowers for imports of capital equipment and other U.S. goods and services.

The U.S. Agency for International Development (AID) makes soft foreign aid loans to less developed countries and requires that the funds be spent on U.S. goods and services.

The International Bank for Reconstruction and Development (IBRD), or World Bank, makes loans on economic assistance terms to foreign countries for financing basic projects and other development activities.

The International Development Association (IDA) makes development loans with very soft repayment terms to less developed countries unable to meet the more conventional repayment requirements of the World Bank.

The International Finance Corporation (IFC) encourages private enterprises in developing countries by providing deed and equity capital in cooperation with private investors.

The Inter-American Development Bank (IDB) makes loans to Latin American countries on conventional economic assistance terms from its ordinary resources and on soft terms from its Fund for Special Operations.

U.S. exporters of capital equipment and other basic goods and services should place these agencies' borrowers high on their lists of potential customers. Most loans offered by these agencies are in U.S. dollars or other convertible currencies and are to finance specific development projects such as dams, electric power plants, highway construction, and cement and fertilizer plants.

Domestic exporters are often placed on these agencies' mailing lists for press releases to keep them informed about projects for which financing has been approved. Many of the projects are so large that a particular U.S. firm can supply only part of the goods under subcontract to the prime supplier. Many loans are listed in *International Commerce,* a U.S. Department of Commerce weekly publication. These agencies do not compete with private capital, however, and will generally not extend a loan if private financing is available on reasonable terms.

Documentation

Each export shipment must be accompanied by specific documents that are used as a basis for financing and may be attached to the draft or other payment instrument related to the shipment. Other forms of documentation are used to comply with government regulations or with the import controls of the country to which the shipment is sent. The principal documents are the *bill of lading,* the *commercial invoice,* the *consular invoice* (when required), a *marine insurance policy* or certificate, and the *export declaration.*

The bill of lading is the carrier's receipt for the goods delivered to it and the exporter's contract with the shipper. This is a negotiable instrument that gives the exporter or his agent control of that shipment until it is accepted or paid for by the buyer. The commercial invoice is merely the exporter's invoice to the customer. The consular invoice is used to clear goods through the customhouse of the country to which the goods have been sent; this kind of invoice is not always necessary. The marine insurance policy protects the shipment against physical damage or loss while the goods are in transit. The export declaration is required by the U.S. government in connection with each foreign shipment. The proper preparation of these documents requires detailed knowledge and is normally done by an agent or an expert in the international marketing division of a company.

Sources of Information and Promotion

A manufacturer considering marketing his product abroad may obtain basic information from sources such as the U.S. Department of Commerce, the foreign departments of domestic banks, commercial attachés, export agents or brokers, and transportation companies involved in international marketing. American Chambers of Commerce in cities abroad, affiliated with the U.S. Chamber of Commerce, will provide information about markets and marketing opportunities in the countries in which they are located.

If a manufacturer wishes to contact foreign distributors or agents in overseas markets, he may begin with the Commerce Department's computer-generated trade lists of companies dealing in specific Standard Industrial Classification (SIC) product categories within given countries. Besides providing the names and addresses of selected distributors, the trade lists highlight the relative size of each firm, the products it handles, the territory covered, and the size of the sales force.

Before making any substantial investment, a manufacturer may obtain information on export markets by exhibiting his products at the Department of Commerce trade centers in London, Bangkok, Frankfurt, Tokyo, Milan, Paris, and Stockholm. These trade centers are permanent sites where specific product line shows are held. The department promotes each of these specialized shows to attract potential buyers and distributors. Another source of information may be the trade fairs that are held in many countries under the supervision of foreign governments and commercial agencies. Often, the Commerce Department sets up a pavilion at the important fairs and permits domestic manufacturers to exhibit.

Many U.S. manufacturers consider international trade fairs and exhibits an excellent way to show their products. A good deal of business is transacted at the European trade shows. In some cases, 50 percent of the annual production may be committed in on-the-spot sales at these manufacturers' exhibits.

Companies exhibiting their products at trade shows may consult a publication entitled *Export Market Guide*, which is put out by the U.S. Department of Commerce. This is issued prior to any trade show, fair, or exposition in which American companies participate or that they may sponsor. The guide includes data on sales opportunities, competition, distribution methods for a specific country, expected attendance, and a review of the technical requirements a manufacturer needs to know before exhibiting.

Trade Missions. In addition to its other services, the Department of Commerce organizes trade missions, which are concerned with specific or related groups of commodities that have a proven sales potential in specific countries. These trade missions are composed of five or six representatives from businesses in the United States plus an official of the Department of Commerce who may serve as a director and trade development officer. All members are volunteers selected for their outstanding leadership, technical competence, and experience in industry. Each member of a mission contributes six or seven weeks of his time a year, during which several hundred business proposals are presented to foreign businessmen and to foreign government buyers. Trade missions penetrate new as well as established markets. Their impact is striking and enduring; it has been reported that the interest they generate continues long after they have visited a foreign country. The Bureau of International Commerce, which is part of the Commerce Department, sends some ten to twenty missions abroad each year.

Position of the United States in International Marketing

Merchandise exports are still the dominant method by which U.S. companies gain a foothold in foreign markets. At the present time, Western Europe is the most important area for investment and export trade; the Latin American countries pose the greatest obstacles to U.S. exports because of the difficulty of obtaining import licenses from their governments.

The fifty markets shown in the table on page 277 accounted for 92 percent of the 1966 imports in all free-world markets and 93 percent of imports from the United States.

A careful evaluation of the figures in the table indicates that probably the greatest potential markets for the United States lie in the so-called undeveloped countries. Currently, the United States exports a large number of items to Western Europe. Further study of the table shows that additional market shares may be gained in Australia, India, the Republic of South Africa, Greece, and New Zealand. If the major obstacles to trade can be overcome in Latin America, this area may become an outstanding market for United States goods and services.

Immediate Outlook for U.S. Exports.   There has been con-

Principal Markets for United States Exports, 1970 (Values in millions of dollars)

Country	1970 Imports From world	From U.S.	U.S. share %	Country	1970 Imports From world	From U.S.	U.S. share %
Germany, Fed. Rep.	29,817	3,293	11.0	Venezuela	1,919	938	48.9
United Kingdom	21,724	2,816	13.0	Argentina	1,685	419	24.8
France	18,918	1,897	10.0	Iran	1,640	218	13.3
Japan	18,883	5,565	29.5	Ireland	1,569	110	7.0
Italy	14,939	1,543	10.3	Portugal	1,556	107	6.9
Canada	14,462	10,268	71.0	Taiwan	1,524	364	23.9
Netherlands	13,391	1,308	9.8	Israel	1,451	326	22.5
Belgium-Luxembourg	11,362	995	8.8	Thailand	1,293	193	14.9
Sweden	7,007	611	8.7	Algeria	1,257	117	9.3
Switzerland	6,483	552	8.5	New Zealand	1,245	167	13.4
Australia	5,086	1,292	25.4	Philippines	1,209	355	29.4
Spain	4,749	897	18.9	Pakistan	1,129	361	31.9
Denmark	4,387	326	7.4	Malaysia	1,111	90	8.1
South Africa, Rep.	3,912	653	16.7	Nigeria	1,059	154	14.5
Norway	3,702	269	7.3	Indonesia	893	158	17.7
Austria	3,549	121	3.4	Turkey	886	172	19.4
Hong Kong	2,905	382	13.2	Colombia	844	390	46.2
Yugoslavia	2,874	160	5.6	Egypt	787	48	6.1
Brazil	2,849	918	32.2	Morocco	686	78	11.3
Finland	2,636	137	5.2	Peru	619	199	32.2
Mexico	2,461	1,568	63.7	Trinidad & Tobago	543	89	16.4
Singapore	2,461	266	10.8	Jamaica	522	226	43.3
India	2,125	622	29.3	Panama	353	139	39.3
Korea, Rep.	1,984	585	29.5	Costa Rica	317	110	34.8
Greece	1,958	116	5.9	Ecuador	248	81	32.6

NOTE: In order to present comparable statistics for all countries, import data have been adjusted from an f.o.b. to c.i.f. valuation for Australia, Canada, Panama, Philippines, Republic of South Africa, and Venezuela. SOURCE: *Commerce Today*.

siderable pressure to stem increasing deficits in the U.S. balance of payments. The devaluations of the dollar in late 1971 and in 1973 were intended to make American goods cheaper in foreign countries and imported goods more expensive in the United States.

The expansion of the European Common Market in 1973 is another significant factor in the American export outlook. The breakdown of these economic barriers, on the one hand, makes it easier for some American manufacturers to expand their European markets but, on the other hand, makes the European competition that much fiercer.

Devaluation has not hurt the multinational firms because they tend to have local production throughout the world and to operate in local currencies.

Conclusion

The proper exploration of foreign markets requires an objective appraisal of the domestic company's prospects, a review of what export marketing will add to the company's return on investment, and some forecast of the long-range opportunities that will be available in these overseas markets. American companies have basic advantages when they consider export operations because, generally, their activities are characterized by four factors: mass production, product-quality control, ability to take advantage of low-saturation markets, and aggressive marketing techniques.

Overseas sales may take up the slack when buying slows down in the U.S. markets as a result of seasonal or other characteristic slumps in this country. The demand for American consumer goods is growing throughout the world, and there is an opportunity for domestic manufacturers to take advantage of this trend. Today, wage earners in Western Europe have more discretionary income to spend than heretofore, which obviously increases sales potential for consumer goods. The European consumer requires the same quality, service, and value in his products as customers in the United States have learned to expect in theirs. This is also true of consumers in Japan, Canada, Australia, Mexico, and Taiwan.

In the foreseeable future, far-thinking businessmen will no longer divide business into domestic sales and export sales but will consider the world their market. It will be their responsibility to evaluate changing potentials for the many communities throughout the world so that marketing plans and strategies may be adapted to fluctuating demands. As economic interdependence grows among the countries of the world, the threat of armed conflicts may gradually diminish.

REVIEW QUESTIONS

1. What are the methods by which an American company can enter a foreign market?
2. What is the Eurodollar, and how is it important in the financing of an American manufacturer's foreign operations?
3. Define the two major methods of financing provided by banks and other financing institutions for foreign trade funds.
4. What public agencies help directly or indirectly to finance exports?

24

THE MARKETING OF SELECTED COMMODITIES

This book has considered marketing from the functional, systems, and institutional points of view. The principles discussed throughout will be supplemented in this chapter by an analysis of the channels through which commodities are distributed. The various steps in the distribution of several basic commodities (steps that are more or less typical of the classes of products they exemplify) will be outlined. Wheat, milk, and other dairy products are good examples of agricultural commodities; woven wire is a good example of a basic material used in the manufacture of industrial equipment; and radios and television sets are good examples of consumer goods.

Cost of Marketing Farm Commodities

When the housewife spends a dollar for food, the farmer usually receives less than half of that amount because most of the food dollar is used to pay the operating expenses and profits of marketing agencies that distribute the food. The accompanying diagram, based on data for a recent year, shows how much the production of food costs in comparison with the cost of each step in its marketing.

The diagram indicates that the major marketing functions, in order of cost, are farm production, retailing, processing, wholesaling, transportation, and assembly. It reveals that the actual growing of food products costs more than any one marketing function, but it also demonstrates that the total cost of all the marketing functions amounts to $.685 of the food dollar.

The magnitude of farm commodity marketing in the United States and its importance to the national economy are indicated by the percentage of national income devoted to the purchase of food. This percentage of per capita disposable income spent for food by the consumer has remained remarkably stable over the

APPROXIMATE DISTRIBUTION OF THE CONSUMER'S DOLLAR
SPENT FOR FARM FOOD PRODUCTS, BY MARKETING
FUNCTIONS AND BY COST ITEMS

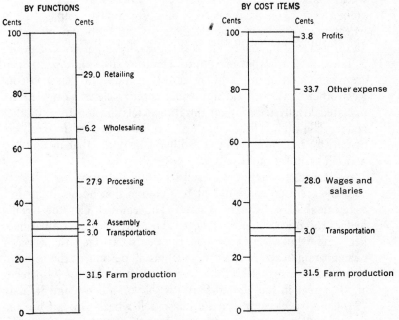

BY FUNCTIONS

Cents		Cents
100		29.0 Retailing
80		6.2 Wholesaling
60		27.9 Processing
40		2.4 Assembly
		3.0 Transportation
20		31.5 Farm production
0		

BY COST ITEMS

Cents		Cents
100		3.8 Profits
80		33.7 Other expense
60		28.0 Wages and salaries
40		3.0 Transportation
20		31.5 Farm production
0		

SOURCE: Economics Research Service, U.S. Department of Agriculture.

years. Since 1929, the highest percentage spent for food in any year was 29 percent, and the lowest was 18 percent, in 1966.

Marketing of Wheat

Hard spring, hard winter, soft red winter, white, and Durham are some of the different kinds of wheat. Since these varieties of wheat grow in different areas, certain minor modifications in marketing techniques may be required for the various types; but generally speaking, all wheat is marketed by means of a definite and quite consistent pattern of distribution. See diagram on p. 284.

Handling of Wheat in the Local Wholesale Market. After wheat is harvested, it is usually brought to the country elevator (a specialized warehouse for grain storage), where it is sold soon after its arrival. Outright sale is the most common procedure because most farmers need cash and also do not care to speculate on wheat market conditions. However, the wheat may be stored in a grain elevator, on payment of a monthly storage charge. In the wheat-growing states of the Pacific coast, the crop may be sacked and stored in warehouses, but this is the only important exception.

There are two types of country elevators: *line elevators*, which are owned or controlled by a central organization that also controls other elevators, and *individual country elevators*, which are operated locally without organizational relationship to any other country elevator. These elevators may be owned by farmers' cooperatives, by a mill, or by individual companies that merely buy and sell grain for profit.

An elevator company may sell wheat in two ways: (1) It may ship the grain on consignment to a commission house situated in a terminal or a primary market. The country elevator usually hedges the price while the wheat is en route to the terminal market. After the wheat arrives in the central market, the elevator owners are allowed to draw as much as 80 percent of the value of the wheat consigned to the commission men. Almost 75 percent of the wheat in the United States is sold on a consignment basis. (2) Country elevator operators also sell wheat through the *on-*

track or the *to-arrive* procedure, in which an acceptable price is set before the grain is shipped.

When a bid is received by the country elevator for sale on an on-track shipment basis, the buyer quotes a price and sets a time limit for delivery of the grain to either a market or a processor. The on-track sale price covers all costs from country elevator to final destination. It will be paid *only* if the wheat arrives within the given period of time.

For sales on the to-arrive basis, the prospective buyer (usually a broker or a manufacturer) mails prices to the country elevator. The price usually holds good until 9:15 on the morning after the mailing. If the quoted price is accepted, the grain must be delivered to the buyer within approximately two weeks. Ordinarily, the price on a to-arrive basis requires the local elevator operators to pay the cost of freightage to the terminal market.

Function of the Terminal Market in Wheat Distribution. When the wheat arrives at the central market, it is stored. The commission men at the central market may act as agents or as merchants. They may buy and sell wheat for speculation, or they may sell it to processors on a brokerage basis. If the transaction is handled on a simple brokerage basis by a broker operating in the central market, his concern with the commodity ends when the wheat changes hands. In either case, the terminal market, which is usually a grain exchange, facilitates distribution of the wheat to the ultimate user.

Distribution of Processed Wheat Goods. Bakery goods are perhaps the most familiar examples of processed wheat products; their marketing channels are shown on page 285. Note that most bakery products are sold by manufacturers to retailers either directly or through manufacturer-owned sales branches. There is also considerable selling directly to the consumer. Only a small quantity is handled by independent wholesalers.

Marketing of Milk Products

The per person consumption of butter is now only 60 percent as high as prewar consumption. This figure is based on current

MARKETING CHANNELS FOR WHEAT

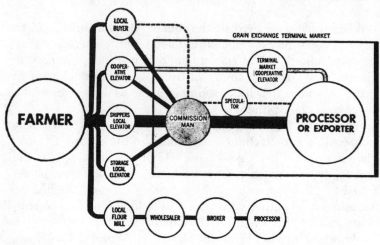

SOURCE: U.S. Department of Agriculture.

levels of production per cow and on a national herd of about 35 million cows. Each decrease of one pound of butter consumed per person per year frees approximately three pounds of milk per year for fluid consumption or other uses. Milk, besides being sold in the usual fluid state, is sold as butter, cheese, and ice cream and in other forms. The table on p. 286 indicates the average consumption per person of milk products in 1966.

Marketing of Fluid Milk. A study completed several years ago showed that 50 percent of all consumer payments for milk and dairy products during a five-year period was for fluid milk and cream. Approximately 60 percent of the milk sold in the United States was delivered to homes. Another 20 percent was consumed in institutions, and the remaining 20 percent was sold to consumers through retail stores.

Milk is usually hauled by trucks directly from farmers' assembly points to city pasteurizing plants. However, some large suppliers deliver most of their milk to country plants first and then reship it in bulk by tank trucks or tank cars to city plants, where it is pasteurized, cooled, and bottled. The bottled milk is distributed to consumers through the retail channels described in the preceding

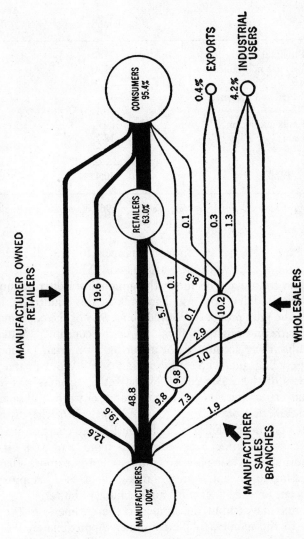

MARKETING CHANNELS FOR BAKERY PRODUCTS

MANUFACTURER OWNED RETAILERS

WHOLESALERS

MANUFACTURER SALES BRANCHES

CONSUMERS 95.4%

EXPORTS 0.4%

INDUSTRIAL USERS 4.2%

RETAILERS 63.0%

MANUFACTURERS 100%

19.6

10.2

9.8

48.8

19.6

12.6

9.8

7.3

1.9

5.7

0.1

8.5

0.1

2.9

1.0

0.1

0.3

1.3

SOURCE: Agricultural Marketing Service, U.S. Department of Agriculture.

Per Capita Consumption of Milk and Milk Products, 1966

	Pounds	Approximate Percent
Total milk fat solids	22.5	5.0
Total nonfat milk solids	41.0	9.1
Cheese	9.9	2.2
Condensed and evaporated milk	10.1	2.3
Fluid milk and cream	300.0	66.6
Ice cream	18.2	4.0
Butter	48.7	10.8
Total	450.4	100.0

Source: *National Food Situation*, February, 1967, Economic Research Service, U.S. Department of Agriculture.

paragraph. The most common channels for the distribution of fluid milk are shown in the diagram on p. 287.

The chart on p. 288 shows the approximate distribution of the consumer's dollar paid for fluid milk in this country in a recent year. The milk producer received about $.55 of the consumer's dollar. Marketing functions took $.45 of the consumer's milk dollar; assembly costs accounted for about $.06; processing, about $.10; and retailing and wholesaling, about $.29. Approximately three-quarters of the $.45 received by marketing agencies was used for the upkeep of vehicles and property and for wages and salaries.

Marketing of Butter. A similar analysis of the distribution of the consumer's dollar spent for butter (See chart on p. 289.) reveals that the farmer received slightly more than $.64. Of the remaining $.357, assembly costs accounted for more than $.03; processing, $.10; and transportation, about $.02. Approximately $.21 went for the wholesaling and retailing of butter.

Butter moves from the farmer to the creamery, to the wholesaler, to the retailer, to the consumer. Approximately 96 percent is churned by creameries from cream milk delivered or shipped by dairy farmers. In a recent year, the creameries sold about 9 percent of their butter directly to household consumers; about one-

MARKETING CHANNELS FOR FLUID MILK

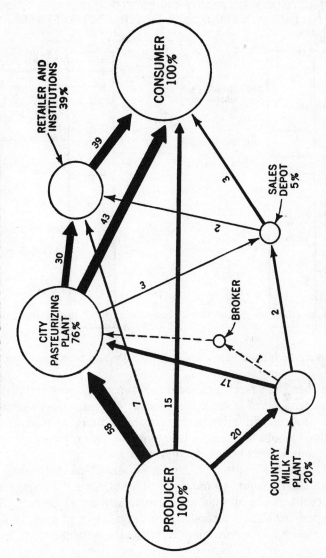

Source: Agricultural Marketing Service, U.S. Department of Agriculture.

APPROXIMATE DISTRIBUTION OF THE CONSUMER'S DOLLAR PAID FOR FLUID MILK IN THE UNITED STATES

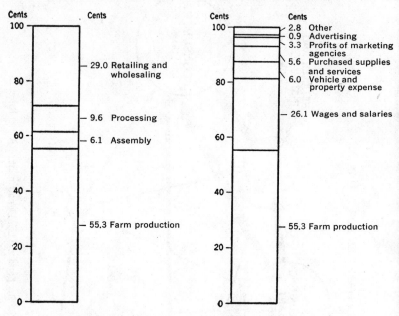

SOURCE: Agricultural Marketing Service, U.S. Department of Agriculture.

fourth of this 9 percent passed through creamery-owned retail stores. Another kind of direct sale was made by creameries to industrial and institutional users, such as manufacturers, railroad commissaries, schools, hospitals, and restaurants. This category amounted to about 3 percent of the total production.

Of the total butter produced, 45 percent passed through the traditional channel to independent wholesalers; 12 percent went to creamery-owned wholesale plants. Another 17 percent passed through retailers' warehouses, thus creating a type of wholesale transaction. The remaining 10 percent was sold directly by the creameries to retailing butter stores, exclusive of those owned by creameries. The diagram on page 290 shows the various marketing channels.

APPROXIMATE DISTRIBUTION OF THE CONSUMER'S DOLLAR FOR BUTTER IN THE UNITED STATES

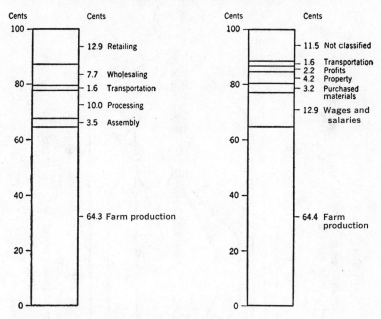

SOURCE: Agricultural Marketing Service, U.S. Department of Agriculture.

Marketing of American Cheese. A government estimate of the portion of the consumer's dollar spent for American (Cheddar) cheese in a typical year shows that, aside from $.49 going to the farmer, the largest single share was $.25 funneled into retailing activities. Wages and salaries comprised the largest marketing cost item, amounting to $.23 of the consumer's dollar. (See p. 291.)

More than 2,600 establishments in the United States specialize in cheese production. About 2,300 of these produce American cheese. Farmers usually either deliver or ship milk directly to the cheese plants. It must be fresh on arrival. After the milk is processed into cheese, approximately two-thirds of it is sold to a special group of merchant middlemen known as *assemblers*. The next most important type of cheese wholesaler is the factory-owned wholesale branch, which receives about 12 percent of the factory's

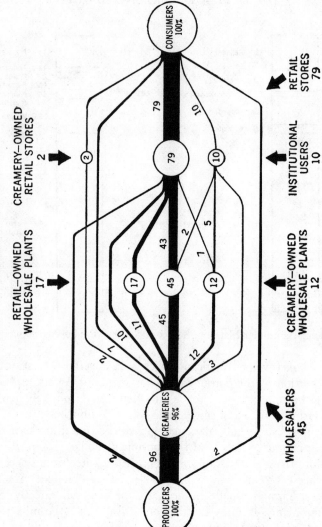

MARKETING CHANNELS FOR BUTTER

SOURCE: Agricultural Marketing Service, U.S. Department of Agriculture.

APPROXIMATE DISTRIBUTION OF THE CONSUMER'S DOLLAR SPENT FOR AMERICAN (CHEDDAR) CHEESE IN THE UNITED STATES

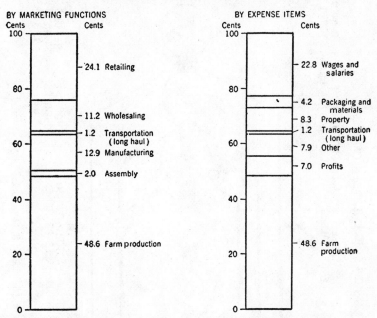

SOURCE: Agricultural Marketing Service, U.S. Department of Agriculture.

total cheese output. To manufacturers making processed cheese, the factory delivers almost 9 percent of its total product.

The unusual aspects of distribution channels for cheese are shown in the diagram on page 292.

Marketing of Evaporated Milk. Fluid milk is processed in a condensery to make evaporated milk. In a recent year, approximately 25 percent of the fluid milk passed through local receiving stations where some reduction in bulk through preliminary condensation occurred. Nearly 50 percent of the evaporated milk was channeled from the condensery to factory-owned wholesale branches for later distribution. About 40 percent moved to independent wholesalers who were usually wholesalers of groceries. See diagram on p. 294.

A government analysis of the consumer's dollar spent for evaporated milk in a typical year revealed that the production of raw

MARKETING CHANNELS FOR AMERICAN CHEESE

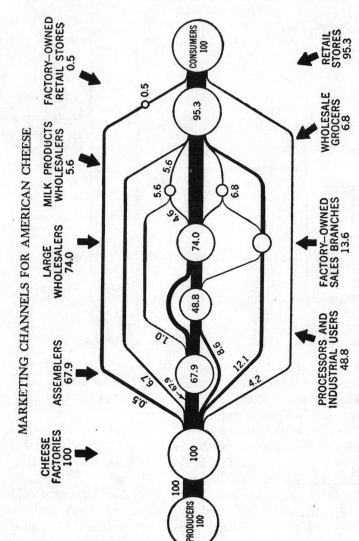

SOURCE: Agricultural Marketing Service, U.S. Department of Agriculture.

milk cost about $.36; $.30 went for processing; $.22, for wholesaling and retailing; $.05, for assembly; and almost $.07, for long-haul transportation. On a cost basis, packaging and other materials took $.185. Wages and salaries, the second largest item, took $.17. See p. 295.

Marketing of Woven Wire

Woven wire is a common industrial item, used primarily by the industrial market but also by the consumer market. Consumer goods include insect screens, hardware cloth, and field and chain link fencing. This market is generally reached via jobbers to hardware outlets.

Marketing of industrial applications is handled by manufacturer salesmen and engineers coupled with commission representatives. Woven wire sold to manufacturers to become part of a manufactured item to be sold (i.e., pump strainers) will be sold directly if in large quantities, but otherwise through the more detailed channels shown on the diagram (p. 296). Woven wire sold as a supply (as in a manufacturer's machine to sort sizes of an item) is typically purchased through a mill supply house.

Marketing of Radios and Television Sets

The past thirty years have seen a phenomenal increase in the number of radios and television sets in the United States; in many large cities, well over 100 percent[1] of the number of families own radios and more than 95 percent have television receivers.

The distribution of radios and television sets is rather simple and follows a well-organized pattern. The manufacturer usually sells to a franchised wholesale distributor who distributes sets to franchised retail dealers for resale to the consumer. However, some manufacturers set up their own wholesale distributing branch as a subsidiary of the parent company. This branch sells to franchised retail stores. See diagram on p. 297.

[1] Multiple ownership by families.

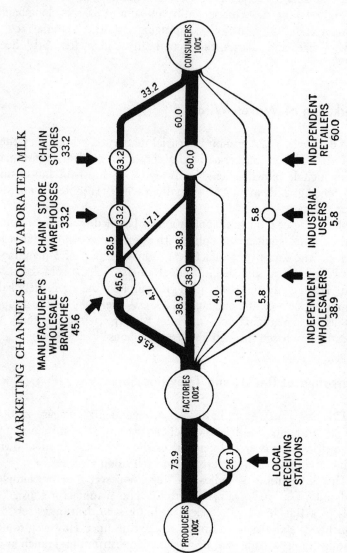

MARKETING CHANNELS FOR EVAPORATED MILK

SOURCE: Agricultural Marketing Service, U.S. Department of Agriculture.

APPROXIMATE DISTRIBUTION OF THE CONSUMER'S DOLLAR SPENT FOR EVAPORATED MILK IN THE UNITED STATES

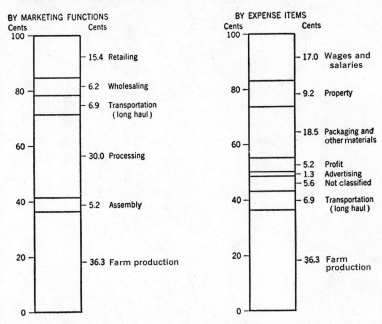

BY MARKETING FUNCTIONS

Cents

	Cents	
	15.4	Retailing
	6.2	Wholesaling
	6.9	Transportation (long haul)
	30.0	Processing
	5.2	Assembly
	36.3	Farm production

BY EXPENSE ITEMS

Cents

	Cents	
	17.0	Wages and salaries
	9.2	Property
	18.5	Packaging and other materials
	5.2	Profit
	1.3	Advertising
	5.6	Not classified
	6.9	Transportation (long haul)
	36.3	Farm production

SOURCE: Agricultural Marketing Service, U.S. Department of Agriculture.

MARKETING CHANNELS FOR WOVEN WIRE

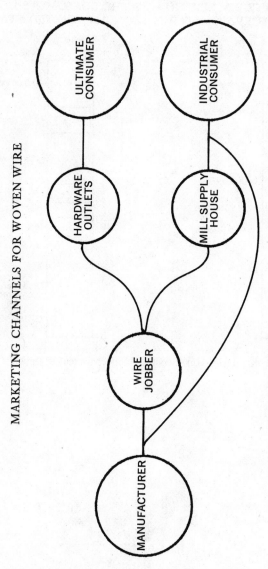

SOURCE: *Agricultural Marketing Service, U.S. Department of Agriculture.*

MARKETING CHANNELS FOR RADIOS AND TELEVISION SETS

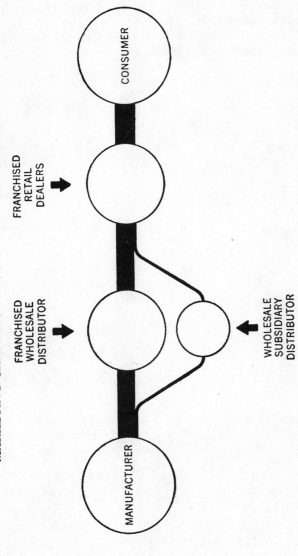

Source: Agricultural Marketing Service, U.S. Department of Agriculture.

REVIEW QUESTIONS

1. Compare marketing of wheat with the marketing of an industrial product and a consumer good.
2. State the distribution channels for the following products: fluid milk, woven wire, radios, and television sets.

25

CHANGING PATTERNS IN MARKETING

The general role of marketing in the American economy has been explored throughout this book. Current trends in this field may be examined by considering what important problems need additional investigation, recent changes in marketing and in the marketing structure, and what factors may be expected to continue to influence marketing procedures.

Important Problems That Need Additional Investigation

The future role of marketing in the U.S. economy will depend upon the efficiency of marketing operations as a means of solving specific problems of distribution.

Marketing Theory. Perfect efficiency in marketing is a theoretical ideal; it has not been and never will be achieved. However, a basic theory of marketing will enable us to approach this theoretical goal of perfect efficiency. There has been very little theory applicable to contemporary marketing practices, most of which have been described in terms of institutions and functions, such as retailing institutions, wholesaling functions, and transportation activities. Instead of this approach, a conceptual framework of theory is needed within which marketing operations can be properly integrated.

Distribution Cost Analysis. Real progress might be made in increasing the efficiency of marketing and thereby contributing to the evolution of marketing theory if the technique of distribution cost analysis were more widely used. This method utilizes cost accounting and various mathematical techniques to pinpoint the costs of commodity distribution. Although this procedure may seem relatively simple, the many products and numerous channels of distribution make it virtually impossible to determine the precise distribution cost by product or by type of outlet. Often, the problem is one of joint costs; and in such cases, it becames extremely difficult to determine accurately the exact portion of cost to be allocated to a particular product.

Pricing. Pricing is also a primary problem in marketing because of the dearth of economic theory applicable to contemporary marketing practices and also because of the confusion arising from conflicting judicial interpretations of the laws on basing points and fair-trade prices.

Effective Sales Promotion. Sales promotion, as the term is used here, includes advertising, public relations programs, the use of special events, and similar activities. The development of a method whereby the effectiveness of sales promotion could be directly measured would greatly increase marketing efficiency. Inability to measure the results of sales campaigns accurately is a problem that has plagued businessmen at all levels, from manufacturing to retailing. For example, would it be more effective to use periodic advertising only in newspapers and magazines than it would be to use such advertising in combination with radio and/or television? Is it best to use direct-mail campaigns (without reinforced selling at the point of sale), or is it preferable merely to advertise a product nationally? In all types of sales promotion, regardless of the media used, the problem of measurement is complex. Because knowledge of this problem is limited, the results of sales promotion campaigns can rarely be measured directly.

Data Processing. Some of the preceding problems may come closer to solution as more companies utilize electronic data processing for analysis of masses of marketing information. In addition, many of the data processing companies have constructed important programs or packages that, when adapted to a company's operation, will permit management to make decisions that are more precise and less intuitive. These operations, plus the work of special institutes in applying mathematics to marketing models, may accelerate the design for a conceptual framework of marketing theory.

Recent Changes in Marketing and in the Marketing Structure

The nature and structure of marketing have changed slowly. The most significant modifications have occurred in the techniques and forms of marketing and in consumer patterns.

Changes in Techniques. The everyday techniques of distribution have undergone great change. Numerous modifications have been introduced in many phases of marketing; for example, various improvements have been made in physical handling. Here we shall consider only a few innovations that profoundly affect marketing efficiency.

Two of these—self-service merchandising and automatic merchandising (vending machines)—have been previously discussed (see pages 108 and 110).

Another development is the return to *scramble merchandising*. Formerly characteristic of the general store, it is today associated with almost every type of marketing outlet. The drugstore, originally an apothecary's shop, now carries an inventory of electrical household appliances, books, costume jewelry, foods, toys, and so on.

An old promotional method is the use of trading stamps. The use of stamps has declined in recent years, though changing needs of retail outlets, not decline of consumer interest, is the reason. The objectives of this technique are to increase store traffic and the size of the average retail transaction.

Still another development, also mentioned earlier (see page

5), is the beginning of replacement of the cash register with the computer terminal. This will mean, from the retailer's viewpoint, a far better inventory control and, from the consumer's viewpoint, getting past the check-out counter much more quickly (because price charging will be done automatically with an optical scanner, rather than through the mechanics of the checkout clerk punching the cash register).

If the cashless society becomes a fact, the habits of both consumer and retailer will be changed. Already successfully tested in an Ohio community, the cashless method makes it possible for the consumer to make retail purchases at many different stores through use of a credit card. The consumer gets current sales slips and is billed for all retail purchases at the end of the month; the retailer is immediately (the same day of the purchase) advanced the funds by the bank sponsoring the charge cards.

In another Ohio community, there is a hardware store that has been converted to automatic retailing. Just one of each item for sale in the store is on display, with a deck of punched cards in front of it. The purchaser selects a card for each item wanted and takes these to a cashier, who, while totaling the cost, feeds the cards into a computer that assembles the entire set of purchases for the customer. The set of items is usually ready (at a window) by the time the customer has paid the bill.

Perhaps the greatest single change in retailing is almost here: being able to do in-store buying at home. The hardware is already available whereby the customer can look at store merchandise by means of a television connection and then punch into a keyboard those items wanted; the retailer accumulates them and delivers them to the home (presumably automatically debiting the customer's bank account for the purchase). Of course, it is impossible to say whether consumers will like this system well enough for it to become popular; some people enjoy the physical aspects of the shopping process.

Still another marked change seems due in retailing. This is the trend to rentals as opposed to purchase. The day may come when the consumer will be able to rent almost everything, including furniture. He will be able to rent his appliances and replace them with new rentals as more advanced machines and designs appear. He may even rent his clothing.

Changes in Form. The form of marketing has changed in three major ways: increased vertical integration, increased horizontal integration, and the rise of the discount house.

Vertical integration has been particularly noticeable in direct marketing. The chain store and mail-order house have increasingly purchased goods from the manufacturer, thereby assuming many of the functions of the wholesaler. Conversely, the manufacturer has absorbed certain wholesaling functions through the opening of branch houses. Moreover, there has been a trend toward selective distribution whereby the manufacturer carefully selects wholesale or retail outlets, a type of franchised distribution that has led to the manufacturer's handling of the sales promotion and advertising formerly provided by the distributors.

Horizontal integration has also expanded, as evidenced by the increasing number and sales volume of chain groups, including supermarkets and branch stores. Part of this growth is accounted for by the development of suburban shopping centers, which parallel population shifts from the central cities to the suburbs. As a result of the growth of horizontal integration, the dollar volume of sales has steadily been concentrated in a smaller number of outlets. In a very real sense, this type of concentration has made retailing more large scale than heretofore.

Changes in Consumer Patterns. Three levels of change are readily noticeable in the consuming pattern of the United States: (1) A marked increase in consumer information has resulted from consumerism. (2) This movement has been buttressed by legislation. (3) Consumers have shown increased interest in the products they buy, probably the result of better consumer education. These changes have developed a more critical and efficient consumer, who shops more carefully and demands reasonable value for his money.

With an increase in public information about nutrition, communicated through schools and other media, the pattern of consumption has changed. In the early 1900s, the American family consumed many more foods containing a high concentration of carbohydrates than it does today. Today, Americans consume more citrus fruits, green vegetables, and fruit juices but less potatoes and other starchy foods. Naturally, the food inventories of distributors have reflected this change in consumption, which may also partially explain the apparent overproduction of certain farm products.

With a higher standard of living has come the widespread consumption of certain products formerly regarded as luxuries. Today, refrigerators, radios, television sets, and washing machines are considered staples in the American home. The use of mass production, a concomitant reduction in prices, and the development of an alert consumer have brought about a level of prosperity unsurpassed by any other country.

Factors That May Be Expected to Continue to Influence Marketing Procedures

The major factors affecting marketing are size of population, level of income and spending, techniques of production, government programs, methods of communication and transportation, and use of automation and mechanization.

Size of the Population. Over many years, the population of the United States increased steadily at a rate of 1.1 percent to 2.5 percent annually. Now there are suggestions that within a few years, America may reach zero population growth. Ecologists believe that this is vitally necessary if we are not to drown in an increasing sea of waste. Sociologists maintain that it is vital if we hope to cure some of the social ills caused by overcrowding.

Up to this time, there has always been an increasing market because of expanding population. If zero population growth is in sight, it will probably mean that some companies will continue their rate of growth by capturing markets now held by less aggressive firms.

It will be more important than ever for the businessman to see where (i.e., in what segments) population is growing and where it is dropping. If the growth segments can be charted, then the firm can exploit emerging new markets for services and commodities.

Distributors also consider the age-groups within the total population. For example, for many years, the proportion of the aged has steadily risen as medical science has increased longevity and eliminated certain disabling diseases of youth and middle age. The youth market (under twenty) constituted 34 percent of the population in 1950, 39 percent in 1960, and 38 percent in 1970. Young adults are the economic backbone of the country. Because they are starting family life, they will become a major market for homes, appliances, baby items, furniture, automobiles, and diversified services. As a result of the growth of the youth market, a large variety of products and services must be developed to meet their particular needs. The older market augments the demand for pensions, insurance, and safe places for the investment of surplus savings. It also enlarges the demand for personal services, comforts, and conveniences. In localities having a large aged population, this trend could mean a revival of retail stores offering personal service by clerks. There could be increases in the sale of books, magazines, and television sets, in the provision of entertainment and adult education (useful in view of the trend toward early retirement), and in the renting of small apartments.

During recent decades, the geographic distribution of population has changed in the following respects: (1) The number of people residing in *suburban areas* has increased notably. From 1920 to 1930, there was an increase of 27 percent in urban population. Since then, the rate of increase has been 8 percent in each subsequent decade. The continuing shift in population led to the establishment of many suburban branch stores. Suburban shopping centers and suburban supermarkets have multiplied almost everywhere. (2) The proportion of the population living on *farms* has declined from a maximum of 95 percent in pioneer America to approximately 5 percent in 1970. This decline may be expected to continue; moreover, at the same time, the growing population in the cities will demand a larger volume of farm products. The dwindling farm population can meet this demand only by means of additional mechanization and improved farming methods, which would also increase the farmer's income. (3) The population of the *Pacific states* rose 25.1 percent during the years 1960 to 1970, while the *total* population of the country rose only 13.3 percent. The growth of population in the Pacific region has modified the marketing structure of the economy.

Another element in the changing patterns of population is the growth of what is called the *contiguous city*. Some experts believe there is developing in the United States a *megalopolis*, such as the continuous stretch of urban and suburban areas from southern New Hampshire to northern Virginia, and from the Atlantic Coast to the foothills of the Appalachians. A region such as this becomes the financial, business, and governmental hub of the nation. It also may embrace large manufacturing and agricultural activities. The population of such a megalopolis is on the average among the richest, best educated, best housed, and best serviced groups in the world. With increasing concentration of population in the United States, there probably will be concomitant growth of megalopolises.

Level of Income and Spending. Consumer buying habits have been affected by the gradual rise in the real income of the nation. For example, the median income of families increased 34 percent from 1960 to 1970; whereas the prices of consumer goods have gone up approximately 31 percent, the net result being a higher standard of living and augmented bank accounts.

Various studies of consumer buying patterns indicate that approximately 20 percent of the income of an American family goes for food; 19 percent, for expenses of operating the home; 12 percent, for clothing; 5 percent, for medical and personal care; 9 percent, for home furnishings and equipment; 5 percent, for recreation; 14 percent, for automobiles; and the remainder, for miscellaneous expenditures.

Techniques of Production. Techniques of production have been modified in two ways: by an increase in mechanization and by changes in the sources of energy.

As a result of increasing mechanization, the average rise in production per man-hour in the United States in recent years has been about 3 percent per year. Except for minor fluctuations, production has risen steadily since 1940, resulting in more take-home pay and a shorter workweek. Prior to the Civil War, producers depended almost exclusively upon human labor and the use of animals as sources of energy; oil, water power, and natural gas supplied less than 6 percent of their requirements. Today, fuel and water power contribute more than 98 percent of the energy consumed. Marketing procedures had to be adapted to this change in the sources of energy, which affected location and exploitation of markets. In view of the probable development of atomic and solar energy for production, the distribution system as described in this text may be expected to change radically; the whole concept of productive efficiency will have to be reexamined.

Government Programs. Certain activities of government have affected the marketing structure, and it appears likely that they will continue to affect it even more in the future because the federal and state governments have been increasing controls over marketing institutions by means of laws and administrative regulations.

At present, government expenditures consume about 22 percent of the GNP. In view of the gradual extension of government controls over business, the costs of wars and defense programs, and public demand for various government services, the federal and state budgets will undoubtedly keep rising for many years to come. Consequently, to ensure a stable, balanced economy, producers and distributors will have to depend mainly upon substantial increases in productive capacity and distributive efficiency. Eventually, with a larger national income, a decline in the percentage allocated to government services may be hoped for.

Aid to the farmer is a notable illustration of government services demanded by the public. The federal government has guaranteed parity prices for certain farm products. These constitute, in fact, a type of government program of insurance for farmers. The guarantee of minimum prices makes the price structure for agricultural goods more rigid. Nevertheless, parity prices, having become a part of the American economic pattern, are likely to remain. The level of parity prices and the selection of specific commodities subject to them may change periodically, but the program as a whole will be maintained. Consequently, distributors anticipate relatively stable prices for these agricultural goods, inasmuch as the forces of supply and demand will be restrained by this type of government regulation.

More recently, the soil-bank program was established, guaranteeing the farmer a certain income for not cultivating a portion of his land. The object of the soil-bank program was to reduce agricultural surpluses.

Methods of Communication and Transportation. Improvement in communication and transportation is constantly being achieved, with marked effects upon the techniques of distribution.

Recently, there has been a notable expansion in air transportation. With an anticipated reduction in costs of operation, the aviation industry will undoubtedly become a primary factor in the distribution of commodities. And the development of the interstate highway system has further speeded truck transportation.

Much progress in communication has also been achieved. The use of direct-dial telephoning for long-distance calls (without the aid of an operator) is a development exemplifying the continuous effort to improve services. Advances have been made in the use of communication media such as radio and television, particularly color television; television, as an effective advertising medium, is currently shortening the fashion cycle. More recently, the development of interstellar satellites and the advances made in transistorization of international cables presage that international television will become an important factor in world communication.

Use of Automation and Mechanization. The perfecting of electronic computing machines has made it possible for many industries to incorporate automatic features in their production processes and thus to produce more goods with fewer people. Even intricate manufacturing processes may be controlled by an electronic data processing system.

Mechanization in agriculture has helped to increase production and has brought about a steady decline in the number of workers engaged in farm labor. Moreover, in certain phases of storage and transportation in both industry and agriculture, power trucks, fork-lifts, conveyor belts, and other mechanical devices are employed to reduce actual handling of products.

The tremendous growth of automatic merchandising is also having a significant effect upon the economy. As pointed out in Chapter 10, vending machines have become characteristic of contemporary marketing and account for $4.2 billion in sales per year.

Undoubtedly, the continuing shift to automated production and mechanized distribution methods will result in a further rise in the very high standard of living enjoyed by the American community.

Marketing Management Concept.   Companies that were once product-oriented have changed their structure and have become consumer-oriented. As discussed in Chapter 5, the result of this change is that the wealth of goods and services that the economy can produce cannot be consumed unless corporate management recognizes that any good or service produced must have a ready market which can be penetrated by appropriate marketing strategy.

REVIEW QUESTIONS

1. Discuss some of the basic problems of marketing that remain to be solved.
2. What fundamental changes in the marketing structure have recently occurred?
3. What factors may be expected to continue to influence marketing procedures?

APPENDIXES

APPENDIX A
DEFINITIONS OF MARKETING TERMS

Little progress can be made in the development of marketing as a systematized body of knowledge unless the terminology has been established and accepted by those practicing and teaching in the field. The definitions in this appendix have been taken from *Marketing Terms*, by Irving J. Shapiro, published by S-M-C Publishing Company, West Long Branch, New Jersey, in 1973. The authors are grateful for permission to use selected definitions from this authoritative source and recommend *Marketing Terms* for a far more comprehensive list of definitions.

ACCESSORY EQUIPMENT. Major units of processing equipment of a general nature, useful in a variety of plants. Usually of a type to facilitate plant operations rather than to determine the product. See: INSTALLATIONS.

ADVERTISING. A nonpersonal, paid message of commercial significance about a product, service, or company made to a market by an identified sponsor. It is the aspect of the selling function which can pave the way for the salesman's activity. It has recently become common to include messages promoting ideas and causes. Contrary to popular belief, advertising can cause people to act only in a manner to which they were predisposed. Advertising *can* cause the realization and recognition of wants not previously known to the market, and it can lead directly to the sale where personal contacts are not involved.

ADVERTISING CAMPAIGN. A coordinated advertising effort over a certain period of time in carefully selected media with a specific objective, such as by a bank to announce a new savings plan, or by a manufacturer to persuade the market of the superiority of his product's benefits so that his market share will rise. See: CAMPAIGN PLAN.

ADVERTISING MEDIUM. The class of vehicle by means of which the advertiser's message is carried to its audience. Commonly considered to be advertising media are: newspapers, billboards, car-cards, magazines, radio, point-of-purchase displays, television, direct mail, advertising specialties, house organs, and trade shows. This list is intended to be illustrative rather than inclusive. Advertising media are often classified into (1) print media and (2) broadcast media.

AGENT MIDDLEMAN. Same as: FUNCTIONAL MIDDLEMAN.

AMA. (1) Abbreviation for: American Marketing Association, a professional organization of marketing teachers, executives, and research practitioners, devoted to bettering the state of the discipline. It publishes the foremost publication in the field, the *Journal of Marketing*, numerous books, and a newsletter. It sponsors an International Congress in the Spring and an Educator's Conference in the Fall. It issues a detailed and categorized roster of members. (2) Abbreviation for: Automobile Manufacturers Association, a trade association of domestic makers of motor vehicles, about ten firms. Founded in 1913, its main objectives are research in all areas of vehicle safety and pollution, liaison with government agencies, and compilation and dissemination of industry data.

AMERICAN MARKETING ASSOCIATION. Same as: AMA (1).

ASSEMBLER. A merchant middleman whose economic justification lies in his performance of the activity of assembly.

ASSEMBLY. (1) The process of bringing together the produce of a number of farmers into a unit of economical shipping size. (2) The process of bringing together the products of a number of manufacturers so that a limited number of each item may be available to the user, e.g., as in wholesaling.

BRANCH OFFICE. See: MANUFACTURER'S SALES BRANCH, MANUFACTURER'S SALES OFFICE.

BRANCH STORE. An arm of a central business district store extended into another area of the market.

BRAND. A word, mark, symbol, device, or a combination of these used to identify some product or service. See: FAMILY BRAND, INDIVIDUAL BRAND, NATIONAL BRAND, PRIVATE BRAND, TRADEMARK.

BRAND IMAGE. How people in the market perceive the identifying marks of the product, rather than the characteristics of the product itself. Thus, the brand may convey an impression of economy, status, high value, etc. Recognizing this aspect, many marketers engage in considerable study before deciding on a name for a product which they intend to use as a brand.

BRAND LOYALTY. The faithfulness displayed by a user toward a brand, measured by relative length of time or regularity of the item's use. It is known that much switching occurs. A considerable amount of research is devoted to finding the reasons for and the volume of the switches.

BRAND NAME. Often used when referring to words, numbers, or initials used as a trademark of a product. Usually means the vocalizable portion of a trademark.

BROKER. A functional middleman whose distinguishing features are: his services to a principal are intermittent, he has limited authority to make terms, and he finances his principal only under unusual circumstances. He may represent either the buyer or the seller.

BUYER. In a department store, the key person who is really a department head responsible in his department for buying, selling, pricing, and controlling his lines of goods, as well as managing his area and his personnel. (2) In an individual firm, usually equivalent to purchasing agent, although an assistant may be so designated for a specific material or class of materials.

BUYER'S MARKET. A condition of the market in which buyers are able to bargain and to be selective because there is an overabundance of goods available in relation to demand. See: SELLER'S MARKET.

BUYING. (1) A marketing function devoted to the efficient acquisition of the materials and services needed for the operation of a business. Includes the determination of the suitability of goods, the proper price, an adequate source, and economic order and inventory quantities. Creates possession utility. (2) Although the consumer usually does not analyze as painstakingly as the industrial user, he always has a reason valid to him for making his decision, e.g., to reach a goal, solve a problem, or otherwise achieve some personal satisfaction.

CAMPAIGN PLAN. A series of mailings of a variety of pieces over a period of weeks, all designed to arouse interest in a coming event, such as the opening of a new facility or the introduction of an innovation. This type of plan ends with a final mailing presenting the announcement for which interest and curiosity have been built. Plans of this sort must be of duration not so long as to create boredom, since that would negate the intent of creating suspense. Sometimes called, as applicable, a "Teaser Campaign." See: DIRECT MAIL ADVERTISING.

CANNIBALIZING A MARKET. What happens when a new form of a product, instead of producing new business from market segments not before reached, eats into the volume already enjoyed from the existing product, so that no sales increase occurs. This did occur with Maxwell House Instant Coffee when Maxim Instant was introduced, until steps were taken to correct it.

CASH-AND-CARRY WHOLESALER. A wholesaler exhibiting the following features: customers call to pick up the merchandise, cash is required with the purchase, salesmen are not widely used to call on prospects.

CHAIN STORE. One of a system of two or more stores of similar type which are centrally owned and managed. In U.S. Census definition four or more such stores are needed to constitute a chain. See: RETAILER.

CHANNEL OF DISTRIBUTION. The course taken by the title to goods as it moves from producer to consumer through middlemen. For some products the channel has been so shortened that the producer acts himself as a middleman, selling directly to a user.

CLASSIFIED ADVERTISING. One of the two broad divisions of advertising in newspapers and some magazines. It appears in special columns of pages where the advertising is assembled by product or service. Usually the selection of type faces and sizes is very limited, as is the freedom of layout. The other broad division is display advertising.

COGNITIVE DISSONANCE. A type of perceptual bias which causes feelings of regret after an important purchase has been made as alternative opportunities that were considered seem to compare more favorably. The normal course is that the buyer will tend to resolve the tension by finding more advantages in support of his action and downgrading the advantages of the rejected alternatives. If anticipated by the marketer, the first decision can be reinforced and the buyer be made a more enthusiastic supporter of the product, although there is some evidence that this may happen anyway as the tension-resolving process goes on. However, it will take longer without positive action by the seller, who can benefit if he acts to include reinforcing evidence in all his advertisements.

COMMISSION AGENT. A functional middleman who accepts shipments of goods, mainly perishables, to sell for a principal. Usually has authority to set price. Service to the principal is intermittent.

COMMODITY APPROACH. An approach to the study of marketing characterized by the following of a product through all the ramifications of its movements from producer to users.

COMMODITY EXCHANGE. (1) An organization or association of individuals which provides a place for trading in an item such as wheat under uniform rules and with facilities for gathering and disseminating information. (2) Frequently used to designate just the facilities provided.

COMMON MARKET. Same as: EUROPEAN ECONOMIC COMMUNITY.

CONSENT ORDER. An action taken by a government agency prohibiting a respondent from doing what the agency considers improper. When agreed to by the respondent, it becomes binding. Such an agreement is for settlement purposes only and does not constitute an admisson by the respondent that he has violated the law. Numerous such orders are currently being issued by the FTC to effect respondent's refraining from restraints of trade, deceptive sales practices, misleading advertising, etc.

CONSIGNMENT. A stock of merchandise advanced to a dealer and located at his place of business, but with title remaining in the source of supply.

CONSUMER. (1) A person who purchases for personal or household use. (2) Anyone who uses up the utilities embodied in goods or services. In marketing, one must consider the motives and habits inferred in (1), and at the same time take into account the influence of (2). Industrial and institutional purchasers should be called *users*.

CONSUMER CREDIT PROTECTION ACT. A Federal law passed in 1968 to stop abusive practices in the field of consumer credit and collections. Same as: TRUTH-IN-LENDING ACT.

CONSUMER GOODS. (1) Goods bought for personal or household satisfactions. (2) Goods used directly in satisfying human wants. See: CONSUMER.

CONSUMERISM. An increasingly prominent activity by consumers and government to take the necessary measures to protect the general public from misrepresentation, poorly made goods, bad service, and obscure warranties. It is forcing business to assume a real responsibility for its product.

CONSUMERS' COOPERATIVE. A voluntary association of consumers, organized to fulfill some of their needs for goods and services. A credit union is an example of this type of organization. See: ROCHDALE PLAN.

CONTRACT CARRIER. A transportation company serving on an individual contract basis. Some states require that these be licensed.

CONTROLLED CIRCULATION. The circulation of specialized publications delivered free to individuals selected by some relevant criteria. There is a trend toward calling it *qualified circulation*. To meet BPA standards, the publication must be issued quarterly or oftener, and must contain no less than 25% editorial matter.

CONVENIENCE GOODS. The type of item which the consumer usually desires to purchase with a minimum of effort at the most convenient and accessible place. While products may be so classified on a broad base, a specific item may be classified only if the attitude of the consumer toward the item is known. See: SHOPPING GOODS, SPECIALTY GOODS.

COOPERATIVE CHAIN. An organization in which a group of retailers become the stockholders of a wholesale company established to serve themselves. See: VOLUNTARY CHAIN.

COPY. In a broad sense, all verbal and visual elements which are included in a finished advertisement. Used more narrowly to designate the verbal elements only. The latter is probably more common.

COPYWRITER. A person who writes advertisements.

CORPORATE ADVERTISING. Same as: INSTITUTIONAL ADVERTISING.

COVERAGE. (1) The number of households or individuals who are exposed to a specific advertising medium in a given area. (2) The sum of the total circulations of all the different media used.

CPM. Abbreviation for: cost per thousand. Must be specified as referring to readers, viewers, circulation, etc. Used in comparing the costs of alternative vehicles of advertising.

CREDIT. The attribute of a buyer which enables him to gain immediate possession of a product or service on his promise to pay at some determinable later date.

CUSTOMARY PRICE. The price of certain goods has become fixed not by deliberate action on the seller's part, but as a result of having prevailed on the market for so long a time that customers have developed a habit of relating that price to that product. Changes in price of such items may sometimes be effected by changing the package quantity at the usual price.

CUSTOMER. Someone who has bought a certain product or service from a source. Most often thought of as being a repeater. A customer may be a prospect for a product or service he has never before bought from that source.

DEMAND CURVE. The plot of the schedule which shows for all possible prices the quantity of goods the market will absorb, considering the factors prevailing at any one time.

DEMOGRAPHICS. The statistics of an area's population, or a market, with distinguishing characteristics such as age, sex, income, education, marital status, occupation, etc. delineated. Includes all vital statistics.

DEPARTMENTALIZED SPECIALTY STORE. A specialty shop in essence, which has become large and in which the various types of merchandise carried are accounted for separately for profit knowledge and general managerial decision making.

DEPARTMENT STORE. The retail institution that probably offers the largest variety of goods under one roof to customers who are invited to the establishment to make their selections. Highly departmentized for sales and accounting purposes. By Census of Business standards it must have at least 25 employees and its merchandise must include apparel, appliances, furniture, home furnishings, and dry goods.

DEPTH INTERVIEW. A research interview in which the respondent is encouraged to speak freely and in full about a particular subject. The interview is conducted without the use of a structured questionnaire.

DERIVED DEMAND. A very significant characteristic of the market for industrial goods which severely affects manufacturers of installations. Denotes a demand for one product which arises from the demand for another product. Explains that the industrial market fluctuates with the demand for final products.

DESCRIPTIVE LABELING. Labeling goods by characteristic, but without reference to recognized standards or grades. See: LABEL.

DESK JOBBER. A merchant wholesaler operating out of an office who in the course of business rarely takes physical possession of the goods he sells. Same as: DROP SHIPPER.

DIRECT DISTRIBUTION. Selling by a manufacturer to industrial users through his own salesmen, sales branches or offices, and/or warehouses. Sometimes used to apply to the consumer level.

DIRECT MAIL ADVERTISING. That ADVERTISING which asks for the order to be sent by mail. Delivery of the order is by mail. Also the medium which delivers the advertising message by mail. Provides greatest control of direction to a market, flexibility of materials and processes, timeliness of scheduling, and personalization. Its biggest problem is getting the recipient's attention. A part of direct advertising.

DISCOUNT HOUSE. A retail establishment characterized mainly by its sale of a large selection of well-known brands of merchandise at less than list prices. The distinction between the discount house and the department store is becoming obscure as each adopts concepts from the other.

DISCRETIONARY BUYING POWER. Same as: DISCRETIONARY INCOME.

DISCRETIONARY INCOME. That part of a consumer's income which he has the choice of spending or saving. Usually considered to be that portion above an amount required for essentials.

DISPOSABLE INCOME. Money left over after paying taxes, union dues, pension contributions, and the like. Not to be confused with discretionary income. Same as: PERSONAL DISPOSABLE INCOME.

DISTRIBUTION. Used generally as a synonym for marketing, but often refers in a restricted sense to the activity of physical movement of goods.

DISTRIBUTION ORDER. An order placed with a supplier for timed and quantity shipments of a product to multiple destinations, as is frequently done for some types of merchandise by central buyers for chains, specifying how many to each store.

DISTRIBUTOR. Essentially the same as: SERVICE WHOLESALER. See: INDUSTRIAL DISTRIBUTOR.

DISTRIBUTORSHIP. A form of franchising in which the franchisee takes title to goods and further distributes them to subfranchisees. This franchisee acts as a supply base for the subfranchisees, whom he usually oversees.

DOOR-TO-DOOR SELLING. Same as: HOUSE-TO-HOUSE SELLING.

Drop Shipment. Essentially the same as distribution order but more frequently applied to a single order and shipment. See: DESK JOBBER.

Drop Shipper. Same as: DESK JOBBER.

Drummer. An American salesman of former times who called on retailers or greeted them as they arrived at buying centers. Many of the methods he used are now considered unethical.

Economic Man. The concept of a buyer who makes rational decisions only, balancing all relevant factors in his objective mind, and who buys only when the price is right and the quality acceptable. The traditional concept of the older economics.

80–20 Principle. Much empirical evidence points to the fact that most firms get the largest proportion of their business from customers on whom they expend a small proportion of their marketing effort, and vice versa.

Elastic Demand. See: ELASTICITY OF DEMAND.

Elasticity of Demand. Demand is generally said to be *elastic* when a reduction in unit price increases total revenue from a product or service. Demand is said to be *inelastic* when a reduction in unit price produces a decline in total revenue. Demand is said to be *unitary* when a reduction in price produces just enough increase in volume so that total revenue from the product or service remains the same.

European Common Market. Same as: EUROPEAN ECONOMIC COMMUNITY.

European Economic Community. An organization established by a treaty in Rome in 1957 by Belgium, France, Italy, Luxembourg, the Netherlands, and West Germany to integrate the economic activities of the six countries and to establish a common tariff wall against outside nations. At the end of 1972, Denmark, Great Britain, and Ireland gained admission. Same as: EEC.

Exchange. The entire system by means of which preferences for goods or services are evidenced in the economy through the way work or monetary units are given up in order to acquire goods or services. If exchange did not increase the total satisfactions of all parties, it would not occur. (2) See: COMMODITY EXCHANGE.

Exclusive Dealing. The dealer agrees to refrain from handling competing products in consideration for his being supplied with the manufacturer's goods. Such an agreement may not be legal under existing laws if it may result in a substantial lessening of competition. See: EXCLUSIVE SELLING.

EXCLUSIVE DISTRIBUTION. Same as: EXCLUSIVE OUTLET SELLING.

EXCLUSIVE OUTLET SELLING. Confining the carrying of a particular service or brand in an area to just one retailer or one wholesaler, usually with some type of contractual agreement. The seller who wishes to use such an arrangement generally anticipates maximum promotional cooperation from his dealers. Same as: EXCLUSIVE DISTRIBUTION.

EXCLUSIVE SELLING. A manufacturer or other supplier agrees with a particular wholesaler or retailer not to sell to other wholesalers or retailers in the same market. May not be legal if it can be construed as a restraint of trade. See: EXCLUSIVE DEALING.

EXTENSIVE DISTRIBUTION. Same as: INTENSIVE DISTRIBUTION.

FABRICATING MATERIAL. Raw material which has been processed into a stable form which requires only dimensional changes to permit incorporation into a product. Examples: lumber, leather, cloth. A few liquids, such as mercury and alcohol, may be so classified under certain conditions.

FACILITATING FUNCTIONS. The marketing functions of standardization and grading, risk-taking, financing, and market information are usually grouped under this classification.

FACING. A shelf stock one unit wide extending to the top and back of a shelf in a display. Used to determine space allocation for packaged items in a retail store. Example: a facing for canned asparagus might be two cans high and five cans deep for a total of ten cans.

FAIR CREDIT REPORTING ACT. A national law effective April 25, 1971, which is designed to protect people from erroneous credit information exchanged among credit agencies, banks, corporations, and others. The law gives an individual the right to examine the information in his file, to have it deleted if found inaccurate, file a report of his side of the story if reinvestigation does not settle the problem, and to have previous recipients of his file informed of any deletions and additions. In general, any adverse information, except bankruptcy, more than seven years old may not be reported.

FAIR TRADE LAW. A law which permits a manufacturer to establish under certain conditions a minimum resale price for his product. Enacted on the state level where desired, as authorized by Federal enabling legislation. Few states have such laws now, and the use of the privilege, where permitted, is diminishing.

FAMILY BRAND. One brand applied to several or a large number of products of one seller, e.g., White Rose, Heinz, Alcoa, G.E. The major advantage of using this type of brand is that goodwill built up for one product that has caught on may be applied by consumers or industrial users to other products in the family. The major disadvantage is the loss of crisp identity of any one product. See: INDIVIDUAL BRAND.

FASHION. A style which happens to be popular at a given time with a significant portion of the market. Usually endures for a lengthy period of time.

FASHION CYCLE. This is a misnomer, implying a regularity or predictability of recurrence or pattern which actually does not exist. Basic styles do move in and out of popularity, sometimes very slowly, other times very rapidly, occasionally with lengthy periods between times of popularity. Attempts to chart these movements have but shown how erratic they are.

FASHION GOODS. Frequent change in design is the major appeal of such items. They are in a sense opposite in character to staple goods. See: FASHION.

FCC. Abbreviation for: Federal Communications Commission, the government agency that licenses broadcast stations and regulates broadcasting.

FDA. Abbreviation for: Food and Drug Administration, the government agency directly charged with controlling the harmful effects of certain foods, drugs, and food additives. Has the authority to forbid interstate commerce in items deemed harmful.

FIELD WAREHOUSING. A plan in which a marketer leases to a warehousing firm that portion of his plant or branch in which his inventory is stored. The warehousing firm takes legal custodianship of the premises and the goods, issuing warehouse receipts to the marketer who can then obtain financing with the warehouse receipts as collateral.

FINANCING. A marketing function which includes the provision and management of money and credit necessary to get goods to the consumer or user, excluding those applicable transactions resulting from manufacturing.

FIXED COSTS. Those costs which remain essentially the same regardless of the firm's production level within the relevant range.

FOOD AND DRUG ADMINISTRATION. Same as: FDA.

FOOD BROKER. One of the most important categories of functional middlemen, he sells grocery products to those who buy in large quantities. Same characteristics as other brokers.

FORECASTING. Estimating future magnitudes and trends of elements of business activity on the basis of historical data and/or predictions of coming environmental conditions. Commonly used to help plan the sales and sales-related needs of a business in the following year. May be projections for a five-year period, in which revisions or reviews would be needed periodically. A few firms attempt a ten-year forecast which they review for the next one-year, five-year, and ten-year periods on a rolling basis.

FORM UTILITY. The characteristic of a product which makes it possible to satisfy a human want because processing has converted it into a usable state which makes it desirable for an intended purpose.

FRAGMENTATION. The current trend of marketers to designate and to isolate portions of the total market as to common characteristics and specialized demand. See: SEGMENTATION.

FRANCHISING. An arrangement whereby an organization which has developed a successful retail product or service extends to others for a fee the right to engage in the business, provided they agree to follow the established pattern. It is a special form of exclusive distribution. Some abuses have appeared, such as failure by the franchiser to keep his promises of training, merchandising assisance, and advertising. There have been a few instances of outright fraud. All of these are being attacked through legislation, publicity, and judicial channels. Anyone contemplating entering into a franchising contract would do well first to investigate fully.

FTC. Abbreviation for: Federal Trade Commission. Brought into existence by an Act in 1914, it is an independent administrative agency of five commissioners appointed by the President with the advice and consent of the Senate for terms of seven years, the terms overlapping. The President designates the Chairman. No more than three of its members may belong to the same political party. Its functions include research and publication of reports; promotion of compliance; investigation of unfair methods of competition, deceptive practices, agreements in restraint of trade, and monopolistic mechanisms; and prosecution of violators. Also, it enforces the Wool Products Labeling Act of 1939, the Fur Products Labeling Act of 1951, the Flammable Fabrics Act of 1953, and the Textile Fiber Products Identification Act of 1958.

FUNCTIONAL MIDDLEMAN. An independent business the major operations of which are to assist in the passing of title to goods without taking title to the goods in the process. Same as: agent middleman. See: BROKER, COMMISSION AGENT, SELLING AGENT.

FUNCTIONS OF EXCHANGE. The marketing functions of buying and selling are often grouped under this classification.

FUNCTIONS OF PHYSICAL SUPPLY. The marketing functions of transportation and storage are often grouped under this classification.

GENERAL ADVERTISING. National or other nonlocal advertising in newspapers.

GENERAL-LINE WHOLESALER. A merchant wholesaler characterized by his attempting to carry a complete stock of merchandise within a given field.

GENERAL MERCHANDISE WHOLESALER. A merchant wholesaler who carries goods in a number of unrelated lines.

GENERAL STORE. A retail store that handles a large number of lines of merchandise without any significant degree of departmental organization. It is usually small scale and heavily oriented toward groceries.

GNP. Abbreviation for: Gross National Product. Equals the total market value of the output of goods and services of the nation's economy at "final" prices.

GRADE LABELING. Indicating on the label the grade of the product as determined by qualified comparison of the product's characteristics with those of an unvarying standard.

GROSS PROFIT. (1) The entire difference between the purchase price of an item and the sale price of that item. (2) The total of the differences in (1) for all the items a firm sells.

HORIZONTAL INTEGRATION. Acquisition by one company of another in the same or related lines of business and on the same level of the channel of distribution, the consumer considered as the base. See: VERTICAL INTEGRATION.

HOUSE-TO-HOUSE SELLING. A form of direct retailing in which employees are engaged to solicit business by cold canvass from door to door. See: HUCKSTERING, PARTY SELLING.

HUCKSTERING. A method of house-to-house selling ordinarily used by farmers in which the goods are brought with the seller for immediate delivery.

IMPULSE BUYING. An act of purchasing, made on the spur of the moment, impelled by some thing or happening in a store.

INDEPENDENT STORE A retail store controlled by its individual ownership. It may enter into limiting agreements, such as that of a voluntary chain, without impairing its status as an independent.

INDIVIDUAL BRAND. A distinctive identification for a single product. In contrast to family brand. Its major advantage is the sharpness of its recall to a consumer, once established. Its major disadvantage is that it can get little or no help from other products of the same firm which have gained consumer acceptance.

INDUSTRIAL DISTRIBUTOR. A merchant middleman primarily engaged in selling industrial goods. See: MILL SUPPLY HOUSE.

INDUSTRIAL GOODS. Any goods bought for motives other than personal or household satisfactions.

INDUSTRIAL USER. Anyone or any firm buying goods or services for purposes other than personal or household satisfactions. In contrast to: CONSUMER.

INFORMATIVE LABEL. An affix to a product telling about the product.

INNOVATION DIFFUSION. The general process by which anything in the market perceived as new by some group becomes adopted for regular use. Sometimes this process is divided into the stages of awareness, interest, evaluation, trial, and adoption. Note that people differ greatly in their willingness to try new products, and may be classified on this basis as innovators, early majority, late majority, and laggards.

INSTALLATIONS. In a plant, the major equipment which determines the product to be produced, and which sets the scale of operations.

INSTITUTIONAL ADVERTISING. Advertising intended to build goodwill for the advertiser rather than to stimulate immediate purchase of a product.

INSTITUTIONAL APPROACH. An approach to the study of marketing which considers the various middlemen and facilitating agencies which perform the marketing functions.

INTEGRATION. The extension through ownership by a firm of the control of a formerly separate business so that it becomes part of a single business unit.

INTENSIVE DISTRIBUTION. Maximum exposure of goods to buyers in the market. Uses as many different types of retailers and retail locations as possible. See: EXCLUSIVE DISTRIBUTION, FRANCHISING, SELECTIVE DISTRIBUTION.

JOBBER. Generally same as: wholesaler. Sometimes more narrowly used to designate a middleman who buys in relatively small lots and sells to a retailer. A firm may be so called in an industry as a matter of long-standing custom.

JOB-LOT. An incomplete assortment of odds and ends of merchandise, bought as a unit usually at an exceptionally low price.

LABEL. That part of the product as it is sold which conveys verbal information about the product or the seller. It may be affixed directly to the product itself, may be a part of the package, or may be a tag securely attached to the product. See: DESCRIPTIVE LABELING, GRADE LABELING.

LAISSEZ FAIRE. A philosophy of government in which it is held that the interference of government in business affairs should be at a minimum consistent with protection to contracts, the physical premises, and the physical safety of society.

LEADER. A dealer offer conditioned by a unit volume-purchase.

LEADER PRICING. See: LOSS LEADER.

LEASE-BACK ARRANGEMENT. Used frequently where the site is important to the supplier or franchiser, it is an arrangement whereby the party of major interest signs the primary lease on the property and then subleases the property to the dealer or franchisee.

LEASED DEPARTMENT. A business operated within the physical space of another business, usually on a rental agreement based on sales. Sometimes called *concession*.

LEASING. An increasingly popular plan whereby a firm may acquire the use of equipment without the necessity of taking title. Of particular import where rapid changes in technology are taking place, highly specialized services may be required, or where the firm may employ its capital more advantageously in some other investment.

LIFE CYCLE OF PRODUCT. The pattern of the sales volume of a product as competition and natural processes (such as the introduction of a new or better product) bring the product through maturity to decline and, eventually, extinction. The time extent of the life cycle has varied greatly among products in the past and may be expected to continue to vary in the future. Increasing emphasis is being placed on the use of this concept to guide decision making about capital investment planning, advertising and promotion planning, the probability of acceptable ROI for new products, the elimination of a certain products based on a rationale, and to assist in integrating management's thinking in all functional areas. It is increasingly recognized that all of these vary greatly according to each product's progress through the stages of its life cycle.

LIFE-STYLE. The characteristic mode of living in its broadest sense of a segment of or the whole of a society, especially as it is concerned with those unique qualities which distinguish one group or culture from others.

LIMITED DISTRIBUTION. Selection of the number of dealers in an area that a firm considers will produce maximum profitability, taking into account all factors. No more dealers are accepted when that number have been activated. Same as: SELECTIVE DISTRIBUTION. See: INTENSIVE DISTRIBUTION, EXCLUSIVE DISTRIBUTION, FRANCHISING.

LIMITED-FUNCTION WHOLESALER. The general category applied to wholesalers who do not grant credit, or who do not carry stock, or who do business only by mail. Some one or more services ordinarily supplied by the regular wholesaler are lacking. See: CASH-AND-CARRY WHOLESALER, DESK JOBBER.

LIMITED-LINE STORE. A nondepartmentized retailer handling but one major line of merchandise.

LINE. (1) In advertising, a unit of space measure equal to one-fourteenth of a column inch. (2) In retailing, generally associated with goods of a related type bought to resell at a single, predetermined price. (3) In industry, the group of items related in use which are offered for sale by a firm. (4) In a firm's organization, those positions assigned the responsibilities and the authority to act directly to achieve the defined goals of the firm.

LIST PRICE. (1) The full price before any applicable discounts. (2) The suggested selling price set by a manufacturer. (3) A price set to be the permanent base from which percent deductions are allowed to various buyers who qualify for different functional discounts. In many instances the simplest way of reflecting price fluctuations affecting an extensive catalog.

LOCAL ADVERTISING. Advertising paid for by a retailer at a local rate. The message of such advertising is usually "Buy this product here!"

LOCAL BRAND. Any brand used in a limited geographic area by either a manufacturer or a middleman. See: NATIONAL BRAND, MANUFACTURER'S BRAND.

LOSS LEADER. An item offered by a merchant at an unusually low price with the full intention of selling it to all who wish to buy. The purpose is to induce a larger customer traffic than would be possible at the normal price. The loss factor is now not legal in those states having unfair trade practices acts. Use of this promotional device results in a continuing situation of special sales.

LOWER-LOWER CLASS. See: SOCIAL CLASSES.

LOWER-MIDDLE CLASS. See: SOCIAL CLASSES.

LOWER-UPPER CLASS. See: SOCIAL CLASSES.

MALL. An increasingly popular type of shopping center which may be a number of shopping blocks closed to vehicular traffic; or more recently, a shopping center of the usual type but with walkways entirely closed against the weather and air-conditioned, or the same in the form of a building with inside parking provided, sometimes near a particular department area. See: SHOPPING PLAZA.

MANUFACTURER'S BRAND. Same as: NATIONAL BRAND.

MANUFACTURER'S SALES BRANCH. An establishment owned and operated by a manufacturer apart from his plants out of which his salesmen may work, and which houses stocks from which deliveries may be made to customers.

MANUFACTURER'S SALES OFFICE. Except that no stock is housed, essentially the same as a manufacturer's sales branch.

MARGIN. The percent of selling price whch gross profit is. Used generally by retail establishments. Distinguish from: MARKUP.

MARGINAL COST. The addition to total cost occasioned by the manufacture of one additional unit of product. See: MARGINAL REVENUE.

MARGINAL REVENUE. The addition to total revenue resulting from the sale of one additional unit of product, considered from the point of view of sliding down the demand curve. See: MARGINAL COST.

MARK. A blanket term which includes any trademark, service mark, collective mark, or certification mark entitled to registration under the law, whether registered or not.

MARKDOWN. (1) A reduction in the retail price of merchandise. (2) In the retail method, a reduction from the price at which the merchandise was offered originally.

MARKET. The totality of those who can benefit from the producer's product or service and who can afford to buy it. More technically: a sphere within which price-making forces operate, and in which exchanges of title tend to be accompanied by the actual movement of the goods affected.

MARKETING. All business activities necessary to effect transfers of ownership of goods from producers to consumers except those normally regarded as manufacturing operations. In the field of services, all those activities required to make the services desirable and available to those who can benefit from their use and have the purchasing power to acquire them. In recent years the same activities as those used for goods and services have been applied to ideas, political candidates, and social philosophies. Because of the dynamic nature of marketing, all techniques employed are necessarily under continuous development. See: MARKETING FUNCTION.

MARKETING CONCEPT. Focusing of all company activity on what will best serve the consumer. Requires an internal marketing organization in which all marketing activities are consolidated under the leadership of one executive placed in top management.

MARKETING FUNCTION. A major economic activity which is inherent in the marketing process, and which tends to become specialized through a continuous division of labor. Generally classified into: buying, selling, storage, transportation, standardization and grading, risk taking, financing, market information.

MARKETING INFORMATION. A marketing function characterized by the accumulation and dissemination of intelligence concerning market developments and other market data.

MARKETING MIX. The total complex of the firm's marketing effort. The central problem in planning this is to find that combination which will produce the maximum net cash inflow. Usually considered to include: personal selling, advertising, delivery, pricing, quality, promotion, special jobs, and technical service.

MARKETING RESEARCH. The use of the scientific method in the solution of marketing problems. A tool for management, not a substitute for experience and judgment. It involves the gathering, organization, and analysis of market data as a branch of a marketing intelligence system which makes studies of specific problems for the guidance of management in the making of marketing decisions of lowest risk.

MARKETING RISKS. These are the various ways in which losses may be incurred by a marketer. They include: obsolescence, waste, damage, physical deterioration, shoplifting and other thefts, credit, discontinuity of supply, discontinuity of demand, changes in supply and demand factors resulting in price declines, and "acts of God." To a varying degree these may be passed on to others through insurance. Others may be minimized only through the effects of good management action.

MARKET POTENTIAL. The total sales of all manufacturers of a product that a market is estimated to be able to deliver during a given period.

MARKET PRICE. (1) The price at which a good is exchanged in the market from day to day. (2) The current ruling price of a commodity in the market.

MARKET PROFILE. A demographic description of the people or the households or both, of a product's market. Sometimes includes the economic information applicable to a geographic area.

MARKET SEGMENTATION. Same as: SEGMENTATION.

MARKET SHARE. One firm's proportion of the industry's total actual volume. Sometimes the base is potential volume rather than actual volume.

MARK-ON. The difference between the cost, and the retail price of an item as originally established.

MARKUP. The percent of cost which gross profit is. See: MARGIN.

MEDIA MIX. The combination of the various media to be used in an advertising campaign.

MERCHANDISING. The activities of manufacturers and middlemen which are designed to adjust the merchandise produced or offered to sale to achieve maximum customer acceptance.

MERCHANT MIDDLEMAN. A middleman who takes title to goods while performing marketing functions.

METROPOLITAN AREA. An area which includes at least one major city of at least 50,000 inhabitants, the county of such a central city, and adjacent counties that are found to be metropolitan in character and economically and socially integrated with the county of the central city. For greater detail refer to *Standard Metropolitan Statistical Areas* published by the Bureau of the Budget.

MIDDLEMAN. Any individual or business firm operating between the producer or seller and the consumer or industrial user for the purpose of passing title to goods and being paid for this service. See: FUNCTIONAL MIDDLEMAN, MERCHANT MIDDLEMAN.

MILL SUPPLY HOUSE. A type of industrial distributor handling as many as 20,000 items in over 600 product lines such as fasteners, bearings, fittings, tools, beltings, valves, and metal rods, bars, and tubing.

MISSIONARY SALESMAN. An employee of a manufacturer who often works with a middleman's salesmen for the purpose of assisting them in introducing new products or to render technical advice. Frequently works alone through a territory when primarily engaged in persuading the use of various dealer aids, leaving samples, or explaining the use of his firm's products.

MOTIVATION. (1) The psychological manifestation that appears to an observer as activity directed toward a goal. (2) All the forces that activate human behavior. See: MOTIVE.

MOTIVE. Anything which makes a person act as he does, such as the need for peer approval, fear, love of family, etc.

NATIONAL ADVERTISING. (1) That kind of advertising the basic message of which is "Buy my product (or service) somewhere." (2) Advertising placed in newspapers by firms who present the message as in (1) and who are most often charged a higher rate than firms who are in business locally. Same as: GENERAL ADVERTISING.

NATIONAL BRAND. A brand owned by a manufacturer. Same as: MANUFACTURER'S BRAND.

NONPRICE COMPETITION. Generally, any competitive activity except price reduction. Trading stamps, games, advertising of brands, and packaging innovations are examples.

NONSIGNER CLAUSE. In those states which have one, the fair trade law usually contains the proviso that all resellers are bound by the minimum price established by a product's manufacturer once any reseller so contracts.

OBSOLESCENCE. The loss in value of an asset due to the advent of superior technology, a better product, or a change in fashion.

OPINION LEADERS. Members of a group who are able in a given situation to exert personal influence on the group. Of interest to marketers because successful appeals to these people have the effect of successful appeals to the group, thereby reducing the cost of the promotional campaign and the time of securing acceptance for the product. It is not always easy to identify these people.

OTC. Abbreviation for: over the counter. Frequently used to apply to those items of medicinal use which may be sold without prescription. Advertising for this type of item is under attack as misleading, and even harmful in that people may be induced to use preparations which may have no real help for them while delaying proper medical attention. The FDA is very close to this situation, already having removed many products from sale.

OUTDOOR ADVERTISING. An advertising medium in which the message is not delivered to the audience as it is with those media which enter the home, but the units are, rather, placed in strategic locations where they can be seen by an audience on the move. Messages in this medium must be brief and easy to read and grasp because the average viewer is exposed to the message for a few seconds only.

PACKAGE. (1) That which serves as a protective device for the product as well as a vehicle to carry the brand and the label. A container. (2) In broadcast media, a combination assortment of time units, sold as a single offering at a set price. (3) In broadcast media, a program that includes all components ready for the addition of commercials. It is bought as a unit for a lump sum.

PARENT STORE. The main store of a retailer operating one or more branches.

PARTY SELLING. A form of house-to-house selling in which a hostess is persuaded through the promise of a gift to invite her friends to an afternoon or evening gathering at which the salesman can demonstrate his wares.

PERSONAL DISPOSABLE INCOME. Personal income after the payment of income taxes.

PERSONAL INCOME. The total money income received by all individuals in an economy during a given period of time. See: DISCRETIONARY INCOME.

PHYSICAL DISTRIBUTION. A term employed in manufacturing and commerce to describe the entire range of activities associated with the efficient movement of goods from producer to consumer. Sometimes used to refer only to the movement of materials from sources of supply to producers. It includes various modes of freight transportation, warehousing, materials handling, protective packaging, inventory control, plant and warehouse site selection, order processing, market forecasting, and customer service.

PHYSICAL DISTRIBUTION CONCEPT. Frequently referred to as the PD concept, it is a business theory which requires that all physical handling and the trade channel system be considered parts of one total system in the firm. A rather old idea, but as yet adopted by few firms in spite of demonstrable advantages, because it requires special and rare managerial talent able to coordinate all the aspects of a business into a unified system.

PIONEERING STAGE. The stage a product or service is in, according to a certain classification, when prospects for it either do not know of its existence or are not yet convinced that there are benefits to them in adopting it. Most often applied where a completely different type of benefit is offered. Any offering may skip this stage if the benefits are obvious to a significant number of prospects.

PLACE UTILITY. The characteristic of a good which makes it possible to satisfy a human want based on geographical considerations, i.e., the item has been moved to where it is desired as distinguished from where it was made or grown or mined. Transportation creates place utility.

PLANNED OBSOLESCENCE. While this concept is a fully acceptable one as applied to business investment, in the sense that a firm should not provide a facility that will last longer than it is anticipated will be useful because resources are wasted thereby, in recent years this term has become associated with the idea of change for consumption's sake, as in the practice of frequent model changes in consumer goods. In the latter sense this is a controversial issue.

POINT-OF-PURCHASE ADVERTISING. Signs and displays at the point of final sale. POP is very flexible as to permanency, format, position, location. Its greatest problem is persuading the dealer to use it. Much of this problem is caused by the advertiser's failure to determine in advance the realistic probability of the dealer's being *able* to use the piece as the advertiser intends.

POLICY. A rule of action adopted by an operating organization to insure uniformity of procedures under similar, recurring circumstances.

POSSESSION UTILITY. The characteristic of a good or service which makes it possible to satisfy a human want based on the need to have the right to use the good as required. Marketing creates possession utility through its title-passing activities.

PREPRICING. The manufacturer prints the retail price (sometimes as "suggested") on the item or the item's package. The effect of this, while it saves the dealer the cost of pricing if he sells for the marked price, is to lock him into a situation where he cannot sell the item for a higher price despite the willingness of his customers to pay. Indeed, the item might be more acceptable at the higher price in that location. Sometimes criticized for the infrequent, unethical practice of putting fictitious, extra-high prices on items so that a reduction in price seems to indicate a bargain, which is not true.

PRERETAILING. A policy of requiring that retail prices be established prior to or at the time of purchase of goods for resale. In many stores the retail prices are placed on a copy of the purchase order at the time the goods are bought and this copy is used as a price authorization for marking when the goods reach the marking stage in the flow to the selling area.

PRESTIGE PRICING. Setting the price of an item high to attract those who find satisfaction in owning expensive and relatively exclusive items, or those who equate high quality with high price. If the demand is enough and the product lives up to expectations for the buyer, this practice may prove successful.

PRICE. The amount of something for which something else can be acquired. In our modern society the something is the legal tender in the form of money. In more primitive societies it may be and has been expressed in cows, horses, wives, beads, etc.

PRICE LEADERSHIP. Other sellers fix their prices by accepting the price announced by a leading firm. The leadership may change from time to time.

PRICE LINING. Buying merchandise to sell at a limited number of predetermined selling prices.

PRICE MIX. The total pattern of a firm's policy regarding raising and lowering prices to meet competition, and the lines on which it will take actions.

PRIMARY BUYING MOTIVE. A product motive applicable to a product the concept of which is new to the market or which has not yet been generally accepted. For example, when commercial air travel was first introduced, it was necessary to convince people that benefits were to be found in flying that were superior to those found by using other means of personal transportation. To this day, the vast majority of people in the United States have never flown. Much work remains toward activating primary motives with respect to air travel. See: SELECTIVE BUYING MOTIVE.

PRIVATE BRAND. A brand name owned by a middleman. Sometimes called: PRIVATE LABEL.

PRODUCT. The totality of every aspect of a firm's offering which the prospect perceives as giving value. May involve psychological as well as physical aspects.

PRODUCT DIFFERENTIATION. The situation in which two products of similar characteristics and end use, usually made by different producers, acquire divergent images in the minds of segments of the market. Ordinarily comes about through promotional activities by the respective producers.

PRODUCT IMAGE. How the consumer perceives the characteristics of a product. What really counts for the marketer is not what the product really is, but what the consumer thinks of it as being.

PRODUCT LIFE CYCLE. Same as: LIFE CYCLE OF PRODUCT.

PRODUCT PLANNING. The company activity which involves the screening and appraisal of an idea, analysis of the market, and the development and testing of a product before production is committed. Although specific organization for this effort varies from company to company, it is almost uniformly recognized as belonging in the top management echelons.

PROMOTIONAL MIX. The combination of all means used to effect sales. It should be recognized that a great deal of substitutability exists among the various means. Traditional mixes may not produce the greatest efficacy at the lowest cost, usually a desired outcome.

PROSPECT. Anyone not now using a firm's product or service, who can benefit from owning it, who has the purchasing power to acquire it, and who has the authority to make the decision. Someone who is not qualified as indicated above should not be subjected to a selling effort. In the industrial field where multiple purchasing influence is a significant factor, persons who can influence the purchasing decision are often called prospects.

PSYCHIC INCOME. A flow of satisfactions over a period of time. There is no standard unit of measurement for this. However, everyone is able to achieve for himself a measure of the satisfaction from one group of experiences relative to another group of experiences.

PSYCHOGRAPHIC MARKET SEGMENTATION. The strategy of segmenting a market by selecting people who react in the same way to a particular emotional appeal, or who share common behavioral patterns. In contrast to demographic market segmentation.

PUBLICITY. Unpaid exposure to the market, by an unnamed source, of commercially significant information about a product or company.

PUBLIC RELATIONS. A planned program of policies and conduct designed to build confidence and increase the understanding of one or more of a firm's publics. These publics may be classified as: (1) customers, (2) suppliers, (3) competitors, (4) employees, (5) stockholders, (6) creditors, (7) local community, (8) the government. It should be noted that these are *not* mutually exclusive.

PURCHASING AGENT. (1) A functional middleman characterized by representation of the buyer. (2) Applied to an employee of an industrial firm who is delegated the authority to commit the firm for acquisition of materials and equipment. (3) In a department store, the person authorized to acquire materials needed for operation and maintenance of the premises.

PUSH MONEY. A cash reward offered by a manufacturer or owner to retail sales personnel for selling that manufacturer's products. Has recently come under attack as an unfair practice when initiated by a manufacturer. Commonly abbreviated: PM.

RACK JOBBER. A limited-function wholesaler who supplies merchandise and sets up displays, and who receives payment only for actual items sold.

RAW MATERIALS. Products of nature which enter into the physical product being made, and which have been processed only enough for convenience in their distribution. Distinguish from the accounting usage which includes all items entering the final product whether processed by the firm or not. See: FABRICATING MATERIAL.

REAL INCOME. The actual group of products and/or services that a person's money income will permit him to acquire. See: DISCRETIONARY INCOME.

REGIONAL SHOPPING CENTER. The largest of the shopping center types. One or two department stores provide the main drawing power, supplemented by many smaller stories. They are set up to serve 100,000 to 250,000 people living in a radius of 6 to 10 miles; they may draw from much farther away. They are usually located outside a business district in an area of easy access by roads.

RETAILER. A business mainly concerned with selling to consumers.

RETAILING. That business activity mainly concerned with selling to consumers.

RISK-TAKING. A marketing function characterized by the presence of the possibility of losses inherent in the nature of economic activity.

ROBINSON-PATMAN ACT. Enacted in 1936, this revision of the Clayton Act was an attempt to clarify prohibited discriminations. While still not entirely clear, it does provide additional strength for the law. Its main provisions: to prohibit fees by sellers to brokers acting for buyers, supplementary services such as advertising allowances by sellers disproportionately to buyers, price differentials to competing buyers not justified by savings to sellers, knowingly to induce or receive a prohibited discrimination in price, and pricing for the purpose of destroying competition or eliminating a competitor.

ROCHDALE PLAN. Developed by a group of flannel weavers in Rochdale, England, who organized as the Rochdale Society of Equitable Pioneers, this plan was the first to incorporate the principles which led to the success of cooperatives: open membership, democratic control, sale at prevailing prices, patronage dividends, limited interest on capital, sale for cash, and educational activity.

SALES FORECAST. An estimate of sales for a future period assuming certain economic conditions and other pertinent forces, such as a proposed promotional program. May be in dollars or in units. May be for an individual item, a product line, or the firm's total sales. See: FORECASTING.

SALES MANAGER. Usually the individual in a firm who makes and carries out sales policies, and who is responsible for recruiting, training, and controlling an inside salesforce and/or a field salesforce.

SALES PROMOTION. (1) In a general sense, all types of marketing activities designed to increase demand. Sometimes called *demand creation* or *demand stimulation*. (2) In a narrower sense, applied to all the above activities except advertising and salesmanship. The inclusiveness may vary with the user.

SAMPLE. (1) A collection of units chosen in such a way that it represents the whole. A vast literature exists on the procedures for developing samples and on tests for judging their usefulness. (2) A unit of a product which is representative of all units of that product.

SAMPLING. (1) In promotion, the technique by means of which a market is exposed to new products, packages, or package sizes through the sending or giving to prospects of a miniature or an actual unit. (2) A blanket term covering a variety of techniques in marketing research all designed to provide information about a large population from data assembled about relatively few units from that population.

SCRAMBLED MERCHANDISING. A condition in retailing in which a store takes on merchandise to sell that is unrelated to the regular lines of the store, e.g., greeting cards in a hardware store.

SECONDARY SHOPPING DISTRICT. A well-developed cluster of stores outside the central business district that serves a population of several thousand people. Found in larger cities, it has characteristics similar to those of the main shopping districts of smaller cities. While the sale of convenience goods predominates, shopping goods and specialty goods are of considerable significance.

SEGMENTATION. Division of a market into subgroups with similar motivations. May be a tactic to increase product acceptance by recognizing product appeals, but there is a danger of overconcentration in a particular segment to which selling effort is applied to the extent that the firm is blinded to other possibilities. The

most widely used bases for segmenting a market are: demographics, geographics, personality, use of product, preference,
attitudes, values, and benefits. Usually a coarser division than
fragmentation.

SELECTIVE BUYING MOTIVE. A product motive applicable to the market situation which obtains once a product concept has been
generally accepted and competition has set in. It then becomes
necessary for the consumer to choose among the products offered
to provide that type of benefit. See: PRIMARY BUYING MO-
TIVE.

SELECTIVE DISTRIBUTION. Same as: LIMITED DISTRIBUTION.

SELF-SELECTION. Merchandise is so arranged in a retail store that the
customer can make a choice without the aid of a salesclerk. Once
the choice is made, the merchandise is handed to a nearby salesclerk who takes whatever steps are necessary to complete the sale.
Differs from *self-service* in that under self-service the customer
not only makes an unaided decision, but brings the choice to a
check-out station where payment is made and the purchase
wrapped. Many stores provide services such as credit, and assistance of a technical nature in departments such as cameras, although the organization is basically on a self-service pattern.

SELF-SERVICE. See: SELF-SELECTION.

SELLERS' MARKET. A condition of the market in which vendors are
able to prescribe the conditions of a transaction because demand
exceeds supply. See: BUYERS' MARKET.

SELLING AGENT. An intermediary in the title transferring process who
is characterized by the fact that he is responsible for disposing of
the entire output of his principal, usually with considerable lati-
tude in setting prices and terms of sale. The only functional middleman who is frequently involved in financing his principal,
whom he represents in the market continuously.

SERVICE MARK. A mark used in the sale or advertising of services to
identify those of one person or firm and to distinguish them from
those of others. Titles, character names, and other distinctive
features of radio or television programs may be registered as service marks notwithstanding that they may advertise the products
of a sponsor.

SERVICES. (1) Work performed by individuals or firms for others
where no goods or commodities are transferred. Banks and utilities
are among those said to create services. (2) Privileges extended to

customers of a firm beyond the merchandise itself, such as wrappings, credit, returns, assortment, delivery, and pleasant environment.

SERVICE WHOLESALER. A merchant selling to retailers, industrial users, and other wholesalers, and performing the usual complete services of such a merchant. These services include credit, delivery, redress for faulty or damaged merchandise, significantly large variety and assortment, information and education through salesmen, and assistance with dealer aids and displays.

SHARE OF MARKET. The percent of the total industry sale of a product or service in a given market which is achieved by an individual firm.

SHOPPING GOODS. The type of item for which reasonable alternates exist and which the consumer usually wishes to purchase only after comparing price, quality, and style in a number of sources. See: CONVENIENCE GOODS, SPECIALTY GOODS.

SHOPPING PLAZA. A large building erected in a shopping district to act as a vertical controlled shopping center. The various areas of the building are rented to different retailers. See: MALL.

SMSA. Abbreviation for: STANDARD METROPOLITAN STATISTICAL AREA. See: METROPOLITAN AREA.

SOCIAL CLASSES. Groups of people who are more or less equal to one another in prestige and community status; they readily and regularly interact among themselves formally and informally; and they share the same goals and ways of looking at life. W. Lloyd Warner and Associates have distinguished among six social classes, now widely accepted:

1) *Upper-Upper* or "Social Register" consists of locally prominent families, usually with at least second or third generation wealth. Basic values: living graciously, upholding family reputation, reflecting the excellence of one's breeding, and displaying a sense of community responsibility. About ½ of 1% of the population.

2) *Lower-Upper* or "Nouveau Riche" consists of the more recently arrived and never-quite-accepted wealthy families. Goals: blend of Upper-Upper pursuit of gracious living and the Upper-Middle drive for success. About 1½% of the population.

3) *Upper-Middle* are moderately successful professional men and women, owners of medium-sized businesses, young people in their twenties and early thirties who are expected to arrive at the managerial level by their middle or late thirties. Motivations:

success at a career, cultivating charm and polish. About 10% of the population.

4) *Lower-Middle* are mostly nonmanagerial office workers, small business owners, highly paid blue-collar families. Goals: respectability, and striving to live in well-maintained homes, neatly furnished in more-or-less "right" neighborhoods, and to do a good job at their work. They will save for a college education for their children. Top of the "Average Man World." About 30%–35% of the population.

5) *Upper-Lower* or "Ordinary Working Class" consists of semi-skilled workers. Although many make high pay, they are not particularly interested in respectability. Goals: enjoying life and living well from day to day, to be at least modern, and to work hard enough to keep safely away from the slum level. About 40% of the population.

6) *Lower-Lower* are unskilled workers, unassimilated ethnics, and the sporadically employed. Outlooks: apathy, fatalism, "get your kicks whenever you can." About 15% of the population, but have less than half of the purchasing power.

Note that these classes are not entirely homogeneous. They include subgroups many of which overlap the class lines as shown due to considerable upward or downward mobility. For a discussion of the marketing significance of these classes see the still fresh: Richard P. Coleman, "The Significance of Social Stratification," in *Marketing and the Behavioral Sciences*, Perry Bliss, ed. (Boston: Allyn and Bacon, Inc., 1962) pp. 156–171.

SPECIALTY GOODS. The category specifying an item which has such an attraction for a consumer that he will go considerably out of his way to buy it. Applies also to an item for which no reasonable substitute exists and which provides benefits which are in demand.

SPECIALTY SELLING. Applied generally to the sale at the home or place of business of merchandise or services not available in stores, e.g., home improvements, insurance, and encyclopedias. The men who accomplish the selling are called specialty salesmen. Advertising is placed to get leads for them. Should *not* be considered in the same concept as specialty goods.

SPECIALTY SHOP. A relatively small-scale retail store which makes its appeal on a broad selection of a restricted class of merchandise. Has no necessary relationship to specialty goods.

SPIRAL. According to the classification held by a number of advertising theorists, the way a product or service evolves with relation to its acceptance by its prospective public. This is a continuous process, moving to a new beginning point in the spiral as acceptance increases; however, it is recognized that some products or services will not advance further after some point is reached.

STANDARD METROPOLITAN STATISTICAL AREA. Same as: SMSA.

STORAGE. (1) A marketing function characterized by the creation of time utility by holding and preserving goods for varying periods of time. Storage is inherent in all goods handling except in those few instances where the item is put into its next use immediately upon being produced. (2) Preferred as a term in EDP to "memory" it is a device in which data can be stored and from which data can be obtained on call as needed.

STORE. A business establishment into which customers and prospects are invited to visit and to select purchases.

STORE TRAFFIC. The flow of customers into and throughout a store. Placement of merchandise in various store areas must take into account the natural and the desired pattern of customer movement to and from these areas.

SUPERMARKET. The retail institution of the present which is most similar to the small general store, but in magnified dimensions. From its start in the 1930s it was the factor which united the automobile, the mechanical refrigerator, and good roads into a system of food use and shopping which voided the corner grocery store and changed American habits of buying and eating goods, with marked effects on the food industry. To be officially classified a supermarket, a food store must have eight or more employees. The typical supermarket sells a large number of nonfood items.

SYSTEMS APPROACH. A way of studying marketing which examines and analyzes the behavioral interrelationships among the various elements of the marketing structure, including the power structure and the communications network.

TEST MARKETING. The new product and its marketing program are tried out in a small number of representative customer environments. Validity is subject to various problems, such as competition's activities, total cost of testing, and representativeness of the locale to the rest of the market.

TIME UTILITY. The characteristic of a good which makes it possible to satisfy a human want based on time preference. Storage creates time utility. See: UTILITY.

TRADE ADVERTISING. Advertising directed at retailers and wholesalers.

TRADE CHANNEL. Same as: CHANNEL OF DISTRIBUTION.

TRADEMARK. Any word, name, symbol, device, or any combination of these adopted and used by a manufacturer or merchant to identify his goods and distinguish them from those of others. It is a brand name used on goods *moving in the channels of trade*. Rights in a trademark are acquired only by use, and the use ordinarily must continue if the rights are to be preserved. That provision is made to register a trademark in the Patent Office does not imply that such registration in itself creates or establishes any exclusive rights. However, registration is recognition by the government of the right of the owner to use the mark in commerce to distinguish his goods from those of others. Brand is the everyday term; trademark is the legal counterpart. Trademarks are registered for twenty years and may be renewed every twenty years thereafter if not abandoned, cancelled, or surrendered.

TRADE NAME. A name that applies to a business as a whole. The same name may be used to identify a product, when it will be a trademark, too.

TRADING AREA. A region around a firm or a shopping district whose limits are set by the costs of selling or delivering goods.

TRADING UP. A legitimate business activity in which a salesman tries to interest prospects or customers in goods of higher price which the salesman feels can be proved to provide superior benefits.

TRANSPORTATION. (1) A marketing function characterized by the physical movement of goods. Creates place utility. (2) Applied broadly to the types of services provided and performed by the different kinds of carriers.

TRUCK JOBBER. A type of merchant wholesaler who combines the activities of salesman with those of deliveryman, who usually sells for cash, and whose stock is usually limited to nationally advertised specialties and fast-moving items of a perishable or semi-perishable nature. Also occurs in a few areas of the industrial market.

TRUTH-IN-LENDING ACT. An Act of Congress requiring that every borrower be informed clearly of the total charges or interest he is to pay on his loan or installment plan, and the equivalent rate of simple interest applicable thereto. Same as: CONSUMER CREDIT PROTECTION ACT.

ULTIMATE CONSUMER. Same as: CONSUMER. Although frequently used to make a distinction between the "final user" and intermediate "consumers" who do something that provides the "final user" with a product or service, the term is really redundant. When one reflects that the *consumer* is always the "final user," there is no point to designating him "ultimate." See: INDUSTRIAL USER.

UPPER-LOWER CLASS. See: SOCIAL CLASSES.

UPPER-MIDDLE CLASS. See: SOCIAL CLASSES.

UPPER-UPPER CLASS. See: SOCIAL CLASSES.

UTILITY. The capacity of a good or service to satisfy a human want. See: FORM UTILITY, PLACE UTILITY, POSSESSION UTILITY, TIME UTILITY.

VARIABLE COSTS. Those costs which depend on and change with the production level. When the plant is not operating, these costs are zero. See: FIXED COSTS.

VARIETY STORE. A retail store offering a wide assortment and variety of articles mainly of relatively low price. It is usually departmentized as to merchandise, but not necessarily as to accounting unless of large size. The purchase of the typical customer is small.

VENDING. A system of selling merchandise through coin-operated devices.

VERTICAL INTEGRATION. Acquisition of a company operating at a different level in the channel of distribution than the acquiring company, the consumer considered as the base. It is *backward* if the acquired company is farther away from the consumer, *forward* if nearer to the consumer. See: HORIZONTAL INTEGRATION.

VOLUNTARY CHAIN. A group of stores organized by a wholesaler around a common interest in the goods or services the wholesaler can provide. The wholesaler usually owns the common name under which the stores operate, and the relative responsibilities of the stores and the wholesaler are delineated in a written contract. The wholesaler most often provides private label merchandise. Such organizations have been quite effective in a number of lines of goods in permitting small, independent retailers to compete with the large retail chains. See: COOPERATIVE CHAIN.

VOLUNTARY GROUP. If intended as a permanent arrangement, essentially the same as either: COOPERATIVE CHAIN or VOLUNTARY CHAIN.

WAGON DISTRIBUTOR. Same as: TRUCK JOBBER.

WAGON JOBBER. Same as: TRUCK JOBBER.

WHOLESALER. A business mainly concerned with selling to those who buy for resale or industrial use; in other words, for purposes other than for personal or household use.

APPENDIX B
FINAL EXAMINATION

Part I. True-False Problems

The following statements are either true or false. The statement is false if any element in that statement is false. The correct answers are in the key on page 355.

Check One

T　　F

1. The fundamental approaches to the study of marketing are the commodity approach, the institutional approach, the systems approach, and the functional approach.　　　——　——

2. Convenience goods are goods selected on the basis of comparisons with regard to suitability, quality, price, and style.　　　——　——

3. Middlemen are not included in the group that makes up the industrial market.　　　——　——

4. The purchasing agent always makes the final decision regarding the purchase of an industrial good.　　　——　——

5. Small-scale purchasing is characteristic of the consumer market.　　　——　——

6. Engel's law describes the fashion cycle in the United States.　　　——　——

7. The terms *agent middleman* and *merchant middleman* are synonymous.　　　——　——

8. The following are merchant wholesalers who perform lim-

ited services for their customers: cash-and-carry wholesaler, drop shipper, truck wholesaler, and mail-order wholesaler.

9. Unlike the manufacturers' agent, the selling agent handles the entire output of one producer.

10. The central wholesale market performs all the marketing functions in the distribution of agricultural commodities.

11. *Jobber market* and *mill market* are synonymous terms that refer to one kind of secondary wholesale market used in the distribution of agricultural commodities.

12. A federated association of local cooperatives is an association wherein the major policies and decisions are channeled from the top down.

13. Unlike the single-line store, the specialty shop distributes only a portion of a single, larger line of products.

14. The operations of a large-scale retailer may be classified into four basic activities: merchandising, publicity, store operation, and control.

15. A voluntary (or contract) chain is a cooperative undertaking organized to aid the small-scale retailer to compete effectively with large-scale retailing enterprises.

16. One advantage of direct marketing is that it eliminates competition with private brands.

17. Government regulations affect virtually all phases of marketing.

18. In contrast with discrimination in international marketing (through the use of tariffs and quotas), there is no discrimination shown by the various states of the United States with regard to goods shipped from one state to another.

19. *Standardization* and *grading* have been defined as the "setting of basic limits in the form of specifications to which manufactured goods must conform."

20. Quantitative factors (such as size, weight, quantity, and packaging) are used more often than qualitative factors as a basis for standards.

21. There are four types of quantity buying: anticipation, advance buying for the season's needs, contract for future delivery, and control of the source of supply.

22. The elimination of middlemen automatically reduces distribution costs.

23. The small-scale retailer usually purchases his goods from wholesaling middlemen, but chain stores and department stores generally buy directly from manufacturers.

24. In an economy characterized by pure competition, advertising and other sales promotional activities would be useless. ___ ___

25. The demand for a particular commodity or service may be inelastic at one time and elastic at another. ___ ___

26. Service competition is one method whereby the effects of price competition may be minimized. ___ ___

27. Quantity discounts are normally offered to large-scale purchasers, thereby giving them an advantage over small-scale operators. ___ ___

28. AIDA is the term used to signifiy the four basic elements in personal selling. ___ ___

29. The basic appeals of advertising may be said to include the following categories: hunger, love, vanity, and fear. ___ ___

30. Publicity is a form of sales promotion. ___ ___

31. Storage creates only two kinds of utility: time utility and place utility. ___ ___

32. Bonded products are usually stored in customs warehouses. ___ ___

33. Special rates for LCL service may be obtained through the use of the package car, the pool car, the consolidated car, or the mixed car. ___ ___

34. All users of railroads for the transportation of freight must pay a special tax called the *demurrage charge*. ___ ___

35. Pipelines (unlike railroads, trucks, and ships) cannot be regarded as part of the transportation system of the United States because they do not move with the commodity. ___ ___

36. Marketing research is the only way in which the cost of distribution may be evaluated and therefore reduced. ___ ___

37. In a sampling survey in which individuals are questioned, the only kinds of data that can be obtained are those concerned with knowledge, opinion, or behavior. ___ ___

38. The extension of credit to consumers may have the paradoxical results of raising standards of living and of encouraging overspending. ___ ___

39. Long-term loans to business are most frequently made for capital outlay; whereas short-term loans are used only to finance current needs. ___ ___

40. Risk in business can always be either completely eliminated or reduced or shifted. ___ ___

41. In a hedging transaction, the gains and the losses are always equal. ___ ___

42. Commodity exchanges not only provide facilities for others

to transact business but often trade on their own account in order to minimize sharp fluctuations in prices.

43. A complete theory of marketing has now been developed that will serve as an adequate criterion for the evaluation of individual marketing activities.

44. One of the most important achievements of the market research executive is his ability to measure accurately the results of sales campaigns.

45. Consumer motivation is one of the more complex problems in marketing.

46. If population growth is considered an important element of the market, it can be said that in the foreseeable future there will always be an expanding market for goods and services.

47. Improvements in communication and in transportation have shortened the fashion cycle.

48. *Market potential* is the expected sale of a commodity, of a group of commodities, or of a service for an entire industry in a market during a stated period.

49. *Market policy* is a course of action established to obtain consistency in marketing procedure under recurring and essentially similar circumstances.

50. *Selective selling* is the policy of selling only to those dealers and distributors who meet the seller's requirements with regard to such matters as size of orders, volume of purchases, profitability, or area or type of operations.

51. The advanced mathematics applied to decision making produce a highly precise and dependable answer to marketing problems.

52. To be termed a *model*, the structure must be highly organized and integrated.

53. Business problems are always characterized by uncertainty.

54. The major reason for failure of American firms in international marketing is the attempt to use marketing methods that worked well in the United States.

55. The first step for an American firm interested in the possibility of marketing in a particular foreign country is to arrange for financing of the operation.

56. The letter of credit provides bank funds for use of the exporter.

57. In foreign purchasing, the promissory note is often used in buying heavy equipment and capital goods.

58. Buying cycles tend to vary around the world.

59. The brand image of a product may be colored by the marketing channels which handle that brand.   —   —

60. Although each person has a self-image, this is essentially unrelated to buying, where the brand image is overriding.   —   —

61. The marketing concept holds that all the firm's efforts should be built around consumer wants.   —   —

62. Market segmentation is the process of dividing a broad market into heterogeneous units.   —   —

63. Market segmentation may require a producer to change his channels of distribution.   —   —

64. Franchising is a major tool accounting for the growth of services in the American economy.   —   —

65. Since 1960, there has been more government activity protecting consumers than in all preceding years.   —   —

Part II. Multiple-Choice Questions

This part consists of multiple-choice statements. For each statement select the one alternative that most accurately completes the statement. The correct answers are in the key on page 355.

Selection

66. A package of cigarettes is a   (1) raw material   (2) convenience good   (3) shopping good   (4) specialty good.   —

67. An agent middleman is one who   (1) takes title   (2) does not take title   (3) sells convenience goods   (4) acts as a purchaser.   —

68. In the marketing of consumer goods, the merchandise most often goes from   (1) producer to consumer   (2) producer to one middleman to consumer   (3) producer to agent middleman to wholesaler to retailer to consumer   (4) producer to wholesaler to retailer to consumer.   —

69. Which of these types of purchaser may be a part of either the industrial or the consumer market?   (1) producers   (2) institutions   (3) government   (4) none of these.   —

70. The beginning of the consumer cooperative is generally traced to (1) publication of consumer books in the 1920s   (2) the depression of the 1930s   (3) the New Deal   (4) the Rochdale Society of Equitable Pioneers.   —

71. On the basis of volume, which of the following types of wholesale middlemen is the most important?   (1) cooperative marketing associations   (2) commission men   (3) brokers   (4) wholesale merchants.   —

72. Most of the extractive raw materials are sold to (1) retailers (2) ultimate consumers (3) manufacturers of other products (4) farmers.

73. The total number of wholesale establishments is about (1) 200,-000 (2) 300,000 (3) 400,000 (4) 500,000.

74. The wholesale middleman most likely to perform all the marketing functions is the (1) selling agent (2) mill supply house (3) mail-order wholesaler (4) drop shipper.

75. The wholesaling middleman most likely to emphasize private brands is the (1) drop shipper (2) regional wholesaler (3) mill supply house (4) direct jobber.

76. The wholesaling middleman most likely to have a long-term contract with his principal is the (1) broker (2) commission merchant (3) selling agent (4) auction firm.

77. Which of the following is *not* a major point of difference between the auction and the commodity exchange? (1) nature of the products being handled (2) failure to take title (3) rigidly defined rules of exchange (4) emphasis on functions of buying and selling.

78. The secondary wholesale market for agricultural goods may be subdivided into (1) the auction and the commodity exchange (2) the jobber and the mill market (3) the local market and the central market (4) none of these.

79. Which middlemen are found only in the local wholesale market? (1) retailers (2) cooperatives (3) central market wholesaling firm (4) none of these.

80. Which of the following characteristics is *not* generally typical of the supermarket? (1) location in a central shopping district (2) minimum annual business of $1 million (3) wide aisles (4) self-service.

81. The small-scale retailer has tried to meet large-scale competition mainly through (1) cooperative enterprises (2) private branding (3) store modernization (4) all these methods.

82. Which of the following is *not* a typical major division of the department store? (1) personnel (2) merchandising (3) publicity (4) operation.

83. Which of the following effects is generally associated with direct marketing? (1) faster movement of goods (2) reduction of distribution costs (3) simplification of servicing problems (4) reduction of inventory.

84. Which conditions are *not* conducive to direct marketing? (1) limited production (2) limited capital (3) diversified markets (4) all of these.

85. Direct marketing is generally most feasible in the distribution of (1) manufactured business goods (2) agricultural business goods (3) shopping goods (4) convenience goods.

86. Which of the following acts was primarily concerned with pricing? (1) Pure Food and Drug Act   (2) Standard Barrel Act   (3) Miller-Tydings Act   (4) Lanham Act.   ___

87. Which of the following acts constituted the first federal step against monopolies?   (1) Clayton Act   (2) Sherman Antitrust Act   (3) Federal Trade Commission Act   (4) Robinson-Patman Act.   ___

88. Which of the following acts was aimed primarily at chainstore practices?   (1) Capper-Volstead Act   (2) Robinson-Patman Act   (3) Miller-Tydings Act   (4) Webb-Pomerene Act.   ___

89. Standardization control at the production level is most effective among   (1) manufacturers   (2) farmers   (3) extractive industries   (4) all of these.   ___

90. The most important factor governing a manufacturer's selection of standards is generally the   (1) inventory on hand   (2) need for quality at a reasonable price   (3) nature of competition   (4) channels of distribution available.   ___

91. The marketing function most affected by standardization is   (1) selling   (2) transportation   (3) storage   (4) equalization.   ___

92. Which of the following is *not* a characteristic of business buying? (1) a small number of purchasers   (2) the small size of the average purchase   (3) buying by specification   (4) reciprocal buying.   ___

93. Which of the following buying methods would most probably be used by a large-scale industrial buyer?   (1) buying office   (2) use of a jobber's services   (3) buying on purchaser's premises   (4) none of these.   ___

94. An agent middleman is most likely to be used in the purchasing of   (1) convenience goods   (2) specialty goods   (3) raw materials   (4) manufactured industrial goods.   ___

95. Selling that is restricted to a single selected middleman within a specific sales area is known as   (1) selective distribution   (2) exclusive distribution   (3) reciprocal distribution   (4) integrated distribution.   ___

96. If a manufacturer utilizes exclusive distribution, which of the following pricing policies is he most likely to follow?   (1) no resale price control   (2) fair trading   (3) suggested resale prices   (4) dictated resale prices.   ___

97. Which of the following is *not* a factor in the seller's determination of prices?   (1) cost of the goods   (2) competitive price levels   (3) the level and the nature of demand   (4) none of these.   ___

98. Resale price maintenance was legalized by   (1) the McGuire Act   (2) the Robinson-Patman Act   (3) the Federal Trade Commission Act   (4) the Miller-Tydings Act.   ___

99. Chain discounts are a form of   (1) trade discount   (2) quantity discount   (3) cash discount   (4) seasonal discount.   ___

100. Department store advertising that lists goods and prices is

chiefly an example of   (1) institutional advertising   (2) direct selling copy   (3) reminder copy   (4) none of these.

101. The advertising agency is paid by   (1) the advertiser   (2) the advertising medium   (3) both of these   (4) neither of these.

102. In field warehousing, the goods are stored on premises owned by (1) the owner of the goods   (2) a warehouse company   (3) government   (4) a transportation carrier.

103. A customs warehouse is used in the storage of goods   (1) only where the goods are bonded   (2) where there is a tax dispute between the government and the owner of the goods   (3) where the tax is not to be paid until the goods are marketed   (4) none of these.

104. Goods whose transportation cost is high relative to their value are known as   (1) diverted goods   (2) high-cost goods   (3) bulky goods   (4) none of these.

105. The least costly form of transportation is by   (1) train   (2) plane   (3) water   (4) truck.

106. The procedure whereby a manufacturer can process his goods somewhere en route and pay transportation costs that are lower than normally expected is known as   (1) diversion   (2) demurrage   (3) LCL   (4) transit privilege.

107. A marketing study is   (1) one that helps the overall study of marketing   (2) one that defines a market   (3) one that analyzes methods of distributing particular goods   (4) all of these.

108. The panel method usually makes use of   (1) personal interviews only   (2) mail questionnaires only   (3) personal interviews and mail questionnaires   (4) none of these.

109. Market research is   (1) an exact science   (2) a social science (3) a method of social investigation   (4) none of these.

110. Cash credit is equivalent to a   (1) functional discount   (2) cash discount   (3) brokerage discount   (4) seasonal discount.

111. The credit exchange   (1) exchanges credits from one bank to another   (2) solicits charge accounts among consumers   (3) collects and disseminates credit information   (4) is none of these.

112. A firm that handles completely the manufacturing of a product and its distribution to the ultimate consumer is thus providing an example of   (1) horizontal integration   (2) vertical integration   (3) cartels   (4) none of these.

113. Hedging may be defined as   (1) speculation in the cash or futures market   (2) an attempt to balance gains and losses resulting from price fluctuations   (3) the marginal balancing of losses   (4) none of these.

114. The on-track sales price must be paid   (1) only if the commodity arrives within a specified period   (2) only during transit   (3)

only while the seller restricts his activities to selling (4) in none of these cases. ___

115. Scrambled merchandising is an apparent reversion to (1) the apothecary shop (2) the general store (3) tent merchandising (4) all of these. ___

116. Select the one choice that is a mathematical model: (1) game theory (2) the implicit model (3) the control model (4) management science. ___

117. The reason that activities such as advertising, public relations, and certain buying patterns may be difficult to put into a symbolic model is (1) they change so quickly (2) they are not easily qualified (3) they are subject to human error (4) their relationship to marketing success is difficult to determine. ___

118. Linear programming is (1) a system in which two or more decision makers are in competition with one another (2) a system that utilizes the concept of people in a line (3) usually applied to allocation problems (4) the critical path followed by those in a line. ___

119. Markoff analysis is most often applied to (1) distribution analysis (2) advertising analysis (3) brand share prediction (4) quantifying qualitative data. ___

120. The combination export manager is (1) an agent middleman (2) a single executive who acts as export manager for all divisions of his corporation (3) an executive who parallels the group product manager in domestic marketing (4) an export manager who represents a syndicate of companies who are combined in exporting. ___

121. Eurodollars are dollars that (1) are underwritten by the European Common Market (2) are spent in Europe for marketing by an American manufacturer (3) are underwritten in all European countries by the banks of the particular country (4) are American dollars deposited in Europe to the accounts of governments, companies, and individuals abroad.

122. The documentary sight draft is (1) a promissory note (2) a draft due on presentation (3) a predated check (4) a bank deposit to the credit of the borrower. ___

123. Which one of these is not a public agency that will help exporters? (1) Export-Import Bank (2) Commodity Credit Corporation (3) International Monetary Fund (4) World Bank. ___

124. Which one of these is *not* a characteristic of brand or company image? (1) images are constant (2) images are psychological (3) images are sociological (4) images are physiological. ___

125. Which one of these marketing functions is most closely associated with image formation? (1) buying (2) financing (3) risk taking (4) selling. ___

126. Which of the following is *not* a method of market segmentation (1) psychographics   (2) semantics   (3) demographics   (4) geography.   ___

127. Which one of these is an example of both an industrial and a consumer service?   (1) a travel agency   (2) McDonald's   (3) a marketing consultant   (4) an amusement park.   ___

128. When an organization contracts for a charter flight and then sells space to ultimate consumers, the organization is acting as a (1) merchant middleman   (2) broker   (3) commission man   (4) selling agent.   ___

129. Probably the key name in the development of consumerism in the 1960s was   (1) Vance Packard   (2) Jessica Mitford   (3) Upton Sinclair   (4) Ralph Nader.   ___

130. In 1962, President Kennedy enumerated four basic consumer rights. Which of the following was *not* in the list?   (1) product safety   (2) to be heard   (3) to choose   (4) to get one's money's worth.   ___

131. Of these functions, which has been most frequently attacked in the consumerist movement?   (1) pricing   (2) advertising   (3) product   (4) storage.   ___

KEY TO FINAL EXAMINATION

Part I. True-False Problems

1. T	12. F	23. T	34. F	45. T	56. T
2. F	13. T	24. T	35. F	46. F	57. T
3. F	14. T	25. T	36. F	47. T	58. F
4. F	15. T	26. T	37. T	48. T	59. T
5. T	16. T	27. F	38. T	49. T	60. F
6. F	17. T	28. T	39. T	50. T	61. T
7. F	18. F	29. T	40. F	51. F	62. F
8. T	19. F	30. T	41. F	52. F	63. T
9. T	20. F	31. F	42. F	53. T	64. T
10. T	21. T	32. F	43. F	54. T	65. T
11. F	22. F	33. T	44. F	55. F	

Part II. Multiple-Choice Questions

66. (2)	77. (2)	88. (2)	99. (1)	110. (2)	121. (4)
67. (2)	78. (2)	89. (1)	100. (2)	111. (3)	122. (2)
68. (4)	79. (4)	90. (2)	101. (2)	112. (2)	123. (4)
69. (4)	80. (1)	91. (1)	102. (1)	113. (2)	124. (1)
70. (4)	81. (4)	92. (2)	103. (2)	114. (1)	125. (4)
71. (4)	82. (1)	93. (3)	104. (3)	115. (2)	126. (2)
72. (3)	83. (1)	94. (3)	105. (3)	116. (1)	127. (1)
73. (2)	84. (4)	95. (2)	106. (4)	117. (2)	128. (1)
74. (2)	85. (1)	96. (4)	107. (3)	118. (3)	129. (4)
75. (2)	86. (3)	97. (4)	108. (3)	119. (3)	130. (4)
76. (3)	87. (2)	98. (4)	109. (3)	120. (1)	131. (2)

INDEX

This index is primarily designed for reviewing any broad topic or specific facts, concepts, and terms. The broad topics have been indexed in considerable detail by means of numerous subtopics. All important terms have been included. Entries referring to items found in Appendix A (pages 313–344) appear in boldface type.

74 75 76 77 78 10 9 8 7 6 5 4 3 2 1